Africa and the Olympics

Ohio University Research in International Studies

This series of publications on Africa, Latin America, Southeast Asia, and Global and Comparative Studies is designed to present significant research, translation, and opinion to area specialists and to a wide community of persons interested in world affairs. The series is distributed worldwide. For more information, consult the Ohio University Press website, ohioswallow.com.

Books in the Ohio University Research in International Studies series are published by Ohio University Press in association with the Center for International Studies. The views expressed in individual volumes are those of the authors and should not be considered to represent the policies or beliefs of the Center for International Studies, Ohio University Press, or Ohio University.

Executive Editor: Rick Huard

Africa and the Olympics

WINNING AWAY FROM THE PODIUM

Todd Cleveland

Ohio University Research in International Studies
Global and Comparative Studies Series No. 20

Athens, Ohio

Ohio University Press, Athens, Ohio 45701
ohioswallow.com
© 2024 by Ohio University Press
All rights reserved

To obtain permission to quote, reprint, or otherwise reproduce or distribute
material from Ohio University Press publications, please contact our rights
and permissions department at (740) 593-1154 or (740) 593-4536 (fax).

Printed in the United States of America
Ohio University Press books are printed on acid-free paper ∞ ™

Library of Congress Cataloging-in-Publication Data available upon request.
Names: Cleveland, Todd, author.
Title: Africa and the Olympics : winning away from the podium / Todd
Cleveland.
Other titles: Research in international studies. Global and comparative studies series ; 20.
Description: Athens : Ohio University Press, 2024. | Series: Ohio University
Research in International Studies. Global and comparative studies series ;
20 | Includes bibliographical references and index.
Identifiers: LCCN 2024017237 | ISBN 9780896803527 (paperback) | ISBN
9780896803510 (hardcover) | ISBN 9780896803534 (pdf)
Subjects: LCSH: Olympics—Participation, African—History. | Olympics—
Political aspects—Africa—History. | Olympic athletes—Africa.
Classification: LCC GV721.5 .C54 2024 | DDC 796.48096—dc23/
eng/20240416
LC record available at https://lccn.loc.gov/2024017237

To my Olympians: Julianna, Lucas, and Byers

Contents

List of Illustrations
vii

Acknowledgments
ix

Summer Olympic Games by Year and Location
xi

Introduction
Africa's Engagement with the Olympic Games
1

1
African Colonies and Newly
Independent Countries at the Olympic Games
Simulating Independence and Fostering National Unity, 1920–1968
25

2
Isolating Racism
African Contributions to South Africa's Olympic Ban
58

3
Africa Protests
Combatting Racial Injustice via Olympic Boycotts
93

4

Parlaying Individual Olympic Success
into Positive Change on the Continent
126

5

The Olympic Games and Personal Improvement Strategies
157

Notes
177

Bibliography
201

Index
211

Illustrations

Map

I.1. Africa   xiv

Figures

I.1 Len Taunyne and Jan Masiana at the 1904 Games in St. Louis   3

I.2 Feyisa Lilesa at the 2016 Games in Rio de Janeiro   7

I.3 Baron de Coubertin and the Olympic flame, Olympic Museum, Lausanne, Switzerland   10

I.4 Identity card prepared for the proposed 1929 African Games   13

1.1 The Egyptian football team—the Pharaohs of Antwerp—at the 1920 Games   31

1.2 Abebe Bikila and Ben Abdesselam Rhadi, 1960 Olympic marathon in Rome, Italy   50

1.3 Kip Keino gold-medal shoes, 1972 Munich Games, at the Olympic Museum   56

2.1 Dennis Brutus testifying before the UN in 1967   76

3.1 African Olympic delegation(s) leaving the 1976 Olympic Games   111

4.1 A South African stamp commemorating Josia Thugwane   130

4.2 Maria Mutola, women's 800-meter event, 2004 Athens Olympic Games   139

4.3 and 4.4 High Altitude Training Centre (HATC), Iten, Kenya 149

5.1 Francis Obikwelu competing for Portugal at the 2004 Athens Games 161

Acknowledgments

I'd first like to thank all of the African athletes, coaches, activists, and supporters who have engaged, in one manner or another, with the Olympic Games. Without their courage, passion, and commitment, this book would never have been written.

Along the research trail I received support from a number of folks and in a number of different ways. Starting close to home, our interlibrary-loan staff once again worked their magic, securing innumerable primary and secondary sources for me to access in the comfort of my office in Fayetteville. Their myriad contributions, which are both immeasurable and, too often, thankless, are vital to every book I write. Also on campus, the Department of History's unrivaled administrative staff—Brenda Foster, Melinda Adams, and Stephanie Caley—helped in so many ways that I've simply lost track; please just know that I'm eternally grateful. Chris Bucknam and Josphat Boit patiently explained the NCAA track landscape to me, enabling me to comprehend how the Olympics has fitted and currently fits with elite college track programs such as the one at the University of Arkansas. The African and African American Studies Program at my home institution provided funding at a key moment during the project. Jackson Critser generated the excellent map that appears at the front of the book. Further afield, I'd like to thank the archival staff and, in particular, Jameatris Rimkus, at the University of Illinois Special Collections, where former International Olympic Committee president Avery Brundage's papers are housed. My time in Champaign was both productive and enjoyable owing to their efforts. Garry Hill at *Track and Field News* helped me gain access and navigate the magazine's invaluable collection of back issues. Bob

x   Acknowledgments

Edelman and Chris Young provided important feedback when this project was still in its infancy, while Jamie Ivey kindly shared with me unpublished work that illuminated the intricacies of the 1980 Olympic boycott. Rita Nunes, from the Portuguese Olympic Committee, assisted me as I began searching for Lusophone African athletes who had competed in the Games for Portugal while still under colonial rule. In Lausanne, Switzerland, the archival staff at the Olympic Studies Centre, including Diego Girod and Estel Timofte, provided relentless support and insight. Over the course of a magical summer, I worked daily at the archive, pouring over Olympic documents while unavoidably intermittently staring out the window next to my desk at Lake Geneva, with the Alps serving as a breathtaking backdrop. That view will forever be imprinted in my brain, and I will never forget the staff's tireless assistance. Edwin, from the High Altitude Training Centre in Kenya, generously provided images for the book. Once again, I'm so grateful to work with the Ohio University Press staff, including Rick Huard, Beth Pratt, and Sally Welch, who supported this project from the moment I shared the idea for this book with them. It always feels like I'm with family when I'm working with OUP. Finally, I'd like to thank my family—Julianna, Lucas, and Byers—who also traveled to Illinois and Switzerland, for their unflagging support. I'll always remember fondly our times together as we pursued and discussed the histories and stories of Africa, Africans, and the Olympic Games. Thank you.

Summer Olympic Games by Year and Location

YEAR	LOCATION
1896	Athens, Greece
1900	Paris, France
1904	St. Louis, USA
1908	London, England
1912	Stockholm, Sweden
1916	Berlin, Germany (canceled due to World War I)
1920	Antwerp, Belgium
1924	Paris, France
1928	Amsterdam, Netherlands
1932	Los Angeles, USA
1936	Berlin, Germany
1940	Sapporo, Japan (canceled due to World War II)
1944	London, England (canceled due to World War II)
1948	London, England
1952	Helsinki, Finland
1956	Melbourne, Australia (equestrian events held in Stockholm, Sweden)
1960	Rome, Italy
1964	Tokyo, Japan
1968	Mexico City, Mexico
1972	Munich, Germany
1976	Montreal, Canada

1980	Moscow, USSR
1984	Los Angeles, USA
1988	Seoul, South Korea
1992	Barcelona, Spain
1996	Atlanta, USA
2000	Sydney, Australia
2004	Athens, Greece
2008	Beijing, China
2012	London, England
2016	Rio de Janeiro, Brazil
2020	Tokyo, Japan (delayed until 2021 due to the COVID-19 pandemic)
2024	Paris, France
2028	Los Angeles, USA

Africa and the Olympics

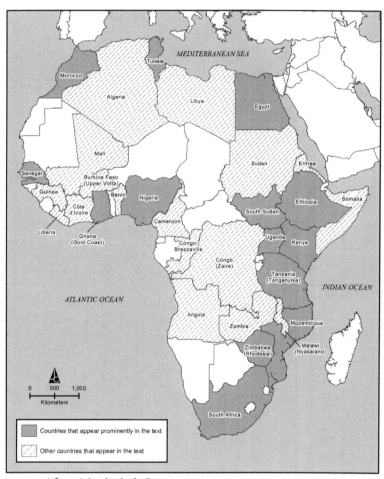

MAP I.1. Africa. Map by Jack Critser

Introduction

Africa's Engagement with the Olympic Games

In Mexico, some time ago, during a discussion of the Games of the XIX Olympiad ... a Mexican friend said in a disappointed tone of voice, "But, we don't win many medals," as if that was the only objective. This same sentiment I have heard expressed in other countries. This is all wrong and one of our most urgent tasks is to convince people that the sole purpose of the Olympic Movement, which I have called the most important social force ... today, is not the winning of medals. That is not even the primary objective! It must always be remembered that the Olympic Games are far more than an ordinary sports competition. They are a great festival of the youth of the world to promote international amity, mutual understanding, peace, and goodwill, as well as to draw attention to the high principles of the Olympic Movement, good sportsmanship, and fair play, the devotion to the task rather than to the reward, and the development of the complete man rather than a narrow specialization. ... We emphasize the basic principle: The most important thing in the Olympic Games is not to win but to take part, just as the most important thing in life is not the triumph but the struggle. The essential thing is not to have conquered but to have fought well.

> —Avery Brundage, International Olympic Committee (IOC) president, in a speech at the IOC's sixty-fifth session, in Tehran, Iran, May 5, 1967

During all my years in detention, I was a keen observer of the campaigns conducted across the entire world against the ignoble

> [South African] apartheid system. . . . The most enterprising
> of these movements . . . whose contribution was crucial for the
> abolition of apartheid was undoubtedly the Olympic Movement.
>
> —Nelson Mandela, South Africa's first
> democratically elected president, 1995

Following the conclusion of the Tokyo Summer Olympics in the summer of 2021, the fifty-four African countries that participated once again finished the tournament with the lowest continental medal haul. In fact, vis-à-vis their continental counterparts, African Olympic teams have collectively accumulated the second-lowest number of medals since the inception of the modern Games in 1896; only the twelve countries that compose South America have earned fewer.[1] Reflective of this relative lack of sporting success, African Olympians—beyond the legions of elite East African long-distance runners—rarely register in the minds of even the most dedicated followers of the Olympics. Nor has an African city ever served as the host location for any Olympic Games. Yet for all their seeming invisibility on the Olympic landscape, African political and sporting officials, athletes, and activists have, over time, effectually used the Games as a vehicle for social, political, and economic change. Indeed, while Western audiences remain transfixed by how many medals their respective teams have earned, Africa has long been "winning" at the Olympics, often far removed from the medal podium.

This book examines the myriad ways that various African actors have achieved these non-sporting victories via the Olympic Games since Len Taunyne and Jan Masiana first represented the continent at the 1904 Summer Games in St. Louis, competing in the marathon for South Africa, which was still a British colony at the time (fig. I.1).[2] Rather than measure the continent's success at the Games in terms of sporting triumphs (i.e., medals), the book adjusts the focus by considering the ways that a wide range of Africans, past and present, have utilized the Olympics to engage in transformative political activity, realize social mobility, and enhance the quality of

Introduction 3

FIGURE I.1. Len Taunyne and Jan Masiana at the 1904 Games in St. Louis.

life for individuals, communities, and entire nations. By reconstructing these historical and contemporary processes and the motivations that precipitated them, the book complicates reductive notions of the Olympics as solely a sporting competition and, instead, considers Africans' various forms of engagement with the Games as a series of strategic measures to improve personal, communal, regional, national, and even continental plights.

A History of Africans Winning Away from the Podium

Arguably, the first of Africa's quadrennial successes "away from the podium" was the initial fielding of Olympic teams by an array of African colonies, including Egypt at the 1920 Antwerp Games, the Gold Coast (Ghana) and Nigeria at the 1952 Helsinki Games, and Kenya and Uganda at the 1956 Melbourne Games, while these colonies were still under European imperial control. This sporting separation from their colonial overlords and the relative success that the African athletes enjoyed at these various Olympic competitions further intensified mounting calls for political independence, which by the 1950s were echoing across the continent.

Meanwhile, already enjoying their status as sovereign nations, Liberia and Ethiopia also sent athletes to Melbourne, while the newly independent countries of Morocco, Sudan, and Tunisia sent teams to the Rome Games in 1960, as did the colonial Federation of Rhodesia and Nyasaland (the contemporary countries of Zimbabwe and Malawi, respectively). In fact, it was in Rome that the first non–South African athletes from the continent—Abebe Bikila from Ethiopia and Rhadi Ben Abdesselam from Morocco—earned medals, finishing first and second, respectively, in the men's marathon. These accomplishments marked the commencement of Africa's dominance in men's distance-running events; African women would begin to exert their own distance-running supremacy some years later, at the 1992 Barcelona Games.

At roughly the same time that these male athletes first began to enjoy distance-running success at the Olympics, the majority of African nations were achieving independence. In turn, these newly sovereign states successfully campaigned for an Olympic ban of South Africa owing to the extreme system of institutionalized racism, known as *apartheid*, that its White minority government had instituted in the late 1940s. Following the limited participation of Len Taunyne and Jan Masiana at the 1904 Games, South Africa fielded its first formal team at the London Games in 1908 and, in the process, earned the continent's first medal: a gold for Reg Walters in the 100-meter dash.[3] Yet although Taunyne and Masiana were Black—and thus their participation was ignored by the South African media—Walters and the other fourteen athletes representing South Africa in 1908 were all White and returned home to great fanfare.

By discriminating against Black athletes and insisting on strict racial segregation, including in the sporting arena, South Africa's apartheid regime eventually earned an Olympic ban, which durably ran from 1964 to 1992. In fact, this was the first such exclusion of any country from the Games. Previously the only countries excluded from the Games were Germany (1920, 1924, and 1948), Austria (1920), Hungary (1920), Bulgaria (1920), Turkey (1920), and Japan (1948), because they fought for the losing side during one or both of the World Wars. Yet the IOC would never have issued this indefinite suspension without a chorus of African voices from beyond, as well as from within, South Africa's borders, including, most notably, the South African Non-Racial Olympic Committee, or SANROC. For these and

Introduction 5

other critics of the apartheid state, the Olympic Games constituted high-profile opportunities to punish and isolate the regime, which the 1964 ban achieved. Subsequently, a wave of international sporting interdictions followed, further isolating South Africa and eventually leading to the dismantlement of apartheid in the early 1990s and the attendant introduction of democratic rule in the country.[4] These profound developments radically transformed not only South African society but also the lives of millions of Southern Africans who had long been living under the shadow of the apartheid state.

Owing to the newfound independence of dozens of African countries and the IOC's suspension of South Africa, the 1960s was a heady period for much of the continent. However, the ensuing chapter in Africa's Olympic history was considerably more fraught, with African states either threatening or actively engaging in politically motivated boycotts of the Games. These sporting protests were again related to the apartheid regime, though only indirectly given the ongoing ban on South Africa. For example, just prior to the 1976 Games in Montreal, twenty-nine of the thirty-one African nations slated to compete withdrew because the IOC had declined to suspend New Zealand after its national rugby team had toured South Africa earlier that year in defiance of the United Nations' call for a sporting embargo of the country. The collective sacrifice made by the African athletes who had been poised to represent their countries drew worldwide attention to the perpetual racial injustice in South Africa and contributed to the expanding, international campaign against apartheid, while also encouraging opposition groups operating clandestinely within the country.

Spurred on by the African boycotts of 1976, the following year leaders of the Commonwealth nations, including many from Africa, unanimously approved the Gleneagles Agreement, which discouraged sporting engagement with South African athletes and teams as part of the broader effort to isolate the regime. Shortly thereafter, the South African national rugby squad—a team that was (and remains) central to Afrikaner culture and served as the sporting symbol of the state—made its last foreign tour prior to apartheid's end.[5] After the tour, the team, known as the Springboks, was not welcome anywhere on the globe.

More recently, individual African athletes have used the Olympic stage as a platform to attempt to engender meaningful change on the continent. For example, just as the raised, gloved fists of Tommie Smith and John Carlos at the 1968 Mexico City Games will forever be etched in Olympic memory, Ethiopian marathon runner Feyisa Lilesa's raised arms and crossed fists as he crossed the finish line (fig. I.2), and again on the medal podium at the 2016 Games in Rio de Janeiro, helped draw international attention to ethnic discrimination and human rights abuses in Ethiopia, which ultimately helped to usher in a more tolerant administration.

Other athletes, such as Kenyan distance runner Tegla Loroupe, have used their Olympic stature to establish charitable foundations that seek to address a broad range of challenges on the continent, which typically disproportionally affect disadvantaged communities. For example, Loroupe's organization, the Tegla Loroupe Peace Foundation, advocates for the peaceful coexistence and socioeconomic development of poor and marginalized communities in northern Kenya and the Greater Horn of Africa Region. To this end the foundation has, among other endeavors, brokered peace deals between local belligerents and established a school for children who have been orphaned owing to regional conflict. Lilesa and Loroupe are but two of the many African Olympians—many of whom never medaled—who have parlayed their participation in the Games to try to effect positive social and political change on the continent.

In other instances African athletes have used the Olympic Games to improve their sporting or financial prospects by switching nationalities. For example, numerous elite East African distance runners compete for adopted countries, often in Europe, North America, or the Gulf States; back in their more competitive home countries, the spots on these Olympic squads would not have been guaranteed, or perhaps even attainable. Moreover, these athletes' adopted nations have the means to financially support them and, by extension, their families. It was through this type of arrangement that Kenyan-born athlete Ruth Jebet became the first gold-medal winner for the Middle Eastern state of Bahrain when she won the 3,000-meter steeplechase at the 2016 Games in Rio de Janeiro.

FIGURE I.2. Feyisa Lilesa crossing the finish line of the marathon at the 2016 Games in Rio de Janeiro. Aflo Co. Ltd. / Alamy Stock Photo

Meanwhile, Kenyan-born distance runner Lonah Chemtai also competed in Rio and, like Jebet, for a country other than Kenya. Chemtai had relocated to Israel in 2008 to work as an au pair for her country's consul. Although she had some distance-running experience as a youth, it wasn't until she met her future husband, Dan Salpeter—a former middle-distance competitor who continues to coach Chemtai—in 2011 that she began to focus on running. Upon marrying Salpeter, Chemtai became an Israeli citizen and proudly competes for her adopted nation, often singing the Israeli national anthem and draping herself in the Israeli flag following a top-three finish. During an interview conducted immediately after her first victory as an Israeli citizen—in the 10,000 meters at the 2018 European Athletics Championship in Berlin—she declared, "Even before, I asked my coach 'When am I going to hold [wear] the Israeli flag?' It's important because I made my new country proud, I made my family proud, I made myself proud."[6]

Collectively, these sustained Olympic achievements in middle- and long-distance running have, in turn, generated economic opportunities in the home countries of the medal winners. In Kenya, for example, an assortment of for-profit organizations offers high-altitude "running safaris," for which foreigners pay to travel to the country and train with elite distance athletes. As one of these organizations touts: "We guarantee an experience of a lifetime for anyone interested in immersing themselves in Kenyan running culture. You will interact and do runs with big-name runners and get to see how they live and train." In turn, this industry has created numerous jobs in rural areas in which stable employment opportunities are otherwise scarce, though some local residents have voiced concerns regarding the objectionable social and environmental impacts that these influxes of sports tourists have had.[7] These concerns notwithstanding, Wilson Kuriungi, the founder and CEO of Run with Kenyans, a company that facilitates running safaris, sees even more opportunity in this realm: "The idea behind Run with Kenyans is to leverage the incredible power of Kenyan athletics to promote a broader Kenyan agenda. I see Kenya as a brand name. . . . Running can be used to invigorate business already in existence by opening up

Introduction 9

markets abroad. Kenya produces a lot of coffee, tea, rose flowers, and other cash crops . . . and they will be marketing [these products] to an audience that's already primed to appreciate 'Kenya' through the runners."[8] Whether Kuriungi's vision will be realized remains to be seen, but the positive economic impact that Olympic-level runners are making in Kenya is already tangible.

The wide array of non-sporting victories cited above suggests that Africans have long been using the Olympic Games to win "away from the podium." These various types of social, political, and financial successes stand in sharp contrast to the marginalization of Africa and Africans in other international bodies, including, for example, the United Nations and the World Trade Organization. Even in FIFA, the world governing body for soccer, African representatives have largely been noted for their ability to provide votes, in bloc form, to help influence internal elections and the sites chosen for the men's and women's World Cup competitions. Yet these recurring efforts have only once benefitted the continent; the men's event in South Africa in 2010 remains the lone World Cup hosted by an African nation.[9]

In contrast to their limited influence elsewhere, Africans have been able to utilize the Olympic Games to effect positive change on the continent, even though they have been relegated to the periphery of the IOC for much of its existence. Indeed, it wasn't until decades after most African nations gained independence that there were African representatives, aside from the long-standing White members from Kenya and South Africa, on the organization's executive committee, where real decision-making power resides. As such, Africans' victories away from the podium, including those outlined above as well as the many others that will be examined in the ensuing chapters, have in many ways been even more remarkable.

Racist Impediments:
A History of Africa's Engagement with the Modern Olympic Games

In 1894, well before Africans were involved in Olympic victories of any sort, Charles Pierre de Frédy—more commonly known as Baron de Coubertin—formed the IOC (fig. I.3). In turn, this sporting body organized the initial iteration of the modern Olympic Games, held

FIGURE I.3. Baron de Coubertin and the Olympic flame in front of the Olympic Museum, Lausanne, Switzerland.

in Athens in 1896, the first Olympics competition of any sort held in some 1,500 years.[10] Yet this initial contest was hardly the global affair that it has since become. Indeed, only fourteen nations participated, and astoundingly, roughly 65 percent of the (all-male) athletes derived from the host nation, Greece. Despite these rather humble beginnings, the Olympic Movement, which the IOC defines as "the concerted, organized, universal and permanent action, carried out under the supreme authority of the IOC, of all individuals and entities who are inspired by the values of Olympism," forged ahead.[11]

The 1900 Olympic Games were held in Paris. The number of nations competing in these games was twenty-six, almost double the number that had competed in the original 1896 Games. The number of participating athletes had quintupled—from 241 in 1896 to 1,226 in 1900—and included women athletes for the first time. The preponderance of local athletes, however, continued; in this case, the French fielded some 720 athletes, whereas the nation with the second most, Great Britain, sent only 102 athletes. Interestingly, four Algerian gymnasts also participated in the Games, but they competed for France, which had forcibly colonized Algeria decades previously.

Introduction

As mentioned above, it wasn't until 1904 in St. Louis that any African athlete competed on behalf of an African nation. Although still a British colony at the time, South Africa received nominal independence in 1910. Going forward, South Africa continued to send athletes to the series of ensuing Olympic Games, as did Egypt, which remained a British territory until 1922. In 1912 Egypt had allegedly sent a single athlete, a fencer, to the Games in Stockholm, though even this minimal inclusion remains uncertain. Consequently, many observers mark the 1920 Antwerp Games as Egypt's initial engagement with the Olympics (the 1916 event was canceled owing to the First World War). In fact, during the opening decades of the twentieth century, the British permitted a handful of colonial territories to form National Olympic Committees (NOCs), but only those that featured meaningful self-governance and a sizable number of European settlers; in Africa only South Africa (1912) and Egypt (1914) met these criteria.

By the 1912 Olympic Games in Stockholm, the number of participating nations had reached twenty-eight. As the Olympic Movement steadily expanded, Coubertin sought to extend its reach into Africa. In order to "conquer the continent," he would need to reach beyond the two nodes—Cape Town (South Africa) and Cairo (Egypt)—that British mining magnate, imperialist, and politician Cecil Rhodes had made so famous.

In eyeing Africa, Coubertin was reconfirming his commitment to the Olympic principle of "all games, all nations."[12] Inspired by the launch of the Far Eastern Games in 1921 and the Latin American Games the following year, Coubertin announced the organization of the biennial African Games in 1923. This sporting event would be formally supported by the IOC and held in Alexandria, Egypt, and subsequently in a collection of other host cities scattered around the continent.[13] Yet as Conrado Durántez has argued, the proposed African Games "were no more than the expression of Coubertin's desire to see the colonial powers of the time promote sport and the Olympic principles among the colonized peoples, including potential athletes in Africa, whom he keenly wished to see partake of 'sporting civilization.'"[14]

For Coubertin sport constituted a promising path of enlightenment for an allegedly backward Africa, the so-called Dark Continent.

These patronizing sentiments were reflected in a piece he wrote the same year (1923) in which he announced the organization of the African Games. "Perhaps it may appear premature to introduce the principle of sports competitions into a continent that is behind the times and among people still without elementary culture—and particularly presumptuous to expect this expansion to lead to a speeding up of the march of civilization in these countries."[15] He continued in this same condescending vein, asking his elite White readership to "think for a moment, of what is troubling the African soul. Untapped forces—individual laziness and a sort of collective need for action—a thousand resentments, and a thousand jealousies of the white man and yet, at the same time, the wish to imitate him and thus share his privileges—the conflict between wishing to submit to discipline and to escape from it."[16]

Although Coubertin was clearly not espousing liberation for Africans living under European colonial rule, he was forced to expend considerable energy trying to convince British and French officials of the innocuous, perhaps even subduing, nature of his proposed African Games. As Coubertin was no champion of the African, with the influence of social Darwinism clearly evident in his writings and articulations, extolling the virtues of colonialism was hardly a disagreeable or disingenuous undertaking for him. Indeed, he had, on at least one prior occasion, openly praised French imperialism in Africa as a "sacred civilizing mission" and spoke patronizingly, albeit indirectly, of the indigenous residents of Europe's imperial territories in Africa. "The colonies are like children: it is relatively easy to bring them into the world; the difficult thing is to raise them properly. They do not grow by themselves, but need to be taken care of, coddled, and pampered by the mother country; they need constant attention to incubate them, to understand their needs, to foresee their disappointments, to calm their fears."[17] Coubertin's African Games were intended to "coddle" these infantilized Africans, while using sport as a tool for broader human development.

The inaugural competition was scheduled for April 1929, the stadium having been completed and official invitation letters distributed the previous year (fig. I.4). Disregarding this momentum, British and French officials ultimately declined their summons to the proposed

Introduction

FIGURE I.4. Identity card prepared for the proposed 1929 African Games

Games, concerned that the racial hierarchy they had imposed in their African territories would be compromised if indigenous athletes were to defeat European participants. They further asserted that, in general, any unnecessary undertaking that could potentially embolden the colonized populations and thereby foment rebellion was best avoided. Clearly, these imperial officials perceived Coubertin's effort to bring Africans into the "sporting civilization," even if not into the Olympic fold, as threatening or potentially even perilous to their hold on power.[18] Consequently, the event was formally canceled in February 1929; the first African Games would have to wait until 1965.[19]

Instead of competing *against* talented African athletes, colonial officials elected to integrate them into metropolitan squads as the French had done with the aforementioned Algerian gymnasts some decades earlier. Indeed, at the 1928 Amsterdam Games, this decision worked to perfection, with Algerian athlete Boughéra El Ouafi, who had obtained French nationality, winning the gold medal in the marathon. Twenty-eight years later, at the Melbourne Games, another Algerian with French citizenship, Alain Mimoun, duplicated El Ouafi's victory. This European inclination to selectively absorb, rather than to compete head-to-head against, skilled African athletes, coupled with the racialism and outright racism that pervaded the Western world—and, thus, the overseers of the modern Games—repeatedly impeded the inclusion of Africans in the Olympic Movement. As John M. Hoberman has compellingly argued, we must discard our contemporary lens in order to understand how the early advocates of the Olympic Games perceived Africans. "It is difficult for us to grasp in its full sense the effortless sense of racial superiority that came naturally to most Europeans and Americans, prominently including the educated classes, at the turn of the century. This is the cultural world in which the Olympic Movement was formed, and it is not surprising that its racial attitudes found their way into the thinking of Coubertin and of other historical actors who formulated the theory and practice of Olympism during its early years."[20]

Indeed, owing to the IOC's durably homogenous composition, which until the 1960s exclusively featured White men of means, there were no voices within the IOC's power structure preaching multiculturalism. Because the IOC came into existence in "the era of the 'Great Powers,' wealthy individuals from prominent European nations were overrepresented in its membership."[21] In 1924, for example, 41 percent of the IOC membership was composed of members of European nobility, while that figure had been an astounding 68 percent in 1908.[22] Moreover, as existing IOC members were responsible for recruiting new colleagues and until the 1980s enjoyed lifelong appointments, its elite Western composition was regularly reinforced and correspondingly perpetuated. Unlike in, for example, FIFA, in which, upon joining, African nations receive one vote, just as do the more established countries in the organization, they enjoyed no such equitable power structure within the IOC. Since it was principally affluent, titled Europeans (who were undoubtedly admirers of their respective colonial empires) running the IOC for roughly the first seven decades of its existence, Africans had little opportunity to influence, or even engage with, the Olympic Movement.

Nor did sentiments that were racialist—or at times outright racist—within the IOC membership dissipate over the decades. As newly independent African nations began forming National Olympic

Committees (NOCs), the elitist circle of IOC directors privately expressed skepticism that Africans could manage their own affairs, questioning their competency and suitability to join this exclusive club. For example, a January 25, 1962, letter regarding monetary assistance for these fledgling African NOCs from then-chancellor of the IOC Otto Mayer to long-standing IOC president (1952–72) Avery Brundage captures this racial condescension: "If the IOC intends to send money to those people, what are they going to do with that money? Can you imagine non-organized people, knowing practically nothing—or not much—about sport, suddenly receiving money, for what? What those people should receive . . . are: educators in sport, trainers, and material. . . . That money should be used for that only: material sent from Europe and Instructors sent from Europe or [the] USA, but certainly not cash money, which will disappear in the pockets of some clever negroes!"[23]

Brundage himself unquestionably shared Mayer's sentiments. For example, during the 1960s Olympic Solidarity campaign, which provides assistance to those NOCs that exhibit the most significant need, the IOC president issued his own racially condescending statements. According to the minutes of a meeting organized by the Commission for International Olympic Aid (CIOA), "Mr. Brundage thought that we should keep ourselves out of all financial considerations that put the IOC in an embarrassing position. Brundage said that it was necessary to educate these people [Africans] and inculcate in them the Olympic ideal. Any sporting undertaking should be built from the foundation upward and the people must be taught to help themselves."[24] Thus, while Brundage and other IOC administrators spoke openly and repeatedly about "Olympic spirit and goodwill" and the "community of nations," they privately demonstrated that they deemed the peoples of some member nations of the Olympic Movement to be more equal than others.

As the 1970s unfolded, however, the power dynamics within the IOC finally began to shift. Delegates from nations on the fringe of the Olympic club began to identify and denounce the array of inequalities within the Olympic tent, including the matter of membership. For example, at the September 1971 meeting in Munich between the executive board of the IOC and the representatives of the NOCs, Prince M. Faroq Siraj of the Afghanistan Olympic Committee formally proposed that there should be an IOC delegate from every country that had an NOC, pointing out that while some countries with an NOC had multiple IOC members, others didn't have any representation within the body.[25] African membership exemplarily underscored this discrepancy. At the time of the Munich gathering, there were thirty African NOCs but only seven of these nations had members in the IOC. Over the ensuing decades more diverse, equitable representation within the IOC was ultimately achieved, though only gradually. At the time of this writing, for example, some 36 of the 102 IOC members are European; however, over half of the members that compose the IOC Executive Committee—8 of 15—are European.[26]

Inextricable Endeavors: Politics and the Olympic Games

The myth of the absence of politics in the modern Olympic Games is enduring within the IOC and can be traced all the way back to its origins. Only in the 1970s did this willful delusion transition to more of an elusive objective or simply an ideal. One of the ways that politics had been manifested in the Olympic Games from the onset was with the foundational ruling that required each participating athlete to be a member of a squad organized by and associated with a formally recognized state. As David B. Kanin has argued, "Using state teams as units meant that the Olympic system would be a part of Western political culture."[27] This landmark policy decision should not be overly surprising given the prevailing global power structures in the 1890s that privileged independent nation-states. This emphasis, in turn, shaped both the composition of the IOC's initial membership and its guiding principles. Indeed, the organizers of the IOC all hailed from recognized political units—that is, states—and thus determined that every athlete participating in the Games had to belong to one of these units.[28] In short, the very structure of the Olympic Games reflected its membership's worldview, which included reverence for the manner in which the Global West was organized politically. As such, attempting to identify the moment that politics and the Olympics first mixed (for

Introduction 17

example, the Nazis' utilization of the 1936 Berlin Games as political propaganda or the boycott of the 1976 Montreal Games by African nations) is, at best, a misguided endeavor, as political considerations have shaped the Olympic contests from their inception.

In fact, this reality is readily discernible dating all the way back to some of the initial versions of the modern Olympic Games. For example, in the early twentieth century, Finland's Olympic fate was decided by its more powerful neighbor, Russia, which required the former, as an autonomous territory within the its empire, to compete under the Russian flag at both the 1908 and 1912 Games.[29] In a similar, though ultimately more severe, case ahead of the 1912 Games, Austria and Hungary prevented Bohemia—a founding member of the Olympic Movement but also an autonomous part of the Austro-Hungarian empire—from participating owing to the political implications of its distinctness from the Austrian and Hungarian squads. Going forward, as Avery Brundage gained influence, power, and eventually the IOC presidency, the alleged insulation of the Olympic Games from politics was trumpeted loudly and relentlessly. His insistence was on full display every time he reminded anyone who would listen that South Africa should not be banned from the Olympics because this proposed exclusion was inherently political in nature. Brundage employed this same argument in the case of Portugal, which obstinately held on to its African colonies until 1975. Even though it openly practiced racial segregation and oppression in these territories, Brundage felt this was an internal political issue and thus not relevant to Olympic considerations.[30]

Beyond his intransigent stance on South Africa and, subsequently, Rhodesia, elsewhere on the continent Brundage regularly bemoaned the influential roles that African governments were playing in NOCs. The IOC president would eventually also target the Organization of African Unity (OAU) for similar reasons, as in Brundage's estimation all these entities were "political" and therefore inherent "interferers" in Olympic sport. For example, a February 1966 letter from Brundage to Jean-Claude Ganga, the Congolese president of the Supreme Council for Sport in Africa (SCSA), which oversaw sport across the continent, highlights the IOC chief's contempt for politics in (African) sport. "The two greatest dangers faced by the Olympic Movements are commercialization and political interference. I hope you will be successful in resisting these perils, which develop from time to time in all sections of the world. . . . More can be done for African unity on the fields of sport than anywhere else, but only if there is no political interference."[31] The following year, Brundage expressed grave concern after discovering that the OAU was providing some $55,000 to the SCSA, suggesting that this infusion could prompt the IOC to withdraw its recognition of the SCSA. Ganga subsequently retorted in a letter to Brundage regarding this concern that "even though we receive a subvention from the OAU, we are not in any way tied to the apron strings of the OAU. In fact, we are prepared to decline . . . their offer the day there is any suspicion of intention to meddle in our internal administration. This will be unequivocally resisted."[32] He further explained to the IOC president that "the OAU was established to foster African Unity. The OAU has to explore all possible avenues to keep Africa United. Accusing fingers are always pointed at Africa, simply because we do not have as much money as developed countries. Had we financiers to contribute some of their millions to our sports under any guise there would be no hue and cry."[33]

Although Brundage was clearly troubled by potential political interference in African sports, boycotts—either realized or even just threatened—profoundly panicked the longtime IOC president, as they unambiguously shattered the illusion that politics and the Olympic Games don't mix. Indeed, as sports historian William J. Baker has argued, "In conservative Olympic circles, where a strict separation of sport and politics was an enshrined myth for the friends and heirs of Avery Brundage, irritation often gave way to infuriation at the constant threat of African boycotts."[34] In fact, during the lead up to the 1968 Mexico City Games, with African nations threatening to boycott if South Africa was readmitted into the Olympic Movement and thereby permitted to compete, Brundage defiantly declared, "A war has broken out between politics and sport, but we will not tolerate that the Olympic Games be directed by politicians. The Mexico Olympic Games will take place, even if I have to be there [alone] along with five South Africans."[35] Despite this pledge, Brundage was

Introduction

eventually forced to relent, as the IOC ultimately upheld South Africa's suspension (examined in greater detail in chapter 2).

At the ensuing Games in Munich in 1972—Brundage's last Olympics in charge—the assassination of Israeli athletes tragically underscored the inextricable mixture of politics and the Olympic Games. Following Brundage's retirement, his successor, the Irishman Lord Killanin, could finally confirm what everyone had known all along, writing in the 1970s that "ninety-five percent of the problems as president of the IOC involve national and international politics."[36] Perhaps Kéba Mbaye, a Senegalese judge, legal scholar, and longtime IOC member (1973–2002), best characterized the relationship between politics and the Olympic Games when he declared some two decades later that "the principle of separating sports from politics is merely theoretical, for sports is by nature the continuation of politics by other means."[37]

Significance and Methodology

Most readers of this book will already have images in their minds of African long-distance runners triumphantly perched atop various Olympics podiums adorned with their hard-earned medals. However, all but the most studied readers would have been unaware of the myriad ways (as outlined above) that African political and sporting officials, athletes, and activists have utilized the Games as a vehicle to realize a range of non-sporting objectives. By expanding and deepening knowledge related to the actions of these historical and contemporary Africans, this book aims to provide insights into a range of topics, including the various roles that the Games have played in African societies; the complex, shifting social, political, and economic dynamics in an assortment of settings on the continent; and the ways that Africans have strategically interacted with international communities and each other through the prism of the Olympic Games.

If many readers will not have previously thought extensively about Africa and the Olympic Games, scholars have been only slightly more engaged with the subject. Although researchers have examined a range of topics related to Africa and the Olympics, most of the scholarship focuses on the South African suspension and ultimate expulsion from the Games.[38] Other works either broadly consider the Olympics and thus engage only minimally with Africa, thereby reinforcing its seeming invisibility, or are limited to particular localities within Africa.[39] As a result, the academic literature related to Africa and the Olympic Games constitutes a patchwork of circumscribed studies dispersed across a range of fields and disciplines. Not since the publication of Ramadhan Ali's concise work *Africa at the Olympics*, over forty-five years ago has a comprehensive history of the continent and the Games been featured in a single volume.[40]

This book, therefore, both updates and expands on Ali's work and, most importantly, reframes the analytical engagement with this topic.[41] It is also the first to assemble content from an array of disparate sources into a single, accessible narrative that centers African sporting and political officials, athletes, activists, and fans. The book's evidentiary base includes reports, correspondence, and other relevant primary source materials resident in the Historical Archives of the Olympic Studies Centre in Lausanne, Switzerland, and in the Avery Brundage Collection at the University of Illinois; global newspaper, magazine, and journal coverage of key Olympic developments; and interviews with African activists, sporting and governmental officials, and Olympic athletes and coaches published in newspapers, in journals, in magazines, and on websites.[42]

Finally, because only relatively few African nations and athletes have participated in the Winter Olympics, and this handful of athletes has not been nearly as profoundly involved in the types of "winning" that this book examines, the engagement throughout is exclusively with the Summer Games. The book also maintains a focus on the Games themselves and their attendant impact as mediated by the actions of a range of African historical and contemporary actors. Although African sports agencies and the IOC sponsor a wide range of workshops, instructional sessions, and developmental endeavors to encourage the growth and quality of sport on the continent as part of the broader Olympic Movement, I deem these endeavors and their associated developments peripheral to the Games, and thus they remain outside the scope of the book.

Introduction   21

Organization and Composition

Following this introductory chapter, Africa's Olympic history unfolds in a series of loosely chronological chapters, enabling readers to grasp the significance of various Olympic-related developments for African individuals, communities, and states across the modern historical period. Certain chapters rely heavily on primary source evidence, while others feature more synthetic reconstructions that draw on the modest collection of relevant scholarship. The ensuing three chapters are diachronically organized so that readers can trace Africans' engagement with the Olympic Games over a series of decades, while the concluding two chapters primarily focus on more contemporary developments.

Chapter 1 examines Africa's initial engagements with the Olympic Games, which primarily began in the 1950s; only Egypt and (White) South Africa enjoyed earlier ties. During this decade European settlers organized NOCs in a handful of colonies, applying for and receiving formal recognition from the IOC. Although Europeans retained control of these NOCs during the remainder of the colonial period on the continent, the squads themselves were either largely or exclusively composed of African athletes. Representing the colonies at the Olympic Games alongside autonomous nations intimated the political independence that these athletes and their compatriots sought to realize. Upon achieving sovereignty, the governments of these and other fledgling African states assembled NOCs and attempted to use Olympic and other forms of national sport to unify their often-divided nations. Closely monitoring these developments, IOC leadership remained conflicted. Although the organization's directors earnestly aspired to expand the Olympic Movement around the world, the racism that many of the IOC's administrators harbored in practice impeded and retarded this process of athletic inclusion. These formidable challenges notwithstanding, African delegates gradually ascended into the upper echelons of the IOC, while athletes from the continent began regularly besting international competitors, legitimizing the participation of African nations in the Games.

Chapter 2 reconstructs the protracted struggle to ban, suspend, and ultimately fully expel South Africa from the Olympic Games. Even as dozens of African nations jubilantly shed colonial rule in the 1960s, following some eighty years or more under European imperial control, South Africa's apartheid regime remained a humiliating reminder for Black Africans of life under White minority rule. In turn, an assortment of African activists, politicians, and sporting officials lobbied the IOC to force the regime to remove apartheid from sport or be expelled from the Olympic family. Given the White, aristocratic composition of the IOC's leadership, it's not surprising that this body exhibited great patience and, at times, even overt empathy for the apartheid government. But as racial violence in South Africa increasingly prompted global condemnation, supporting the embattled regime became increasingly untenable. Ultimately, even Brundage acknowledged that South Africa's intransigence was grounds for the country's removal from the Olympic Movement. But this expulsion would never have come to fruition without the unflagging efforts of a committed group of activists and politicians who coordinated the agendas and corresponding actions of an array of African sports organizations.

Chapter 3 examines African efforts to ban Rhodesia and, subsequently, New Zealand from the Olympic Games. Having successfully orchestrated South Africa's expulsion, African activists and officials next turned their attention to Rhodesia, a rogue colony featuring a White minority regime that had illegitimately declared sovereignty from Great Britain. The campaign to oust Rhodesia resembled the earlier endeavor against South Africa, but as the former fielded a multiracial Olympic squad for the Games, this struggle featured a somewhat divergent set of challenges. Assisted by a series of punitive United Nations resolutions against Rhodesia and the unwillingness of the Mexican authorities to disregard them, African activists succeeded in keeping the rogue state away from the 1968 Games. The ensuing Munich Olympics, however, required much more extreme measures and potential sacrifices. Ultimately, though, the African campaigners prevailed, efficaciously threatening a boycott of the 1972 Games. Desperately wanting to avoid the chaos and embarrassment that an African withdrawal might precipitate, the IOC banned Rhodesia on the eve of the Games, even though its athletes had already assembled in Munich. Next, African activists turned their attention to New

Zealand, which had maintained sporting ties with the otherwise isolated apartheid regime but which was poised to participate in the 1976 Montreal Games. Once again, African nations threatened to boycott. However, the absence of racial discrimination in New Zealand sport, coupled with the country's democratic traditions, convinced the IOC's leadership to uphold New Zealand's inclusion in Canada. Regardless, most African nations honored their commitment to keep their athletes away from the Montreal Olympics, thereby leading a principled protest against racism in sport.

Chapter 4 shifts the focus away from the series of international lobbying campaigns orchestrated by African activists, politicians, and sports officials to the Olympic athletes themselves. The mere participation of these athletes in the Games has contributed in innumerable ways to the well-being of the continent's residents, while Olympic success has typically amplified these positive impacts. For example, on various occasions, these competitors' accomplishments at the Olympic Games have effectively generated national unity, especially in deeply divided states. Similarly, the Olympic Refugee Team, formed in 2015 ahead of the Rio de Janeiro Olympics the following year, has fostered community among athletes who have fled conflict in their home nations, including many in Africa. The chapter also explores the various charitable initiatives and foundations that these athletes have launched, parlaying their Olympic credentials to effect meaningful, positive change on the continent both domestically and further afield. These organizations' efforts, including facilitating access to education and clean water, often target the most vulnerable in African societies, including women and children. Other charitable initiatives have utilized a familiar activity—sport—to empower women, cultivate gender equity, build confidence among youth practitioners, and even secure scholarship opportunities for aspiring African student-athletes at colleges and universities in the Global West, among other objectives. Finally, the chapter considers the sporting and social achievements and tribulations of the South African athlete Caster Semenya. Beyond the fame she has garnered via success at the Olympic Games, her status as an intersex woman, meaning that she was born with a combination of male and female biological traits (which in Semenya's case includes elevated testosterone levels), has generated considerable athletic and political controversy. Refusing to capitulate and resolutely identifying as a woman, Semenya has used her Olympic platform to champion athletes who have faced similar adversity while also spearheading a wide range of social improvement programs in her home country.

Chapter 5 maintains the focus on African athletes but instead considers the various ways that they have used the Olympic Games to enhance their own lives. These personal improvement measures have included switching nationalities, either by defecting or by licitly competing for other countries for athletic, financial, or other purposes. The chapter also considers the (in)famous case of Zola Budd, who avoided the international sporting sanctions on South Africa by expeditiously securing British citizenship in order to participate in the 1984 Los Angeles Olympic Games. Ultimately, this stratagem backfired, as her feet became entangled with American favorite Mary Decker-Slaney's during the women's 800-meter event, exacerbating the villainous status she had already earned owing to her repeated refusal to condemn apartheid. The chapter concludes with an examination of the trend of African Olympians parlaying their success at the Games to earn scholarships at American colleges and universities from the 1960s until the 1980s. Despite a litany of challenges associated with these strategic arrangements, which provided educational and athletic opportunities to African athletes and propelled otherwise middling US college track-and-field programs to national prominence, the practice persisted for roughly two decades. Ultimately, the allure of elevated amounts of prize money available on the professional circuit; the newly sanctioned ability to retain one's eligibility for international athletic competitions, including the Olympic Games, even after turning professional; and increasingly tightened regulations regarding these scholarships collectively drew these elite athletes away from American institutions of higher education.

1

African Colonies and Newly Independent Countries at the Olympic Games

Simulating Independence and Fostering National Unity, 1920–1968

The little band from Nigeria felt proud, indeed, that for once Nigeria was brought into the limelight of international recognition and admitted into the fellowship of the brotherhood of sport. . . . In my opinion, the success of these International Carnivals [Olympic Games] is to be judged not by how high a Davies jumps or how fast a McKenley runs, but how far International and Race harmony have been fostered through this intercourse. . . . Although we won no gold medals, we are still proud that our Country was represented in Helsinki [at the 1952 Olympic Games]. We now know that Nigeria has an untapped and unexplored potential of athletic talents.

> —B. A. A. Goubadia, a Nigerian athlete who competed in the 1952 Helsinki Olympic Games, while Nigeria was still a British colony, 1953

While every country hopes to win some of the coveted Olympic medals, the fact of participation in the Games is of the greatest importance. Uganda is hoping that the team will come home with some medals, but this is not the only reason for sending the team. Support for the ideals of the Olympic Games is fundamental and Uganda's consistent support of them, both before and after independence, is being continued by the dispatch of a team to this year's Games.

> —Editorial in the *Uganda Argus* newspaper ahead of the 1968 Mexico City Olympic Games, September 24, 1968

The decade of the 1950s marks the formal entry of Black sub-Saharan Africa into the Olympic Games. African athletes from the British colonies of Kenya, Gold Coast (Ghana), Nigeria, and Uganda participated in the 1952 Helsinki Games and, again four years later, in the Melbourne Games.[1] The inclusion of these African competitors in successive Games, distinct from their colonial overlords' squads, dovetailed with mounting calls for self-rule that, by the 1950s, were echoing across the continent. As such, the dispatch of these teams to Finland and Australia, respectively, intimated the political autonomy that these and other African nations hoped to realize in the very near future. As Pascal Charitas has contended, the mere presence of African athletes competing for their own National Olympic Committees (NOCs) at the Olympic Games constituted a significant step in the protracted course of decolonization.[2]

This sports-generated optimism was tempered, however, due to the continued oversight of these African NOCs by White officials who had earlier founded them. Moreover, International Olympic Committee (IOC) leaders considered some of these administrators as ideal candidates for lifetime membership in the body, even though—or perhaps because—African independence was clearly on the horizon. Consider the case of Reginald Alexander, once the mayor of colonial-era Nairobi and a founding member of the Kenyan NOC. When contemplating possible IOC membership for Alexander, Otto Mayer exclaimed in a 1959 letter to the Marquess of Exeter and then–vice president of the IOC David Burghley, "My idea is that he would be a very good member for us. He is young, very Olympic minded; he is British (not a coloured man!), and I wonder if it would not be a good idea to have at once a member in that section of the world?"[3] Even following Kenyan independence in 1963, Alexander remained the country's sole representative until his death in 1990 because he was a lifetime member of the IOC.[4] Europeans residing elsewhere in the colonies in the 1950s and 1960s similarly presided over other African NOCs. For example, Nigeria's NOC featured the Englishman P. H. Cook at the helm from 1953 until 1962, even though the country had achieved independence in 1960. Only upon Cook's departure did a Nigerian, Sir Adetokunbo Ademola, assume this leadership position.

Meanwhile, the independent African nations of Liberia and Ethiopia had also sent athletes to the 1956 Melbourne Games. Subsequently, Sudan, Morocco, and Tunisia, each of which had received independence in 1956, all sent teams to the Rome Games in 1960, as did the colonial Federation of Rhodesia and Nyasaland. Collectively, more than two hundred African athletes participated in the 1960 Games, although some, such as Senegalese sprinter Abdul Seye, who won the bronze medal in the 200-meter dash, competed for their colonizing nations, in Seye's case, France. Regardless, with over 5,000 athletes in total (including 611 women) from around the world competing in Rome, the African engagement with, and impact on, the Games remained extremely modest.

Despite their relatively small presence at the Games, for African countries that had recently achieved independence, participating in the Olympics contributed to the initial processes of national unification and nation building. These twin objectives often confounded newly sovereign African states, which were largely artificial conglomerations of disparate peoples thrust together by the European imperial powers at the infamous Berlin Conference in 1884, at which the representatives carved up the continent into a series of colonial empires. As African nations emerged from the darkness of imperial overrule, the leaders of these fledgling states identified sport as a tool that they could utilize to unite diverse populations. And the sporting profile of the Olympics was arguably unparalleled. Participating in the Games also further confirmed the global standing that decolonization had conferred on new African states. As Maureen Margaret Smith has argued, these independent nations "sought to establish themselves as legitimate members of the international community through their close proximity with larger sporting bodies, most notably the Olympic Movement."[5]

Yet not all officials from newly sovereign states on the continent perceived the Western-centric Olympics in the same manner. Instead, many of them retained the bitter taste of European colonialism, while the Cold War further hardened their political sentiments and alignments. In this context, many African politicians deemed participation in the Olympic Games anathema. Consider the words of Tanzanian politician Ngombale Mwiru, commenting on the possibility of his country joining the Olympic Movement as it approached independence: "We knew very well that the idea of the Olympics originated from Europe. Indeed, it came from the very European imperialists who were colonizing us. What is more, at the heart of the Olympic Movement were the imperialist attitudes of its leaders, which were apparent in the actions of the Movement. These people were indifferent to colonialism, they were indifferent to racism.... In such circumstances, how could we even imagine being part of such an organization? Surely, that would have been an act of collaborating with the imperialists."[6]

In this chapter, I examine Africans' initial engagements with the Olympic Games during the waning days of the colonial period and, subsequently, in the heady years immediately following independence. While still under European overrule, the participation of African athletes in the Olympics, competing on behalf of NOCs based on the continent, simulated the autonomy to which Africa's colonized peoples increasingly aspired. Upon finally realizing this freedom, participation in the Games further legitimized African states' newfound status and thus encouraged them to take their seats more confidently at the international table of nations. Regarding this shifting sociopolitical environment, Robert Skinner has contended that "within this context, international sport became a contested terrain in which new values of anti-racism and global solidarities challenged visions of innate social hierarchy that had underpinned colonialism."[7]

Meanwhile, domestically, engagement with the Olympic Games helped to foster national unity in these newly independent African countries, which often featured deeply fractured societies owing to the disparate constituent subpopulations and the deliberately divisive policies pursued by colonial regimes. These and other beneficial sporting impacts were felt even more deeply following success at the Games, which African athletes began enjoying in the 1960s with the emergence of an array of elite middle- and long-distance runners hailing from the eastern stretches of the continent. These Olympic achievements, in turn, engendered both domestic and continental pride and dignity for African populations that were facing significant challenges as they attempted to advance in the wake of European colonialism while simultaneously negotiating the instability and pressures that the Cold War relentlessly generated.

The Origins and Initial Activities of NOCs in Colonial Africa

The origins of African NOCs can be traced back to the original introductions of so-called modern sports by European colonizers. Although these foreigners had taken up residence in various locales in Africa as far back as the 1500s, it wasn't until after the formal, violent colonization of the continent during the latter half of the nineteenth century that these sporting introductions began in earnest. As African societies had a wide variety of their own athletic traditions prior to the arrival of these interlopers, these newly imported sportive activities were planted in fertile ground. Consequently, many indigenous residents quickly embraced the range of athletic endeavors that the Europeans had introduced. Rarely able to compete directly against White settlers owing to imposed racial hierarchies, Africans often formed their own leagues, tournaments, and events. These sporting pursuits were largely sanctioned by the colonial overlords, who mainly considered them to be harmless recreational outlets in which African participants would expend their energies engaged in physical activity, rather than campaigning for improved rights and conditions in the face of oppressive, imperial overrule. In many cases, Africans appropriated these imported sports, modifying the strategies, techniques, and rules and imbuing them with new meanings. Ultimately, the decades-long exposure to, and engagement with, Western sporting activities prepared African athletes to competitively participate in the Olympic Games.

Egypt as African Olympic Pioneer: Sport and Nationalism

Egypt played a pioneering role in representing the continent at the Olympics. Just as a handful of other African nations did, Egypt participated in the Games prior to independence and was similarly reliant on foreign initiative and representation to generate these initial sporting opportunities. However, Egypt's first engagement with the Games, in Antwerp in 1920, occurred decades earlier than other African nations' first taste of the Olympics (with the exception of

South Africa), though political independence from Great Britain would still have to wait two additional years.[8] The initial period of Egypt's sovereignty and its early Olympic performances were deeply intertwined, as the incipient nation identified the Games as a stage on which it could demonstrate to more established—that is, Western—countries that it, too, was a "civilized" nation worthy of respect. As Shaun Lopez has explained, "For Egyptian nationalists, Egypt's intrinsic worthiness for modern nationhood was often cast in relation to both the West and also to other colonized locales, and Olympic competitions thus provided an internationally recognized cultural arena for the performance and evaluation of postcolonial modernity."[9] Accordingly, poor performances by the Egyptian Olympic squads resulted in deep public discontent and dented the nationalism that the sporting events had been expected to deliver.

Some seven years before the first Egyptian squad competed at the Antwerp Games, Prince 'Umar Tusun had signaled in a letter to Muhammad Pasha Said, the president of the Council of Ministers, that he intended to form an Egyptian Olympic Committee. Tusun was convinced that "sport was a unifying element and a key factor in any nation's development," and Egypt was no exception.[10] The formal announcement of the formation of the Egyptian NOC came on January 19, 1914, with Prince Tusun serving as its president and Angelo Bolanachi, a Greek national who resided in the country and had for decades developed and directed sports policy and infrastructure in Egypt, as general secretary.[11] Unfortunately for the fledgling Egyptian Olympic project, the First World War put all Olympic events on hold until the conclusion of the conflict in 1919, with the Games finally resuming the following year in Antwerp.

In 1920 Egypt sent a football team (fig. 1.1), two competitors each in gymnastics and track and field, and one each in wrestling, fencing, and weightlifting. Collectively, the performances were unremarkable, with Egyptian journalists concerned that these showings suggested that Egypt was not presenting itself to the rest of the world as a modern nation but rather as one "walking around naked like the rest of the peoples of Africa."[12] Indeed, as Lopez has explained, these performances and especially those of the Olympic soccer team

FIGURE 1.1. The Egyptian football team—the Pharaohs of Antwerp—at the 1920 Games

were "understood against the backdrop of Egyptian independence and a desire to be seen as modern by their European opponents. Moreover . . . Egyptians also saw these competitions as a way to distinguish themselves from the supposed pre-modernity of other African countries . . . and to reclaim Egypt's place among the great civilizations of the world."[13]

The ensuing 1924 Olympics in Paris produced another largely forgettable performance, which in turn further heightened national frustrations. As these Games were the country's first as an independent nation, the Egyptians had been hoping to achieve legitimacy in the eyes of the Western world via their sporting accomplishments. Owing to the athletic failures in Paris, though, the Egyptian Olympic Committee (EOC) and Bolanachi, in particular, as a foreigner came under strident attack. Critics claimed that these disappointments were obstructing the process of national unity that Tusun had proclaimed the Olympics would foster, while also presenting an image of Egypt that was lacking in both culture and character.[14] An article in the local newspaper *al-Nil* in 1927 reflects this discontent, describing Egypt's two Olympic appearances as "a comedy performed on European world stages" and further arguing that the squad required someone "who could inspire a nationalist consciousness in the athletes."[15] This slight was unsubtly directed at Bolanachi's Greek ethnicity; allegedly, only an Egyptian national could prompt and cultivate these feelings among the country's Olympic athletes.

Yet other Egyptians saw signs of promise, as the performance in Paris had been slightly better than the effort in Antwerp four years previously. For example, one observer, also writing in 1927, said, "That little [improved performance] was a lot in the eyes of others [Europeans], and moreover it was a palpable sign that Egypt had started to move forward."[16] The author's optimism notwithstanding, his focus remains on the connections between the cultivation of nationalism through Olympic competition, the external image of the nation, and its national project. Going forward, the 1928 Games in Amsterdam delivered a gold medal in wrestling, won by Ibrahim Mustafa in the light-heavyweight class, and a fourth-place finish for the soccer team, but even these successes weren't sufficient. The Egyptian public's desire to generate national pride via the Olympic Games only intensified.[17]

A corollary of this fervor was Egyptians' unwillingness to continue countenancing a foreigner leading the nation's Olympic campaign, and thus calls for Bolanachi's resignation correspondingly amplified. Since his initial inclusion on the EOC, the Greek national had subsequently been promoted; by 1928 he was Egypt's sole IOC member. Rejecting Bolanachi's "foreign" representation and also invoking "national honor and dignity," the Egyptian government lobbied the IOC to replace him. However, the Olympic governing body refused (at Bolanachi's request), prompting Egypt to boycott the 1932 Games in Los Angeles.[18] That same year, as part of a broader wave of nationalization, Egypt introduced a policy that required its IOC member to be Egyptian. Two years would pass before the IOC and the EOC fully settled this dispute, in this case by electing Muhammad Taher Pusha to serve as Egypt's IOC member, while Bolanachi had already transitioned to represent Greece on the IOC some two years earlier. Only decades later, in 1955, did the EOC honor Bolanachi by granting him an award of merit for the significant role he had played in the development of sport in Egypt.

By the time the Egyptian government formally recognized Bolanachi's contributions, the country had become a regular participant in the Olympic Games, medaling in each tournament from 1928 to

African Colonies and Newly Independent Countries at the Olympic Games   33

1952 and becoming increasingly competitive in a range of events. It's unclear how this sporting progress may have tangibly contributed to Egypt's national project of social, political, and economic development and, correspondingly, its legitimacy in Western circles. However, it is clear that Egypt's regular participation and moderate success in the Olympic Games fostered national unity during a pivotal period in the country's development. Moreover, this sporting engagement and achievement helped Egypt steadily shed its postcolonial label and join the international community of nations with a more self-assured national identity.

To the South: Sub-Saharan African NOCs and the Olympic Games

Beyond Egypt the eventual establishment of NOCs in other territories under European colonial rule largely reflected the gradual push for political independence on the continent. In the years following the conclusion of the Second World War, the onset of the Cold War, and the establishment of the United Nations, the perpetuation of colonial empires was increasingly viewed as anachronistic. In response, the colonial powers began to listen, albeit begrudgingly, to the growing chorus of voices calling for self-determination on the continent. Colonial officials of all stripes identified some form of African sporting autonomy as an innocuous alternative to this more radical political demand. However, many British administrators, in particular, remained cautious regarding even this seemingly benign endeavor, as "they feared that sporting organizations in the colonies would signify independence from the Empire and the Commonwealth, following the example of India and Pakistan," which had both been granted national sovereignty by Britain in 1947.[19]

The 1948 Olympic Games in London provided something of an opening, however, for IOC officials in favor of increased African participation, even if sporting autonomy or something approximating it would have to wait. For the first time, the British government permitted athletes hailing from the empire to compete as members of its Olympic squad. These participants ultimately included seven Nigerians, including Prince Adegboyega Adedoyin, who placed fifth in the long jump, as well as other athletes from the West Indies. But

34 AFRICA AND THE OLYMPICS

this type of sportive inclusion of the empire would be short-lived. Later that year reforms made to the British Nationality Act newly denied athletes from the empire the opportunity to compete for Great Britain's Olympic team.[20] Moreover, the International Amateur Athletic Federation (IAAF) stipulated in 1949 that, going forward, "only subjects of a country can represent that country."[21] Collectively, these policies spurred the creation of independent NOCs in Africa, even as the colonies that they represented remained under imperial rule.

In 1950 both Nigeria and the Gold Coast (Ghana) participated in the British Empire and Commonwealth Games, in Auckland, Australia, as independent entities separate from Great Britain. This involvement, in turn, signaled the commencement of a process of "sporting decolonization," with political sovereignty proceeding in its wake. Soon afterward, with the IOC's endorsement, Nigeria and the Gold Coast, followed by Uganda, each formed NOCs and also affiliated with the IAAF. National pride predictably ensued. In an editorial in Nigeria's *Daily Times* from 1952, appearing just over a month before athletes from the colony would participate in their first Olympic Games, this sentiment is clearly evident: "The Chairman of the Amateur Athletic Association of Nigeria, in a short speech, assured the country that the team would see to it that the highest tradition of Nigeria's sportsmanship was upheld. The country's prestige would be heightened, not only in the eyes of its fellow countrymen, but also in the opinion of the world by their participation in the XVth Olympic Games in Helsinki."[22]

But not everyone with an interest in these developments was equally as pleased. French officials, for example, influenced by their "assimilationist" approach to imperial governance, wanted to keep African athletes within France's broader sports framework.[23] Moreover, they were also concerned about the sporting autonomy that the colonies would newly enjoy, which they feared would somehow augur political independence. Indeed, while Armand Massard, the French vice president of the IOC, was actively lobbying Brundage against this inclusive move during the early 1950s, his countryman and fellow IOC member François Piétri was busy writing Otto Mayer in 1951 about the potential consequences of permitting Nigeria to form an

NOC: "This Nigerian business is intolerable. If this sort of development continues, the colonial countries will end up with five, ten, or twenty additional votes in the IOC. This is a real plan that must absolutely be thwarted."[24]

Alarmist predictions like this one notwithstanding, the IOC leadership remained at least outwardly committed to this expansion of NOCs, wanting to bring Africa into the Olympic fold and use these initial members as models. These IOC officials correctly understood that at some point these colonies *would be* independent states; and if they featured previously formed NOCs, they would already be a part of the Olympic Movement. Yet despite this public encouragement and seeming goodwill, the IOC brass remained privately wary of adding new NOCs, especially from Africa. These high-ranking members were not only mindful of European colonial overrule, but many of them also harbored thinly veiled racist sentiments toward the continent's indigenous residents. For example, in a 1955 letter from Otto Mayer to Avery Brundage regarding the creation of NOCs in Uganda and Tanganyika (Tanzania), the former cautioned, "As you said in a previous letter, we must help and develop the Olympic Movement, but also pay attention to which countries and people we are taking in[to] it!"[25]

At the fiftieth session of the IOC in June of that same year, this type of racial condescension was overtly audible and much more explicit. During a discussion regarding the formation of new NOCs in the developing world, which included dialogue about how politics could be kept out of this process, an unidentified speaker offered the following haughty commentary:

> Originally, NOCs were always formed by members, who saw that the new organizations complied with Olympic regulations. Today, NOCs are organized by outsiders who often have no accurate knowledge of the Olympic Movement. We must have a rule that will provide some protection. Please remember that this rule is not written for the [Western] nations which are familiar with the Olympic Movement and know very well the Olympic spirit. The rules which we are discussing are particularly intended for remote countries not experienced in Olympic

affairs, such as Liberia, Rhodesia, Nicaragua, Indo China, Bolivia and many others. We should really, of course, send a representative of the IOC to all these countries in order to teach them the Olympic philosophy before they are recognized.[26]

At various times, this pomposity fueled, reflected, or mixed with the exoticization of "remote" Africans as part of the broader "othering" process, the constitutive sentiments of which were instantiated in the presence of over forty Guinean dancers, singers, and musicians at the 1956 Melbourne Games. Invited by the IOC as part of the Olympic cultural program associated with the Games, the official pamphlet that documents these Africans' performance in Australia is replete with photographs of many of the women, topless and adorned in shells and bracelets, entertaining the dapper White audiences, which undoubtedly included IOC officials.[27]

Support for Africa in the Olympics: Public Encouragement and Financial Backing

Far removed from the politics surrounding IOC membership, African sports enthusiasts from nations with newly formed NOCs that were sending athletes to the Olympic Games were deriving both enjoyment and pride via this engagement. For example, although the Ugandan NOC—which had been recognized by the IOC in January 1956—sent just three athletes to the Melbourne Games later that year, even this minimal participation made a significant impact on the nation some six years before the country would achieve independence from Britain. Fondly recalling the fanfare, Ugandan IOC member Francis W. Nyangweso, reported, "[The year 1956] was the first time I had ever heard about the Olympic Games, which were highly publicized in cinemas on the BBC newsreels shown before the main feature films. We were able to watch the opening and closing ceremonies and some of the events in which the . . . athletes took part."[28] And these Olympic participants' social and sporting impact only grew upon their return to Uganda. Indeed, Nyangweso explained that "when the athletes who had participated in the Melbourne Games returned, they went around to the schools, recounting their experiences in Australia. We were thrilled and it inspired me to be among those to be selected for the next Olympics.... Eventually, I made it to the [1960] Olympic Games in Rome as a boxer."[29]

Meanwhile, the European overseers of the various African NOCs had been attempting to tap this public enthusiasm in order to raise funds to train the athletes and, ultimately, facilitate their transportation to the various Olympic venues. It's important to recall that even though these NOCs featured African athletes, the officials who created, composed, and managed these sporting organizations were invariably White settlers. Consequently, these individuals, such as the president of the Nigerian NOC, C. E. Newham, and the Kenyan NOC director, Reginald Alexander, sought to raise money for their budding Olympic organizations primarily by reaching out to well-heeled members of the White settler communities. In many ways, NOCs constituted a vanity project for these expatriates, as these far-flung, oft-forgotten African colonies were newly poised to take a seat at the Olympic table, right next to their European overlords.

In Nigeria fundraising started immediately after the IOC's recognition of its NOC, in May 1951. To assist in the solicitation of sizable public donations, the Nigerian Olympic Committee enjoined the governor, Sir John MacPherson, to issue a "Letter of Appeal." In turn, the governor's entreaty appeared in Nigeria's *Daily Times* on November 10 and read as follows:

> I confidently appeal to all Nigerians, and to all who work in and for Nigeria to contribute—according to their means—to the Fund which is needed to send Nigeria's first representatives to compete in the Olympic Games next year, for the first time in the country's history.... It is estimated that it will cost $400 for each member of the team who travels to Helsinki, and on this basis if we are to send, say, nine athletes and a manager, a sum of at least $4000 will be needed. This is a lot of money but it will pay handsome dividends in placing Nigeria more prominently on the map of world sport. I believe that our chosen athletes, by prowess, conduct, and sportsmanship, will bring new credit to our country in the eyes of the world. It would be a matter for deep regret if one athlete worthy of representing

Nigeria had to be left out of the Olympiad because of a lack of funds. I make this appeal in the confident hope that the public will be prompt and generous.[30]

By May 1952, just months prior to the Nigerian team's departure, donations from individuals, institutions, companies, mercantile houses, and firms, as well as proceeds from a formal ballroom dance, collectively surpassed the Nigerian NOC's target figure. Nigeria was going to Finland.[31]

A Diverse Approach: Multiracial Olympic Squads and Coaches

Ahead of appearances in the 1956 and 1960 Games, the Kenyan Olympic Committee (KOC) appealed to an even wider variety of communities to support its squad due to the nation's multiracial composition, which featured a sizable Southeast Asian population.[32] Although Kenya would have to wait until 1963 for its independence from Britain, its NOC had been recognized in June 1955 and was overseen by the aforementioned Reginald Alexander. The KOC had aimed to send a delegation of thirty athletes to Melbourne for the 1956 Games but ultimately assembled a twenty-seven-person team, including eight African runners; two White riflemen; a White female swimmer; and a sixteen-man, predominately Asian, field hockey team, which also featured an Indian coach. Alexander would later boast to Brundage about this racial diversity in a letter to the IOC president: "So far as Kenya is concerned, the record of the Kenyan Olympic Association is thoroughly clean and above reproach. In fact, we led the way, when we participated at Melbourne in 1956, in showing the world how black, white, and brown could, and do, perform together in one integrated team."[33] The ensuing IOC president, the Irishman Lord Killanin, confirmed the Kenyan NOC director's assertion, remarking that "Alexander had created an extremely good impression in the Olympic world by bringing Black, European, and Indian Kenyans to the Olympic Games in the most integrated teams to come from any country."[34] Regarding the 1960 Rome Games, Kenya again sent a twenty-seven-person, multiracial team, which featured five runners—four African and one Asian—a primarily Asian field hockey squad, and an array of White athletes who represented the nation in the shooting and sailing events. Following independence, in 1963, Kenya continued to send multiracial teams to the Olympic Games, including in 1964, 1968, and 1972, before boycotting the 1976 and 1980 events.

If certain African countries sent multiracial athletic squads to the Games in the years that succeeded their political sovereignty, the coaching ranks for these squads were often even more racially diverse. And in some cases, these training staffs were formed prior to achieving independence. Typically, Europeans filled these positions, such as in Nigeria, where V. B. V. Powell, a British long jumper, served as both the Nigerian Olympic squad's general team manager and its sole coach for the 1952 Games in Helsinki. But a series of preparatory measures to enhance the team's prospects in Finland reveals a more diverse approach. Indeed, in order to help its athletes prepare for the Helsinki Games, the Nigerian Olympic Committee had enlisted two elite Black athletes from the West Indies to augment Powell's training: Arthur Wint, a Jamaican sprinter who had won gold and silver medals at the 1948 Games in London (and who would win another gold and another silver medal in Helsinki), and McDonald Bailey, a Trinidadian sprinter who had competed at the London Games (and who would go on to medal in Helsinki). B. A. A. Goubadia, a high jumper and one of the members of Nigeria's 1952 Olympic team, remarked about the squad's focused and intense preparation to which Wint and Bailey had contributed: "Always the emphasis was on training, and our private likes and dislikes were sub-ordinated to those of the country. . . . Our one solitary determination was to do the utmost of our . . . brawn for the honor of Nigeria."[35]

The Origins, Initial Activities, and Challenges of NOCs in Postcolonial Africa

Following political independence, African nations had a variety of experiences with the Olympic Games. As outlined above, a handful of countries had already participated in these contests, having formed NOCs prior to independence. For example, Nigeria experienced two Olympics prior to becoming a sovereign state—and was close to a third, with independence arriving on October 1, 1960, less than three weeks after the 1960 Games in Rome had concluded. But many nations, especially in the former French empire in which colonial officials had prohibited autonomous NOCs prior to political independence, would only engage with the Olympic Movement after their imperial overlords had departed.

Similar to the African NOCs that had sent athletes to the Games prior to independence, medals were elusive for these newly sovereign participants. Regardless, their mere presence at the Olympics delivered much-desired pride and prestige, with African contenders competing side by side against other elite athletes from around the world as part of an emerging global sports community.[36] Moreover, the heads of these incipient African nations eyed the Olympic Games as ideal opportunities to generate social unity and cultivate national identities, two daunting but vital projects for these largely fragmented countries. As Alfred E. Senn has contended, "Leaders of the new states . . . quickly recognized the usefulness of sport as a quick and effective way to establish national identity and feelings of national loyalty. While some individuals objected to the popularity of the sports of their former imperial masters, a victory . . . could create all sorts of good feelings. As a result, these new governments were quite likely to have sport ministries, sport councils, and articulated sport policies."[37]

Tempering this enthusiasm surrounding Africans' initial sportive engagements with the Olympic Games were a host of complications generated by the Cold War. Throughout this contentious period, the IOC's leadership remained clearly aligned with the Global West and thus treated the multitude of emerging African nations with considerable suspicion, fearful that they would concertedly support the Soviet Union within the body as a form of gratitude for Moscow's assistance in helping to end colonial overrule. Even absent this type of reciprocation, in some African countries such as Tanzania, socialist inclinations and the enduring association of the Olympics with European colonialism also impeded, or at least complicated, initial engagement with the Games. New African states were also forced to navigate relations with their former imperial occupiers.

These erstwhile colonizers sought to utilize the Olympics as part of their broader neocolonial agendas on the continent, which entailed the utilization of their formidable power and influence to engineer considerable political and economic control over their former territories. Only after African representatives began joining the IOC in increasing numbers as formal members of the body from the 1960s onward did the range of aforementioned dynamics gradually shift, rendering the continent's nations more, if still not quite fully, equal participants in the Olympic community of nations.

Tunisia: Intertwining Olympic Sport and National Development

The case of postcolonial Tunisia illustrates well the types of optimistic, sporting-nationalist objectives, strategies, and experiences outlined above. Having gained its independence from France on March 20, 1956, the Tunisian government formed an NOC the following year. The members of this body were selected from a series of national sports federations that the government had established to replace the array of colonial-era equivalents in order to further sever the link with Tunisia's imperial past. Although Avery Brundage invariably loathed governmental intervention in the (Olympic) sports arena, the IOC president acknowledged the Tunisian state's crucial contributions to this developmental process. He expressed these sentiments in a letter to Otto Mayer in May 1957, while also reaffirming his condescension toward the developing world, including Tunisia: "I hope that the organizations in Tunis . . . will understand something about the Olympic Movement. The great trouble is that in these *primitive* countries in Asia, Africa, and South America, which constitute a large part of the world, conditions are such that unless the Government does it, it is not done. Few organizations of any kind are completely independent and free from political control and influence. This is the case also in all Communist countries."[38] Brundage's reservations notwithstanding, roughly four months later the IOC, at its session in Sofia, Bulgaria, officially recognized Tunisia's NOC, signaling the "primitive" country's acceptance into the Olympic Movement.

Emboldened by this development, the Tunisian government moved purposefully to use Olympic sport to cultivate national unity and buttress domestic dignity in the face of considerable social and economic challenges. Indeed, as Maha Zaoui and Emmanuel Bayle have contended regarding sport more broadly, "In Tunisia ... sport is an inexhaustible source of symbolic and identity capital that sporting and/or political leaders readily draw upon ... all of the country's post-independence leaders have been aware of the value of sports as a component of national identity, with the result that politics has played a major role in shaping sport ... sport was a precious ally in the fight against cultural and economic underdevelopment; it was the road that would facilitate Tunisia's entry into the international sphere."[39] Tunisia's first prime minister, Habib Bourguiba, certainly subscribed to this approach, realizing that sport constituted an "excellent vehicle for consolidating and legitimizing the young nation state, thanks to its power in building national unity and obtaining international recognition."[40] As such, early on in his tenure as the country's leader, Bourguiba declared that "We need to be present at sports competitions, whether Arab, Mediterranean, or worldwide. . . . The prestige provided by sporting exploits is undeniable. It rains down on the entire nation."[41] In 1959 the government even established National Olympic Day, which continues to be celebrated annually on the third Sunday in May. For Bourguiba and the citizens of the fledgling nation, participating in the Olympic Games generated national pride and identity, both of which constituted victories for the country far removed from the medal podiums.

Tanzania: Olympic Skepticism Followed by Strategic Tolerance

Not every new African nation embraced the Olympic Movement as ardently, or as immediately, as Tunisia did. In Tanzania, for example, which achieved its independence from Great Britain in 1961, hostility toward the Olympic Games began prior to political autonomy and persisted throughout the first decade of the emergent state's existence. As mentioned earlier in the chapter, many Tanzanians understandably associated the IOC with European colonial overrule, owing to its predominantly Western composition. And with the country's first president, Julius Nyerere, espousing "African Socialism" and viewing allegedly Western activities such as tourism with

African Colonies and Newly Independent Countries at the Olympic Games   43

contempt or at least suspicion, it's not surprising that the Olympic Movement would come under similar criticism.[42] If nothing else, the Olympics were seen as peripheral to the development of the nascent nation, which had scant resources to invest in sporting activity. As Sendeu Titus M. Tenga has explained, for most Tanzanian officials "the promotion of sport, in particular modern sport in the form of Olympic sport, could not be a priority for a newly independent and poor country. . . . In the opinion of the government, what was crucial was the development of its society and the welfare of its people through the provision of education and health services, as well as the eradication of poverty, by improving economic growth. Towards achieving these goals, sports in general, not to mention Olympic sport in particular, were seen to play a negligible role."[43]

These sentiments notwithstanding, Tanzania did send eight athletes to the 1964 Tokyo Olympics, in part because former colonial officials still oversaw a portion of the sporting activity in the country, and the athletes themselves had been formally invited by the Organizing Committee of the Games. Subsequently, the Tanzanian government essentially terminated the operations of the Tanganyika Amateur Sport Federation and Olympic Committee (TASFOC), which had served as the incipient country's de facto NOC.[44] Shortly thereafter, though, the Nyerere administration softened its stance toward the Olympic Movement, concluding that the Games could serve as a useful tool in the fight against apartheid and enduring European colonialism elsewhere on the continent. According to Tanzanian politician Ngombale Mwiru:

> To be sure, the pressure of the international anti-apartheid movement on the IOC awakened and changed the government's stand on the Olympic Movement. Since Tanzania was already seriously committed to the fight against colonialism and apartheid in Africa, the government quickly saw the potential that the Olympic system presented in inflicting harm on the racist regime in South Africa, by isolating it from the international sports community. For the government, this was a good enough reason for the country to join the Olympic

Movement. It broadened the scope of the country's foreign policy, which clearly stipulated that support for the struggle against colonialism, racism, and neo-colonialism was the main principle behind Tanzania's international relations.[45]

Following this adjustment in sporting policy, Tanzania applied to the IOC for recognition of its NOC just in time to compete in the 1968 Games in Mexico City, initially receiving provisional acceptance before finally securing official recognition in 1970.

Olympic Sport and Neocolonialism

In hindsight, perhaps Tanzania's initial cynicism toward the Olympic Movement had been both warranted and prudent, as government officials from the former colonial powers, namely Britain and France, widely considered Olympic sport a vehicle through which they could deepen neocolonial relations with their erstwhile African territories. As sports historian Pascal Charitas has argued, in pursuit of this politico-sporting relationship building, the former colonial powers employed "alternative forms of power: a more flexible domination based on strategies of influence, development assistance, humanitarian actions, and commercial agreements . . . guiding their 'partner' nations' behavior or being able to ensure their preponderance in joint decision-making processes—allied with the power of the Olympic rings."[46]

In practice, French officials engaged in this hegemonic process in francophone Africa more ruthlessly than did their British counterparts in the latter's former territories on the continent. As Charitas has contended, "This colonial reshaping consisted of simultaneously supporting the political independence of the African countries with . . . the blessing of the United Nations, and finally gaining the IOC's recognition of the NOCs from francophone Black Africa."[47] The IOC was apparently mindful enough of France's ongoing, asymmetrical power dynamics with its former colonies that in 1957 Otto Mayer expressly sought French approval to admit Tunisia—which was, by then, an independent country—into the Olympic community of nations. In turn, French officials allegedly replied, "Tunisia is a free

African Colonies and Newly Independent Countries at the Olympic Games 45

country and we have no objection whatsoever. In any case, it does not concern us."[48] This exchange suggests that the IOC was arguably even more invested in colonial-era power relations than was France.

Cold War Considerations

Irrespective of an African nation's former colonial occupier, every one of these new states came into existence during the Cold War, and thus, officials in both Moscow and Washington were acutely interested in the political fates of these countries. Both sides in the conflict actively courted African heads of state and rebel leaders, recklessly lavishing them with money and matériel while also trying to win the "hearts and minds" of the continent's residents. So when observers from either of these Cold War camps commented on sporting developments in these fledging nations, they were interested in far more than just sportive plights. For example, writing ahead of the 1960 Rome Olympic Games, Soviet sportswriters Alexei Dykov and Vitali Petrusenko lauded the new African countries in a piece for *Pravda,* the official newspaper of the Communist Party. "They exude strength. Together with their nations, the athletes, boxers, and gymnasts of Africa recently fought for independence. Now, they march in the Olympics as equals among equals. It is not very important that they have little sports experience. Observers already forecast that the Rome Olympic Games will reveal many new talents among representatives of the black continent."[49]

By invoking the struggle for independence in Africa, which the Soviet Union continued to support both diplomatically and materially, the writers were confirming the importance of sport for international prestige and respectability and their backing for these nascent nations, while also regarding them as novel partners in the ongoing struggle against the West. One way the Soviet Union confirmed its patronage was to immediately recognize the new governments formed in Morocco and Tunisia upon independence in 1957 and in Ghana the following year. The Soviets also "provided political and economic options for Sékou Toure in Guinea," a nation that had abruptly achieved its independence from France in 1958 and quickly embraced socialism, thereby positioning itself firmly in the Soviet camp in the global Cold War struggle. Going forward, the Soviets would constitute a potent ally for the coalition of African nations seeking to exclude apartheid South Africa from participating in the Olympic Games.

The (Unfounded) Fear of an African Voting Bloc

As part of its durable prioritization of the Global West, IOC leadership was keen to prevent the formation of a bloc of newly independent African (and Asian) nations that might support Soviet initiatives within the organization as a reciprocative motion for Moscow's ongoing assistance. Although Brundage and other high-ranking IOC officials outwardly maintained an apolitical, or at least neutral, stance regarding this matter, privately they fretted. In a letter to the Marquess of Exeter in April 1960, for example, Brundage revealed his anxiety regarding the potential for African nations to pursue this type of "political" cooperation. "Since the war, for the first time in the history of the Olympic Movement, we have a group of countries operating as a unit, and from your letter of April 5 it seems that this unit will become more and more active. In addition, it will probably try to enlist other countries to strengthen its forces. This is indeed a most serious situation, particularly since the main objectives, no matter how well they attempt to cover them, are political. We must be alert and watch these developments most carefully."[50] Writing to Otto Mayer some years later, Avery Brundage echoed his earlier sentiments, though in much more hyperbolic fashion, opining, "The IOC faces a serious problem. . . . If every tribe in Africa forms a new country, the IOC will have more African members than the rest of the world put together."[51]

For Brundage and the IOC, this type of intraorganizational cooperation constituted a considerable threat, even if members of Western nations in the body had repeatedly exhibited similar solidarity in the past. Ultimately, although the leadership of the IOC feared that the new African countries would vote as a bloc, in practice, the individual governments of these new states were quickly positioning themselves in either the American or Soviet orbit, reflective of their particular Cold War–era ideological perspectives and associated material interests.

African Colonies and Newly Independent Countries at the Olympic Games   47

The Committee for International Olympic Aid

Irrespective of the IOC's apprehension regarding African solidarity, the multitude of new states coming into existence—in 1961 alone seventeen African countries joined the United Nations—also presented the Olympic organization with an opportunity to extend its ideals of humanism and universalism to the continent. In response, in the early 1960s the IOC created the Committee for International Olympic Aid (CIOA), which aimed to support the integration of newly independent African nations into the Olympic Movement, to assist in the development of their various sports federations, and to foster goodwill among Africa's assortment of fledgling states in general. However, given the Cold War context in which the CIOA was formed, it was inevitable that this organization would become politicized, thereby undermining some of its core objectives.

In particular, the IOC was concerned that it would be exploited or even co-opted by African states in the Soviet sphere. Ahead of the IOC meeting in Nairobi in 1963, which was intended to bring African nations further into the Olympic fold by holding this important annual gathering on the continent, Otto Mayer wrote to Brundage to share his concerns regarding the CIOA and to suggest a means to contain, or perhaps even abandon, the initiative: "In my opinion, you should try to stop that whole CIOA while in Nairobi. First, we cannot allow it to ask for funds all the World round. . . . Without money, that Commission has no reason to live. We must take great care with the African countries and educate them first by sending them information distributed by us. We can also follow our correspondence with them so that they understand our ideas and the Olympic principles."[52] Ultimately, the IOC canceled the meeting in Nairobi, owing to Kenyan authorities' refusal to host members from South Africa and Rhodesia (as well as from the colonies of Angola and Mozambique, both of which remained under Portuguese overrule). After considerable controversy, the IOC moved the gathering to Baden-Baden, Germany, while the CIOA survived, eventually merging with the International Institute for the Development of NOCs in 1971 to form the Committee for Olympic Solidarity.

48   AFRICA AND THE OLYMPICS

Diversifying the IOC: New Voices from the Continent

As the IOC directors continued to cautiously engage these emerging states, Africans were gradually gaining increased influence in the organization's affairs by joining the body as formal members. Although White delegates Reginald Honey from South Africa (elected 1946) and Reginald Alexander from Kenya (elected 1960) both continued to obdurately and, it must be said, anachronistically represent these two African nations, Alexander at least attempted to persuade the West and the IOC to respect the "New Africa." For example, writing to Brundage in 1963, Alexander lamented, "I am fully aware that there are older people, particularly in Europe, who must understandably be unable or unwilling to re-orientate their thinking with the New Africa, and see everything only through the tinted spectacles of disorder or revolution."[53]

Alexander's efforts aside, ongoing White representation of Black Africa in the IOC was inherently problematic, as it failed to reflect the seismic changes on the continent ushered in by decolonization. In response to this continued White representation, the IOC began to diversify its membership from the continent as increasing numbers of African states emerged from colonial rule. Indeed, by the mid-1960s new African members included Ahmed Eldermerdash Touny from Egypt (elected 1960), Hadj Mohammed Benjelloun from Morocco (elected 1961), Sir Ade Ademola from Nigeria (the first Black member of the ICO, elected 1963), and Mohamed Mzali from Tunisia (elected 1965). And prior to the end of the decade, they were joined by Dr. Abdel Mohamed Halim from Sudan (elected 1968), and Louis Guirandou-N'Diaye from Côte d'Ivoire (elected 1969). Although these new members weren't part of the organization's inner circle, their mere presence at the IOC table and their growing numbers signaled the further democratization of the Olympic body. Moreover, they collectively constituted an effective counterbalance to the longstanding support that the leadership of the IOC and Brundage in particular had openly expressed and exhibited toward South Africa.

Long-Distance Success as a Generator of National Pride

In the 1950s both colonized and independent African nations sent delegations to compete in the Olympic Games, though without

African Colonies and Newly Independent Countries at the Olympic Games   49

securing any medals, even though both the participating individuals and teams were becoming increasingly competitive. These African competitors were hindered by a general lack of skilled coaching and other contributory resources, and the relatively small size of their Olympic contingents further reduced their odds of medaling. Yet the 1960 Olympic Games would dramatically feature athletes from the continent mounting the steps of the medal podiums, owing to the accomplishments of a handful of long- and middle-distance runners. These feats would extend to the ensuing Olympic Games in Tokyo in 1964 and on to Mexico City in 1968, granting Africa the sporting respect it had been chasing since it began participating in these contests. More specifically, this sustained success earned East Africa the reputation it still enjoys as the cradle of elite distance runners.

These Olympic achievements in turn generated much-needed pride across the continent, especially as African countries had been struggling in a variety of ways during the early years of their sovereignty. Indeed, as David B. Kanin has argued, "Upon achieving independence, African states found that they could compete more successfully in the Olympic Games than in the struggle for resources and power."[54] Consequently, successful Olympic athletes were often deified and charged with helping to cultivate national esteem, unity, and identity among populations that were often short on confidence as they tried to develop under incredibly trying and disadvantageous circumstances. As such, by the end of the 1960s, these distance runners had become symbols of the continent's significant potential and resolute determination. These individuals, as Baker argues, were highly visible, but "even more than political heroes, they represented a kind of success that was ostensibly within reach of vast numbers of young Africans. In the world at large, they served as unofficial ambassadors. . . . What cultural ambassadors and African representatives to the U.N. attempted, these athletes achieved with apparent ease: publicizing an image of strength and success rather than poverty and instability."[55]

Ethiopia: The Eventful Life of Abebe Bikila

The first and arguably most famous of these landmark Olympic victories came in the marathon at the 1960 Rome Games. In this event,

FIGURE 1.2. Abebe Bikila and Ben Abdesselam Rhadi competing in the 1960 Olympic marathon in Rome, Italy. Smith Archive / Alamy Stock Photo

Ethiopian runner Abebe Bikila ran barefoot through the streets of the Italian capital in what was then record time (2:15:16) to claim the first gold medal for a predominately Black African nation (fig. 1.2). Trailing Bikila to claim the silver medal was Ben Abdesselam Rhadi of Morocco. In fact, four of the top eight finishers in the event were African.

Upon returning home Ethiopian emperor Haile Selassie praised the Olympian's role in promoting the country on the global stage. "We are pleased that you [Bikila] have proven to the world that sports are not a new phenomenon to Ethiopia.... We are definitely pleased to see today the first fruit of the sports organization that we started during our reign. Finding ourselves international victors in such a sport ... makes Ethiopia even more worthy of international recognition. With your achievements serving as a trailblazer, the door has now been opened for future generations to follow in your footsteps."[56] Even more broadly and boldly, Robert Parienté, at the time a writer for the French sports newspaper L'Equipe, wrote that Bikila's success in Rome marked "the emergence of Africa."[57] Bikila's

African Colonies and Newly Independent Countries at the Olympic Games   51

victory was also especially symbolically important, as Ethiopia had previously been violently invaded and colonized by Italy, so the victory in the ancient capital of the former colonial master suggested that the power dynamic between the two nations, at least in the realm of Olympic sport, had irreversibly shifted.

In the aftermath of 1960 Games, Bikila naturally enjoyed elevated status in Ethiopia, but an unexpected political development underscored just how important he had become to the nation. During a failed coup d'état in December of 1960 while Selassie was abroad, Bikila had refused orders issued by the coup leaders orders to execute Ethiopian royals. His demonstrated loyalty notwithstanding, when order was restored, Bikila was arrested and at least questioned, if not worse, for his suspected role in the attempted overthrow of the government.[58] Emperor Selassie's eventual conviction that the star athlete was indeed innocent, coupled with international support for the marathoner—which included pleas from the IOC—ultimately saved his life. Selassie's alleged words upon articulating his mercy signal how important the Olympic champion had become to the nation and how this popularity—and the sporting success on which it was predicated—had helped to protect Bikila.

> We could hang you! We should feed you to the lions! You have dared to defy us. . . . We have given you everything: your position, your very existence—and you have betrayed us! Did you want power for yourself? Is that it? . . . Did your victory in the race go to your head? Did it make you insane? We have decided not to kill you. You are the one they [the Ethiopian public] want now. You are the one they admire in the market. You are like a god to them now. They have heard of your deed and they are amazed. You have beaten all the Whites, all the colonialists, and you are their hero. I suppose we should be grateful that you are too simple to understand what this means. Well, hear this: as long as you run, Ethiopia shall not fall! As long as you run, as long as you win medals, we shall rule![59]

Perhaps inspired by Selassie's rousing harangue, some four years later, Bikila repeated his earlier feat, winning gold in the same event at the 1964 Tokyo Games and again in record time. In fact, this was the first time an Olympic gold-medal winner in the marathon had successfully defended their title. In response, Selassie promoted Bikila to lieutenant in the Ethiopian army (following his 1960 victory, he had also been promoted, which the runner described as "a great thing, greater for me than winning the Olympics").[60]

In practice, this connection between successful athletes from Africa and the military was, for a variety of reasons, reasonably common. As Baker explains, "An overwhelming number of Africa's Olympic victors . . . came from the ranks of police and army forces . . . especially in the early days of independence, as African school and university facilities were woefully inadequate, while police and army organizations provided athletic equipment as well as regular pay and a consistent emphasis on physical fitness."[61] Reaffirming this link between sports and the military, Bikila's superior officer, a colonel, was newly tasked with coordinating the running icon's schedule so that he could be utilized as a "national asset." As one observer noted regarding Bikila's stature within, and his importance to, the Ethiopian nation, "Only the emperor claimed higher status among his countrymen."[62]

Tragically, Bikila was not to serve as a "national asset" for long. Injuries precluded him from finishing the marathon at the 1968 Olympic Games in Mexico City, and a devastating car accident in March 1969 relegated him to a wheelchair for the remainder of his life. Following the crash, Selassie declared to Bikila, "We have decided to make you Ambassador for Sport. We want you to travel to schools and to meetings at home and abroad. We want you to remind them that we are not inferior when it comes to sport. Your example will serve to show them that Ethiopia can catch up and surpass."[63] Although Bikila dutifully and enthusiastically fulfilled this newly assigned role over the ensuing years, on October 25, 1973, at the age of forty-one, he died from a cerebral hemorrhage, a direct complication from the car crash. Subsequently, the Ethiopian government announced a national day of mourning and gave Bikila a state funeral, while the former champion was eulogized across Africa. These testaments emanating domestically and from abroad confirmed Bikila's importance, both within the nation and throughout the continent.

African Colonies and Newly Independent Countries at the Olympic Games   53

Kenya: Fostering National Unity through Olympic Success

If Bikila energized an entire nation and generated pride in both Ethiopia and, more broadly, throughout the continent, so too did an assortment of long-distance runners hailing from Kenya in the 1960s. Today it's well known that this East African nation produces seemingly endless numbers of elite middle- and long-distance runners, but in the 1960s these athletes were just beginning to emerge on the global running landscape. By the conclusion of the decade, though, they were firmly planted in the minds of track fans, practitioners, and officials from around the world.

Although Kenya had competed in three Olympics prior to its independence in 1963, the first Games it participated in as a sovereign nation was the ensuing year in Tokyo. The significance of this participation went well beyond the sphere of athletics, as the Games in Japan constituted an opportunity for the newly independent state to present itself to the world as it took its seat at the Olympic table. Indeed, prior to the team's departure for Tokyo, Jomo Kenyatta, Kenya's first leader (1963–78), addressed the athletes and stressed the magnitude of the occasion. "For the first time, Kenya is going to participate in the Olympic Games as a free and independent nation. I am confident that our team will demonstrate to the world through their performance that the Government and people of Kenya regard social, physical, and cultural advancement as of utmost importance. We want to show that our model of *Harambee* [the Kenyan concept of coming together as one] can be applied to sport, that people of all creeds and colors can pull together. We want Kenya to be an example to the rest of the world."[64]

Despite Kenyatta's inspirational speech, the thirty-seven Kenyan athletes who went to Tokyo won only a single medal at the 1964 Games: Wilson Kiprugut's bronze in the men's 800 meters. This inauspicious start notwithstanding, Olympic success proved less elusive going forward, in large part owing to a pioneering track coach, John Velzian, a British expatriate who had arrived in Kenya well before independence and had been asked to stay on by the new government. Among other divergences with long-standing practices and beliefs, Velzian stressed that racial divisions should no longer

54   AFRICA AND THE OLYMPICS

be regarded and that Kenyan runners did not have to be materially enticed to strive for success. In a 1966 interview Velzian explained:

> The reason it has taken so long for Kenya to come through in athletics is that Kenya was a colony and sport was run by a colonial sports department. Sport was organized for the African, the Asian and the Arab, but there was no integration.... When an African won, you rewarded him with something useful or, the belief was, he would not run at all. When I suggested that the African was capable of running for the pure amateur love of it and would work hard to achieve, I was held up to ridicule.... Oh, yes, I was. To dare suggest that the African athlete would work for the intrinsic value of sport—that was unthinkable. I spent my first four years trying to break down this colonial attitude, and I succeeded. The willingness of the African to compete and to work for the glory of it is now established.... All over the country now there are athletes who go out and train regularly for the sheer joy of training and the knowledge that possibly one day they will represent Kenya. Before independence, they could not have cared less about representing their country.[65]

Employing these novel approaches, Velzian helped to further decolonize Kenyan sport, a process that would continue in the coming years as the team hurdled toward the 1968 Olympic Games.

By the time the Mexico City Games began, the Kenyans were no longer unknowns. Since Tokyo, Kenyan runners, including most prominently Kipchoge "Kip" Keino, had been winning races around the world and breaking records in the process and, thereby, attracting significant attention. That the Kenyans were formidable competitors was now clear to everyone, even to England's Queen Elizabeth, who astonishingly mentioned Keino in a Christmas message to the Commonwealth during this period. Writing in *Sports Illustrated* on the eve of the Mexico City Games, John Underwood outlined the rapid ascendence of Kenya's runners: "Two years ago, and through last year, the runners of Kenya were the talk of the footracing world.

They were a new kind of emerging force in Africa—something tangible out of the new social order. Neither well trained nor well equipped by Western standards, with little to go on but their willing (and often bare) feet, they produced, in the remarkably short time since independence in 1963, a platoon of runners who were capable of giving world-class opponents a case of the discouragements."[66]

Despite the mounting international hype, the immediate buildup to Mexico City 1968 had hardly been encouraging. Some of the elite Kenyan runners were underperforming, and prior to the commencement of the Games, the government had sacked Velzian, replacing him with his assistant coach, a Kenyan. Ironically, the ousted British coach was most likely a casualty of the very decolonization process within Kenyan athletics that he had helped to start. Regardless, by the time the Games began, the Kenyans were ready. It was in Mexico City that Keino confirmed his status as one of the world's greatest, winning the men's 1,500 meters in a contest that teammate Ben Jipcho, who had helped to facilitate Keino's victory by setting the pace, described as "good for Kenya." Keino also earned the silver medal in the men's 5,000-meter race. By the conclusion of the Games on October 27, of the sixteen total medals won by Africans, Kenyans had secured nine of them, all in track events. More broadly, Kenya's elite runners, including Keino, Naftali Temu, and Amos Biwott, had contributed to Africa's sweep of every men's running event over 800 meters.

This on-track success also paid dividends away from the medal podium back in Kenya. As Kanin has contended, "Perhaps the most successful use of sport in Africa for purposes of national orientation has come in Kenya. . . . Kip Keino helped his countrymen say with pride, 'I am Kenyan,' a notable victory for a government seeking to displace more traditional forms of political affiliation," which were largely ethnically dictated.[67] In particular, as many of Kenya's social and political fault lines were (and continue to be) ethnically based, the transcendent reaction to Keino's performances was extremely encouraging for a nation in need of unifying developments.

Upon returning home, the athletes were greeted as heroes. Keino, for example, received the Distinguished Service Medal from

FIGURE 1.3. The shoes Kip Keino wore in his gold-medal performance in the 3,000-meter steeplechase at the 1972 Munich Games, on display at the Olympic Museum.

Jomo Kenyatta and was elevated to elder status—a prestigious and privileged classification—within his ethnic Nandi community. Kenyan running success in ensuing Olympic Games continued, prompting Ramadhan Ali to assert in the mid-1970s, "With these performances, Kenyans have generated immense enthusiasm, self-confidence, and national pride.... Kenya is the most track-conscious nation in Africa today."[68] And this success persisted: across the forty years that followed the 1968 Mexico City Games, Kenyan distance runners won 39 out of a possible 120 Olympic medals in races of 1,500 meters or more.[69] And the sport remains as vital to national identity as ever. For example, an image of a long-distance runner appears on the back of the country's twenty-shilling note. Similarly, amidst the ethnically based unrest in Kenya that threatened the running community in 2008 during the buildup to that year's Games in Beijing, *Sports Illustrated* writer Richard Demak reminded us that "this is a country whose international identity is inextricably tied to athletic achievement."[70] Perhaps even more profoundly, elite Kenyan marathoner Moses Tanui has remarked that "without these athletes, Kenya would be like any other country that nobody knows in the world."[71]

Whether African athletes were competing as members of NOCs that represented colonized African nations or as independent states, their presence at the Olympic Games instilled pride and fostered national unity and identity among domestic populations. When these competitors began winning Olympic medals, their contributions to these processes also transcended national borders, positively affecting communities across the continent.

In fact, these athletes' mere participation facilitated their inclusion in an emerging global sports community that, in turn, expeditiously bestowed the range of fledgling African countries with the type of international credibility they sought. As Skinner has argued regarding this array of benefits that participation in the Games generated for African states, "International sporting competition is a forum for diplomacy, a potent force in nation building, and a means of gaining access to international institutions."[72]

Meanwhile, the Olympics were also contemporaneously offering African nations another opportunity to "win away from the podium" by using the Games and, more broadly, the Olympic Movement to successfully isolate the apartheid regime in South Africa. Eventually, owing in great part to the solidarity that these countries maintained and the incredible persistence that a core group of African activists displayed, this sportive isolation of South Africa transitioned into an outright ban from the Olympic Games and, ultimately, to an expulsion from the IOC. It is to these developments that the book turns in the ensuing chapter.

2

Isolating Racism

African Contributions to South Africa's Olympic Ban

We will not rest content until there is fairplay [sic] for all South Africans and the Olympic Charter is faithfully observed by all national sporting bodies in our country.

> —Dennis Brutus, South African activist, in a letter to Avery Brundage, November 12, 1961

It is in the sphere of sports, the arts, and culture that South Africa can be made to feel the full weight of international moral indignation against apartheid. . . . It is a cynical act of hypocrisy even to suggest that they will march under the same flag and sing the same National Anthem when they [Black and White South African Olympians] are prohibited from doing so inside South Africa. The test of whether there is race discrimination or not against the black people in South African sport can only be demonstrated by what happens inside South Africa. . . . We are paying a very heavy price for apartheid; our only crime is that we were born black.

> —Press release issued by the African National Congress, whose members fought to end apartheid, in anticipation of South Africa's readmission to the Olympic Movement owing to the country's promise to generate a multiracial squad for the Mexico City Games, January 1968

In 1948 the Nationalist Party won the South African elections, and by the following year the new government had begun enacting legislation that, predicated on its apartheid platform, acutely discriminated against non-Whites. Racially discriminatory policies were certainly nothing new in South Africa—White residents had for centuries been engineering society in their overwhelming economic, social, and political favor—but the apartheid statutes were much more invasive, extensive, and severe than anything that had preceded them. Of course, oppressive control of Black Africans by White minority regimes was standard across the continent at this time, as virtually every space on the African map was the colonial territory of one or another European imperial power until the 1960s. But as African nations steadily gained their independence, apartheid became increasingly anachronistic, and South Africa consequently came under heightened scrutiny internationally, even though it could continue to rely on its Cold War ally, the United States, owing to the regime's staunch anti-Communist stance. Undeterred by America's avowed support, by the 1950s an array of domestic and international organizations and activists had identified sport as a site of vulnerability for the regime and consequently applied unrelenting, intense pressure in this area. Most notably, FIFA, the world's governing body for soccer, banned South Africa in 1963, and by the following year, the International Olympic Committee (IOC) had withdrawn the country's invitation to the 1964 Games in Tokyo. Ultimately, the sports boycotts and bans of South Africa, as Scarlett Cornelissen has argued, "had much earlier origins and were, in some regards, more efficiently organized, and held more immediate consequences for the apartheid regime than later forms of [economic and political] sanctions against the country."[1]

These measures to isolate, ban, and ultimately expel South Africa from the international sports firmament would not have come to fruition without the tireless efforts of a number of African and international officials and activists over a period that eventually spanned three decades. Arguably, the most important entity in this broad alliance struggling to exclude South Africa from the Olympic Games was the South African Non-Racial Olympic Committee, or

SANROC. The organization began operations within the country, but its founding members, including the aforementioned Dennis Brutus, were eventually forced into exile in London, where they resumed their activities while also coordinating their efforts with other anti-apartheid groups. As Skinner has explained, "Sport became a political resource for the many groups fighting against apartheid, and the egalitarian claims deeply embedded in sporting discourse became an important tool for those pressing for reform."[2] The resolve of African IOC members, activists, and politicians from across the continent was also vital to these broader efforts. In practice, all these anti-apartheid campaigners faced considerable opposition from within the IOC, as plenty of the body's members, including Avery Brundage, viewed the South African regime empathetically. Although the Olympic Charter explicitly forbade racial discrimination and exclusion in both National Olympic Committees (NOCs) and Olympic squads, these IOC officials instead focused their energies on condemning Black Africa for bringing politics into sports, thereby sullying the alleged, pristine divide between them; of course, this discreteness never existed. Over time, though, even this strategy lost any efficacy it might have had, as South Africa's growing international isolation precluded the possibility of the IOC reinstating the pariah nation. Not until the aftermath of Nelson Mandela's release from prison in 1990 and the dismantlement of apartheid in the ensuing years would South Africa be invited back into the Olympic Movement, just in time for the 1992 Barcelona Games.

Even after the Olympic ban of the country in 1964, these restrictive efforts persisted for another two-and-a-half decades, until the IOC approved South Africa's request to send a multiracial team to Barcelona. Throughout this struggle, sporting isolation served as a proxy for the broader, global condemnation of apartheid, which over time circumscribed the ability of White South Africans to engage with the international community in any fashion. As SANROC activist Dennis Brutus declared, "If you hit the South Africans on international sport, you are going to get the message across that white South Africans are not welcome in the world as long as they practice racism in sport."[3] The protracted, arduous journey to isolate

South Africa was marked by numerous setbacks and impediments, including the fact that there were numerous IOC members who viewed the apartheid regime's cause favorably. Yet the unity and resolve of the individuals and organizations that tirelessly campaigned to ban South Africa from the Olympics and sustain this exclusion ultimately proved to be irrepressible.

Apartheid and Its Initial Impact on South African Sport

Although South African legislators wasted little time enacting racially discriminatory legislation following the Nationalist Party's electoral victory in 1948, sport in the country wasn't officially segregated until June 1956. In many respects it's surprising that it took the regime that long to apply apartheid policy to sport. Indeed, South Africa—and in particular its White population—is acutely sport conscious. Joan Brickhill has described this profound, durable, almost intrinsic regard as follows:

> For the white minority, ensconced in economic privilege and political power, leisure is not an occasional indulgence or a wished-for luxury, but a part of daily life. And in a country with the ideal climate for outdoor activity, sport is the natural occupation for leisure time . . . and has an exceptional importance for white South Africans. It is both the principal means of filling the idle hours, and, more deeply, the expression of white power and physical dominance. . . . Defeat in the sports field is treated as a national humiliation for the whites, success confirms their world view of the master race, their heroic image of themselves, and justifies to themselves the position of superiority they claim and hold.[4]

Prior to the enaction of the assortment of racially motivated sports legislation, only a single sports federation existed for the entire country: the South African Olympic and Commonwealth Games Association (SAOCGA)—changed to the South African Olympic and National Games Association (SAONGA) in 1961 when the country left the British Commonwealth—which was a Whites-only entity. The organization had permitted interracial sporting competitions prior to 1956 but newly prohibited them once the apartheid framework had been applied to the sports arena while also forbidding non-Whites from representing the country in international competitions. South African sport was finally, safely within the apartheid fold.

Yet South African officials continued to try to convince the world otherwise, and with some success. Reginald Honey, for example, the South African IOC member speaking at the fifty-fifth session of the IOC in Munich, Germany, in May 1959, disingenuously declared, "No objection exists in my country to non-white athletes participating in the Olympic Games as long as they have an international or Olympic standing. . . . Should a champion be discovered in my country, it is most certain that he would belong to the Olympic team of South Africa."[5] Of course, in practice, it was impossible for any non-White athlete to secure "international or Olympic standing," considering that they had no access to competitions at which they could have earned either status. But when India's IOC member at the Munich gathering retorted, "The mere fact that they [non-White athletes] are allowed to compete only amongst themselves is a sure sign of discrimination," Avery Brundage objected, stating, "We must take the assurances given to us by Mr. Honey just now into account. Our only course is to accept the promises given to us."[6]

In response to the ongoing racial discrimination within sport in South Africa, which the IOC appeared to be openly sanctioning, Dennis Brutus, who was of mixed racial heritage, and the famous White anti-apartheid author Alan Paton, cofounded the South African Sports Association (SASA) in 1959, the precursor to SANROC. SASA's stated objectives were to "co-ordinate non-white sport . . . to see that non-white sportspersons and their organizations secure[d] proper recognition [in South Africa] and abroad, and to do this on a non-racial basis."[7]

Initially, SASA officials pleaded their case domestically, requesting that SAOCGA offer "fair and equal membership to all South Africans." However, they also threatened to pursue their grievances with the IOC, which could potentially jeopardize South Africa's ability to compete in the Olympic Games.[8] On May 5, 1959, SASA sent a memorandum to the IOC that described aspects of South African sport, "including

Isolating Racism

its development, structure, and organization, with the aim of convincing the IOC to apply pressure on SAOCGA to dismantle its racialist constitution."[9] Yet a SASA circular, also from that year, declared that the organization's mission was solely to achieve racial equality in sport, not to pursue punitive measures against South Africa's White athletes: "SASA must make it clear that we do not wish to see any South African barred from the Olympics next year [the 1960 Rome Olympics]. We simply desire to see all South Africans being given a fair chance to compete on merit and ability."[10] In response, the SAOCGA directors hid behind government policy—as would officials from the other all-White sports bodies in the country going forward—claiming that they were simply adhering to the regime's statutes, which had been imposed on them. Cheryl Roberts describes the organization's justification as follows: "SAOCGA blamed this situation on political conditions prevailing in the country, which were not the prerogative of the sports federations but of the Nationalist government. By presenting such an argument, SAOCGA effectively sheltered behind the racial structure of its affiliates which blocked the entrance of Black sports people into its membership ranks."[11] SAOCGA officials instead invited SASA to form a series of non-White sports entities that the former would both oversee and represent on an exclusively White administrative body.[12] Predictably, SASA rejected this proposal. The organization would now take its fight directly to the IOC.

Unfortunately for SASA, that meant engaging Avery Brundage. Throughout this period, his assertion that sport and politics don't mix went virtually unchallenged by the collection of compliant IOC members. Relatedly, he maintained that the South African issue was both internal and political in nature and thus was "inappropriate for the apolitical domain of sport."[13] The racism that undergirded these opinions was manifest in a letter Brundage sent to the IOC's secretary general, Otto Mayer, in the fall of 1959 on the occasion of SASA bringing its campaign to the IOC: "This man, [Dennis] Brutus, who is writing to us so frequently, is an Indian and not a negro, and probably more interested in politics than sport. Apparently, the most difficulty in relation to his complaints is caused by rivalry between the different negro tribes, the Indians and other Asians, and the half breeds."[14] In the letter, Brundage's insistence that sport and politics are absolutely discrete is clear; the fact that Brutus was neither Indian nor of Indian descent would not have troubled Brundage, as his condescension toward non-Whites of all types was also clear. Regardless of the IOC president's personal sentiments, Dennis Brutus, the alleged "Indian," would go on to become one of Brundage's most persistent irritants, ultimately helping to bring about an unprecedented ban on an IOC nation. But that development would have to wait, at least for a time.

1960–64: An Uncertain Success

Although the dawn of the 1960s constituted a time of hope for racial justice in the South African sporting realm for Dennis Brutus and others, by 1964 the country had been banned from the Olympic Games owing to its uncompromising commitment to racial segregation and discrimination. As outlined above, the IOC suspension was not the preferred outcome for most anti-apartheid activists. Instead, they had primarily been seeking racial inclusion in sport, rather than a punitive exclusion of South Africa from global sports circles. Regardless, the eventual Olympic ban was anything but inevitable. At many key moments during the dramatic years leading up to this outcome, African resolve was repeatedly tested and periodic setbacks—including Brutus's arrest—precipitated profound discouragement. Ultimately, though, shifting international racial and political sentiments toward apartheid, African activists' persistence and rules pertaining to discrimination laid out in the IOC's own charter collectively prompted the ban.

Although the IOC suspension would arrive prior to the halfway point of the decade, the 1960s did not start auspiciously for opponents of apartheid in South African sport. In April 1960, for example, police raided SASA's offices, as well as the homes of the organization's directors, seizing, among other items, a series of allegedly incriminating documents. The South African government also officially "banned" Brutus under the Suppression of Communism Act, which prohibited him from meeting with more than one other person outside his family—in public or even in his own home—thereby precluding him from participating in sports-related meetings or gatherings. As the

Isolating Racism 65

authorities deemed some of the seized documents "subversive," the regime denied Brutus a passport when he applied to travel to the 1960 Olympic Games in Rome. Given the sheer volume of the apartheid state's array of suppressive actions and decisions, it's clear that the authorities were deeply concerned about this nascent nonracial sports movement. And this unease was merited, as SASA continued to pressure the IOC regarding the South African issue. Responding to this unremitting lobbying, at its June 1962 meeting in Moscow the IOC formally warned SAONGA, while the Indian delegation—with the backing of both Brazil and the USSR—called for South Africa's immediate suspension from the Olympic Movement. Ultimately, though, these outspoken critics of the apartheid regime could muster only five votes for the associated resolution. South Africa had again survived.

The Birth of SANROC

On October 7, 1962, SANROC replaced SASA, a move prompted by the frustration that frontline activists, including Brutus, had been experiencing owing to their lack of progress with the IOC and South Africa's NOC. This new multiracial organization, which claimed the support of some sixty thousand athletes opposed to racial bigotry in sports, launched a campaign that was decidedly more aggressive and escalated than SASA's had been.[15] SANROC was newly positioned as a nondiscriminatory rival to SAONGA, which by that time was more commonly referred to as SANOC (South African National Olympic Committee), with Brutus demanding the latter's expulsion from the IOC. As Douglas Booth has explained, "SANROC's objective was to expel SANOC from the Olympic Movement and, thus, it began a full-blooded campaign to destroy the racial structures in South African sport and to replace them with those consistent with Olympic principles."[16] Those structures included merit-based selection for teams and federations. Recalling the mood at the time, Chris de Broglio, an anti-apartheid activist and cofounder of SANROC, said, "The frustration . . . stiffened the determination of the leaders of non-racial sport to fight for the total abolition of racialism from South African sport. . . . It had become apparent that Black South Africans could not rely on the good offices of the white organizations for their international participation. It had become quite clear that the racial bodies would have to be forced into integration or face expulsion from the international organizations. This was the road traced for SANROC at its inaugural meeting in 1962."[17] Three months after the meeting, Dennis Brutus was named president of SANROC and its constitution, drafted in accordance with IOC guidelines, included the following pledge: "Above all, to ensure that the South African team to the Olympic Games in the future is selected without any influence of racial discrimination."[18]

With SANROC's goals firmly in place and its efforts focused, 1963 would deliver the most transformative developments, thus far, related to the apartheid regime's ongoing practice of racialism in sports and, correspondingly, the country's participation in the Olympic Games. Although SANROC was spearheading the international sportive campaign against South Africa, it was the East African nation of Kenya that would brazenly confront the IOC and ultimately refuse to back down.

Kenya on the Frontlines

After having endured decades of colonial overrule, in 1960 Kenyan and British representatives negotiated the end of imperial rule in the country, which they set for December 1963. Prior to the formal transition of power, though, on June 1, 1963, Jomo Kenyatta was named Kenya's first prime minister. This political development had major implications for the IOC, as its annual meeting was slated to be held in the Kenyan capital, Nairobi, during October 1963. In particular, Kenyan officials controlled who could cross the country's borders, even though it was still not yet a sovereign nation. Indeed, as Michelle Sikes explains, "The power to admit South African and Portuguese IOC delegates into Kenya rested not with the colony's British Governor, Malcolm MacDonald, who represented the last vestiges of formal colonial ties, but rather with the newly elected Prime Minister Jomo Kenyatta and his principal immigration office, Minister for Home Affairs, Jaramogi Oginga Odinga."[19] In this matter, Kenyan authorities coupled Portugal with South Africa, because the former still maintained colonies in Africa, refusing to grant independence to any of its five territories on the continent.[20]

Isolating Racism

Influencing the new Kenyan officials' decision was the formation, in May 1963, of the Organization of African Unity (OAU), initially composed of thirty-two independent states. The body tasked itself to, among other aims, promote African unity, respect and defend the sovereignty of African nations, and eradicate colonialism and White minority rule throughout the continent. Odinga attended the organization's foundational meeting in Addis Ababa, Ethiopia, as a representative of African territories still under imperial rule, including Kenya. At the gathering, European colonialism was roundly denounced, as were the White minority regimes in Rhodesia and South Africa. In turn, Odinga left Ethiopia "infused with the spirit of Addis," determined to "isolate and refuse contact with the practitioners of apartheid."[21] Inspired by the OAU, in July 1963 Kenyan government officials declared that delegates from Portugal and South Africa would be denied entry visas ahead of the October IOC meeting. This action complied with the OAU's decision that it would "boycott any conference in the world if South Africa or Portugal was present."[22] In fact, OAU members had already abandoned an International Labour Organisation conference in Geneva, walking out when the South African delegate rose to address the participants.

Although Africans throughout the continent applauded the decision to prohibit the Portuguese and South African delegates from attending the IOC meeting, within Kenya this decision was, perhaps surprisingly, somewhat controversial. Organizers had spent considerable time preparing for the event, tourism was expected to spike (over three hundred representatives from around the world were expected at the meeting, with many more visitors accompanying them), reservations and travel plans had long been solidified, and most significantly, the IOC event was poised to be the first on African soil south of the Sahara. As Sikes explains, though, Kenyan officials remained unconvinced by any of these arguments. "The fundamental principle of the Olympic movement—that no discrimination should be allowed against any country or person on grounds of race, religion, or politics—had yet to be recognized within Kenyan policy-making circles as a distinctive opportunity to hold the South African establishment to a higher standard. . . . [But] excluding South African and Portuguese delegates from high-profile events taking place in Kenya presented a low-stakes way to demonstrate pan-Africanist solidarity and burnish pro-liberation credentials. When the opportunity arose to rebuff Olympic officials representing the two offending nations, they seized it."[23]

Meanwhile, perhaps counterintuitively, African sports activists also pressed Kenyan officials to permit the South African representatives to travel to Nairobi. In practice, although nonracialist sports campaigners around the world, including these activists, uniformly sought the end of racial discrimination in South Africa, they often identified and pursued divergent means to achieve this shared objective. As Simon Stevens has observed elsewhere, "Opposing apartheid meant very different things for different people and served very different purposes."[24] In particular, these activists, including SANROC members, had very few opportunities to engage high-ranking South African sports officials. Moreover, Nairobi constituted a setting to do so safely, beyond the borders of the apartheid state. As such, they implored the Kenyans to lift the visa bans; unmoved by these entreaties, however, Kenyan officials steadfastly rejected them.

These officials' principled resolve notwithstanding, preventing IOC members from attending an annual meeting had, heretofore, been virtually unfathomable and was certainly unprecedented. Indeed, in the fifty-nine previous sessions, the host nation of an IOC meeting had never refused access to delegates. Commenting on this novel action, IOC chancellor Otto Mayer declared, arguably understatedly, "It is most regrettable."[25] Meanwhile, within Kenya, some officials feared IOC recrimination. Just as the IOC had suspended Indonesia, the host nation of the 1962 Asian Games, for excluding Taiwan and Israel from that event on political grounds, some Kenyan authorities were concerned that their own NOC might meet a similar fate, as both banished nations had deliberately and unambiguously mixed sports and politics. Moreover, these officials were keen not to jeopardize their country's inclusion in the 1964 Games in Tokyo, which were poised to be the first Olympics in which an independent Kenya would participate.

Although there is no evidence that Brundage and other highranking IOC officials ever seriously contemplated this type of retaliatory

Isolating Racism 69

measure, Kenyan officials preemptively declared that they would call on all independent African nations to boycott the 1964 Olympic Games should their country be suspended from the Olympic Movement. This threat reverberated across the continent, appearing on the front pages of newspapers in numerous countries, with associated commentary in support of, or railing against, this proclamation. Naturally, South African editorialists were particularly, predictably vocal.

Confronted with the prospect of an Olympic boycott, as mentioned in the previous chapter, the IOC ultimately opted to relocate the meeting to Baden-Baden, in West Germany. With this maneuver, the IOC avoided direct confrontation with the Kenyan government and, by extension, the independent nations of Africa, which strongly supported the decision to deny entry to the Portuguese and South African members and were seemingly in solidarity with Kenya regarding a possible boycott of the 1964 Games.

Victimization-cum-Celebration: Dennis Brutus and the Olympic Ban

Around the same time that these dramatic events were unfolding in Kenya, a related series of developments, in this case regarding Dennis Brutus, was playing out across Southern Africa. In May 1963 Brutus was arrested in South Africa for violating his "banning"; ironically, he did so in order to meet with an IOC official. Brutus was subsequently sentenced to jail time, but while out on bail he escaped house detention, initially fleeing to neighboring Eswatini (then known as Swaziland) on August 7, determined to eventually make his way to the IOC meeting in Baden-Baden. Unfortunately for Brutus, he was betrayed while there, so that when he attempted to enter Mozambique on September 13, he was apprehended by the Portuguese secret police, interrogated, and returned to South African custody. Upon arriving in downtown Johannesburg, he attempted to escape his armed guards, who promptly shot him as he ran away.[26] Bleeding, he waited as an ambulance arrived, but the medics refused to treat him as their services were reserved for Whites. Upon eventually recovering, Brutus was sentenced to sixteen months in the notorious Robben Island Prison, located on the eponymous island off the coast of Cape Town, where Nelson Mandela and so many

70 AFRICA AND THE OLYMPICS

other high-profile South African political dissidents were, over time, detained.

Meanwhile, Brutus's arrest and shooting had prompted both domestic and international condemnation. The South African newspaper, the *Rand Daily Mail*, which often featured content critical of the apartheid regime, declared, "He is not some faceless petty offender whose escape happened to fail. He is the head of an organization that has been working for the elimination of racialism in South African sport."[27] The violence inflicted upon Brutus notwithstanding, there was a silver lining associated with his unenviable plight. As historian Matthew Llewellyn explains, "Ironically, as Brutus lay incarcerated, white South African sport suffered its most debilitating blow. Likely influenced by the fallout from Brutus's capture, shooting, and imprisonment, the IOC voted in January 1964 to rescind white South Africa's invitation to compete in the forthcoming Tokyo Olympics."[28] Brutus himself similarly confirmed the impact that his arrest and shooting had had on the IOC's verdict: "The mere impact of the bullet which had been fired into me, and the publicity surrounding the event and the outcry at the United Nations, in Britain and elsewhere ... created a climate in which it was much easier for the IOC to take the kind of decision which it was most reluctant to take because so many of the Olympic committee countries were sympathetic to apartheid."[29] And regarding the moment he and the other Robben Island inmates learned that South Africa would be prevented from participating in the 1964 Tokyo Games, Brutus recalled, "It gave us great satisfaction. The cheering in the quadrangle ... where we were breaking stones, must have deafened the guards."[30]

Even after suspending South Africa, though, the IOC left the door open for its return. For example, at the sixty-first session of the IOC, in Innsbruck, Austria, held in late January 1964, the Marquess of Exeter delivered encouraging words to the South Africans, offering them a path forward: "The SAOC [South African Olympic Committee] must openly and officially declare itself to be against apartheid in sport and to be the champions of Olympic ideals among its people. Even if it [the SAOC] was not entirely successful, its effort in this direction would be noted."[31] At the same meeting, the

Isolating Racism

president of the SAOC, Frank Braun, said, "I will do my best to satisfy the demands of the IOC before the closing date for entries for the Tokyo Games," suggesting that an avenue to full readmission did indeed exist.[32] Yet far removed from Innsbruck, the apartheid regime remained defiant, declaring that it would not be bullied by the IOC into altering domestic policies, no matter how much the international athletic suspension smarted. In particular, the regime announced, "The South African custom, which is traditional, finds expression in the policy that there should be no competition in sport between the races within our borders, and that the mixing of races in teams taking part in sports within South Africa and abroad will be avoided."[33] In many ways, this recalcitrant language reflected the country's dire, if entirely self-inflicted, position: operating fully outside of the Olympic Movement while faced with the impossible task of reconciling apartheid with the Olympic Charter in order to gain reentry. But that didn't mean that it stopped trying.

Despite this resoluteness, events within South Africa, coupled with transformative global developments, rendered the regime's efforts to be readmitted to the IOC less likely to succeed with each passing year. By the mid-1960s, criticism of the apartheid state regarding its discriminatory sporting policies did not come only from SANROC. Indeed, politicians and sporting officials across Africa, and around the world, increasingly articulated their concerns and, subsequently, acted upon them. This international condemnation of South Africa can be traced back to the Sharpeville massacre in March 1960, during which police fired on thousands of unarmed Black protestors, killing 69 and injuring 180. In turn, this tragedy prompted international scrutiny of racial violence in the country and offered nations, including the United States, space to criticize the regime, even if the administrations in Washington and Pretoria remained Cold War allies, united in the fight against the alleged scourge of Communism. Even more importantly, the array of newly independent African states began to coalesce around the anti-apartheid movement. As Cornelissen explains:

> A coalition of Developing World states emerged that shared, to begin with, few common objectives beyond the desire for

self-determination and the rhetoric of anti-imperialism. By the mid-1960s, however, this coalition had become better organized, more focused, and rallied around specific causes, one of which was the issue of apartheid South Africa's membership in the Olympic movement. Their lobbying and coordination of protest with other Communist and, later, Western allies to expel the country from the Olympic body constituted one of the earliest and most protracted advocacy networks that fed into the wider anti-apartheid movement.[34]

For some individuals in these networks, South Africa's IOC suspension didn't go far enough. Indeed, African IOC members and NOCs further protested the ongoing presence of South Africa's representative, Reginald Honey, at the organization's meetings. Eventually, these objections prompted the IOC to bar any member(s) of sanctioned countries from attending its assemblies. Commenting collectively on this meeting proscription, the broader ban on South Africa from participating in the Olympic Games, and the mounting anti-apartheid pressure applied by African and other nations, Rudolph W. L. Opperman, who would become the president of the country's NOC in 1971, described this grim period as "the years in the cold."

1965–68: Competing Efforts to Maintain and Repeal the Ban

This metaphorical frigidness notwithstanding, periodic thaws elevated the South African regime's hopes of returning to the Olympic Games. The first of these optimistic moments arrived in May 1967 when SANOC announced at the IOC meeting in Tehran that the South African government had agreed to the formation of a multiracial NOC. It's unclear if this decision was made because of or in spite of the presence of SANROC at the gathering, where it was lobbying IOC representatives in the hopes of securing a permanent expulsion of South Africa from the Olympic Movement.[35] Regardless, even Brutus was impressed with the regime's proclamation that it would racially diversify its NOC. He would later recall, "My first reaction on reading the concessions was that they were really quite spectacular. Compared to South Africa's previous position, they represented a real advance."[36]

Isolating Racism

In response, Brundage, who was always looking for an opportunity to readmit South Africa into the Olympic club, committed the IOC to form a commission that would travel to the nation to assess the regime's sincerity to remove sport from its stable of apartheid policies. It was eventually determined that this evaluative team would visit the country for ten days in September 1967 and subsequently issue a report predicated on their findings. Regarding the composition of the commission, Brundage was determined that it include a representative from Black Africa and thus wrote to the Nigerian IOC member Sir Adetokunbo Ademola to encourage him to participate, well aware of how the mission would be perceived if there was not at least one Black member of the delegation: "Your presence on the commission cannot be criticized by anyone.... If you are not on the commission, however, there may be criticism of the fact that the black African countries are not represented. Unfortunately, Amadou Barry, from Senegal, does not speak English and, therefore, his contacts in South Africa would be limited."[37] Brundage was surely relieved when he received Ademola's prompt, affirmative reply, though the Nigerian did express concerns related to possible difficulties while in South Africa:

> I am willing to serve on the delegation to South Africa, but I must confess I share the views of my government that considering my position as the Chief Justice of Nigeria should anything untoward happen as a result of the behavior of the South African Government (or any South African) to me when I am in that country, it will cause a great embarrassment to Nigeria. I should hate to be the center of any dispute which is likely to spark off any bitterness in race relations between Africans (black) and the whites.... Somehow, I have not the necessary confidence in the South African Government.... All I can say at present is that with further and better assurances and undertaking that they will guard against anything unseemly or improper during our visit, I will (subject to my government's consent) join the delegation.[38]

By assenting to serve on the commission, Ademola would join fellow IOC members Lord Killanin of Ireland and Reginald Alexander of

74 AFRICA AND THE OLYMPICS

Kenya (who openly favored South Africa's policy of racially segregating sport) on the investigative mission to South Africa.

With the composition of the evaluative team settled, Brundage next aimed to influence their eventual assessment by reemphasizing to them that, in the case of South Africa, the IOC was solely concerned with the allegedly toxic mixture of politics and sport. For example, in August 1967, prior to the departure of the commission, he had written to its members to stress,

> Our concern is with the [South African] National Olympic Committee and what it is doing to comply with Olympic regulations, especially Articles 24 and 25. We had an analogous situation in 1936, when most of the world condemned Naziism and many wanted to remove the Games from Berlin [Brundage decidedly had not]. Also, after the II World War many of those who were against Communism wanted to keep the Eastern Countries out of the Games. We must not become involved in political issues, nor permit the Olympic Games to be used as a tool or as a weapon for extraneous causes.[39]

Strategic Measures: African Efforts to Maintain the IOC Ban on South Africa

Following the formation of the IOC commission to South Africa, but prior to its departure, a series of influential developments further shaped the campaign against apartheid in sport. In December 1966 alone, the irrepressible Dennis Brutus, who had relocated from South Africa to London following his release from prison, newly reconstituted SANROC in the English capital, while in Bamako, Mali, representatives from thirty-two African nations gathered to form the Supreme Council for Sport in Africa (SCSA). Although the primary objective of the SCSA was to oversee and promote sport throughout the continent, the organization also worked to coordinate the assortment of African movements against apartheid in sport. To this end, at this inaugural meeting the SCSA passed the following resolution: "To obtain the expulsion of South African sports organizations from the Olympic Movement and from international federations should South African fail to comply fully with IOC rules."[40] Predictably,

Isolating Racism 75

Brundage wasn't particularly enthusiastic about this development and, in response, reinvoked his long-standing concerns about mixing sport and politics. As Cornelissen has explained, "Although Avery Brundage publicly supported the aims of the SCSA, he was mistrustful of the political motivations of the council. The incorporation in 1967 of the SCSA as the sport arm of the Organisation for African Unity (OAU)—thereby placing it under the control of African governments—further raised Brundage's suspicion of the body and led to long-term friction between the SCSA and the IOC."[41]

Regardless of whether SCSA officials were aware of the IOC president's sentiments, they raised the stakes at the organization's Second General Assembly meeting in December 1967 in Lagos, Nigeria. At the gathering, the secretary general of the SCSA, Jean-Claude Ganga, vowed, "If, in spite of South Africa's segregationist tendencies in sports, the IOC decides to readmit South Africa, we will withdraw from the world body."[42] This declared intention to leave the IOC, which would inherently preclude participation in the upcoming Mexico City Games, echoed calls for African solidarity against South Africa emanating from across the continent. For example, earlier that year André Hombessa, Congo-Brazzaville's minister of the interior, had asserted that "no matter what South Africa does to cover its apartheid policy, it will not be acceptable to African states." Likewise, the Tanzanian government issued a statement in May 1967, proclaiming, "As long as South Africa adheres to its principle of apartheid in sport, it cannot be allowed to take part in international tournaments. . . . Because South Africa insists on categorizing some sportsmen as human athletes and others as sub-human, she should not be allowed to pollute the Olympic atmosphere. . . . It must be hoped that other members will be persuaded to this line of thinking so that pressures against South Africa's obnoxious policy of apartheid may gain further momentum."[43] Despite these types of resolute avowals, during the SCSA meeting at the end of 1967 Brutus warned his colleagues that the IOC would lift the suspension on the South Africans and that "the commission's report would not keep them out" (fig. 2.1).[44]

Heeding Brutus's forewarning and sensing that the report might indeed constitute the first step toward South Africa's eventual readmission to the Olympic Movement, African sporting officials began

FIGURE 2.1. Dennis Brutus testifying before the UN in 1967 on behalf of SANROC.

openly urging countries to maintain their resolve regarding the eradication of apartheid in South African sport. For example, ahead of the May 1967 IOC meeting in Tehran, Ato Tessema, head of the Ethiopian Sports Confederation, warned that if South Africa was readmitted, Ethiopia would boycott the 1968 Mexico City Games. Tessema further predicted that every African nation would join Ethiopia, while Isaac Lugonzo, head of the Kenya National Sports Council, announced, "We must resist any pressure brought to bear to have South Africa readmitted to the Olympic Games until apartheid in sport in the Republic is broken 100 percent."[45]

Once assembled in Tehran, African officials maintained this campaign. Just prior to the opening of the IOC meeting, for example, African NOCs met to formally confirm their commitment to ending discrimination in sport in South Africa, passing the following motion: "The African NOCs are firmly resolved to use every means to obtain the expulsion of South African sports organizations from the Olympic Movement and from the International Federations,

Isolating Racism 77

should the NOC of this country fail to comply with the IOC rules. The African NOCs reserve their decision to participate in the 1968 Olympic Games in case the South African team would be allowed to participate in such Games without complying fully with the Olympic Charter, of which the IOC is the supreme guardian."[46]

The Return of South Africa? The IOC Moderates Its Stance

If these African sporting officials had hoped that Brutus's predictions would ultimately prove to be unwarranted and that the IOC's fact-finding mission to South Africa would, instead, reaffirm the righteousness of their cause, they were to be supremely disappointed. Circulated in early 1968, the delegation's 113-page report, informed by the commission members' discussions with over sixty sports officials representing the range of racial groups in South Africa, instead expressed hope that the apartheid government would be willing to meet the IOC's demands regarding racial equality in sport. Indeed, the report appeared to both "accept South Africa's contention that meaningful strides had been taken toward full compliance with IOC regulations and find credible South Africa's statement that the construction program for sports facilities for nonwhites was rapidly catching up with that for whites."[47] Moreover, the report was also dismissive of SANROC as a representative body for non-White athletes in South Africa. Most disconcerting, though, was the fact that the "optimism occasioned by this seeming crack in the wall of South African policy was based on a private conversation between Lord Killanin and South African Prime Minister B. J. Vorster" during the visit, at which Reginald Alexander and Adetokunbo Ademola were not present.[48] Opponents of apartheid across the continent were understandably distraught following the release of this surprisingly favorable, or at least encouraging, assessment of the sportive landscape in South Africa.

Perhaps emboldened by the commission's report, the IOC forged ahead, convinced that this evaluative account provided the cover that the body needed to readmit the South Africans. Consequently, a vote on the matter was set for the IOC's annual meeting in Grenoble, France, in mid-February 1968. In the meantime, Brundage continued to frame the South African issue as one that revolved

78   AFRICA AND THE OLYMPICS

solely around the intolerable intertwining of sports and politics. Yet
a series of scholars has posited alternative explanations for the IOC's
durable support for South Africa. John Hoberman, for example, has
identified the "prevalence of colonial thinking and racial attitudes, as
well as decades of predominately white self-recruitment (including
both Nazis and Nazi sympathizers), as explanations for the IOC's
firm loyalty to its white colleagues from South Africa and concom-
itant tolerance of their racial policies," while Matthew Llewellyn
has argued that "for Brundage and the IOC in particular, apartheid
appeared to be more of a political embarrassment than an intrinsic
moral concern."[49] Worryingly for the assortment of anti-apartheid
activists, these formidable sentiments within the IOC were increasingly subordinating dissenting opinions.

1968: A Tumultuous, Historic Year

On February 15, 1968, the IOC Congress voted thirty-six to twenty-
seven to conditionally readmit South Africa to the Olympic Movement.[50] Dennis Brutus's speculation had been accurate, after all.
Outrage from across the continent predictably ensued. The immediate response from the SCSA and countless African sports officials,
politicians, athletes, and citizens included a call to boycott the 1968
Mexico City Games, even as these nations were eager to demonstrate
their athletic prowess on the world stage. Ethiopia was the first to
announce its intent to withhold its athletes, followed by Algeria and
Uganda, and subsequently a host of other African nations, as well as
other countries from beyond the continent. Assuming an even more
extreme position, Kenyan officials declared not only their commitment to boycott Mexico City but also that a separate Olympic Games
for countries that withdrew from Mexico should be organized.

After various political and sporting officials had announced their
intentions, African athletes began weighing in. Roughly a week after
the IOC decision, for example, the famous Kenyan distance runner Kipchoge "Kip" Keino declared, "I'd prefer to give up all hope
of a medal than to have to run with [White] South Africans, who
regard my Black brothers and Coloured brothers as second-class
citizens."[51] Fellow countryman Jackson Mutala, the president of the

Kenyan Boxing Association, similarly opined, "What's the point of Kenya sending a side when other African nations are boycotting the Games? This would show a lack of sympathy with our South African brothers."[52] And the two-time defending champion in the marathon, Ethiopia's Abebe Bikila, offhandedly stated, "I'm in favor of the boycott, and if I can't win my third gold medal this year in Mexico City, then I'll do it in Munich in 1972."[53] Meanwhile, Dennis Brutus accused the IOC members of "betraying their own principles, in full knowledge of the policy of apartheid in South African sport," while the *New York Times* published this succinct, yet biting, commentary: "However you look at it, the IOC decision is a tremendous victory for the apartheid policy."[54]

Despite the considerable international discontent, South African officials were, somewhat surprisingly, largely ambivalent, rather than jubilant. Of particular concern to these governmental and sporting administrators was the series of conditions for readmission that its NOC had committed to satisfy. These concessions included forming an Olympic team without any racial consideration or discrimination (selected jointly by White and non-White officials), featuring a common flag and uniform, and enjoying joint travel and accommodation without racial separation. For strict proponents of apartheid, these mandates were both unpalatable and unacceptable, with some strident observers even claiming that these dispensational measures would mark the end of apartheid and thus the end of the (White) South African nation.

Boycott: The African Rebuttal to South Africa's Conditional Readmission

Seemingly the only person trumpeting the readmission of South Africa without any reservation was Avery Brundage. Speaking in a self-congratulatory manner in the aftermath of the vote, Brundage described it as "a great service performed by the IOC in aid of the Coloured athletes of South Africa" and further lauded the "transcendent triumph" of the Olympic Movement in this scenario.[55] But much to the IOC president's consternation, this victory would prove to be incredibly short-lived. On the heels of Brundage's remarks, the Executive Committee of the SCSA, whose members had gathered

80   AFRICA AND THE OLYMPICS

in Brazzaville on February 23, 1968, in the wake of the decision, announced the following day that thirty-two African countries were
poised to boycott the Mexico City Games. Moreover, the organizing
officials of the Mexico Games had sent a three-person delegation to
the Brazzaville congress to "assure the SCSA of Mexico's goodwill."[56]
Jean-Claude Ganga later described the extraordinarily far-reaching
impact that the Mexican government's overt support of the SCSA
had made:

> As soon as the decision of the SCSA's Executive Committee
> became known, statements began to flood in from all the Afri-
> can capitals. They were unanimous in ex-pressing their refusal
> to take part in the Olympic Games in Mexico City because of
> South African participation. The Mexican Government, for its
> part, declared in a particularly energetic statement that due to
> the implementation of a U.N. resolution prohibiting the grant-
> ing of visas to the holders of South African passports, Mexico
> would refuse entry visas to South African athletes. A number
> of Asian, Latin American and European countries immediately
> took a stance in support of the Africans and indicated to the
> IOC that they were withdrawing from the Games. The entire
> world was shaken by the shock wave of the bomb set off by
> the SCSA in Brazzaville. There were street demonstrations
> and meetings in Kenya, Nigeria, Uganda, and just about ev-
> erywhere else in Africa, to protest against the IOC's decision.[57]

In his closing speech to the SCSA's Executive Committee, André
Hombessa, a former president of the organization, warned that if
South Africa did indeed send any Black athletes, "they [would] be no
more than trained monkeys ... paraded in Mexico City and then sent
back to the jungle."[58] The day after the SCSA's boycott announcement, the Council of Ministers of the OAU voted in favor of this
measure for all member countries.

Meanwhile, on the other side of the Atlantic, a group of prominent African Americans had formed the Olympic Project for
Human Rights (OPHR) as a Black Power initiative. Participants
included Wilt Chamberlain, Kareem Abdul-Jabbar (then known

Isolating Racism 81

as Lew Alcindor), Jackie Robinson, Arthur Ashe, and the leader of the movement, San José State University sociology professor Harry Edwards. The latter had already endorsed a boycott of the Games by Black American athletes owing to enduring, systemic racial injustice in America—while the OPHR formally declared its support for the proposed African boycott. In turn, the chastened Brundage called for an extraordinary meeting of the IOC Executive Committee, which had been formally requested by the Soviet Union, in Lausanne on April 20 and 21, 1968. Regardless, the imperious IOC president continued to defiantly declare that the Mexico City Games would go on and that they *would definitely include* South Africa: "The Mexico Olympic Games will take place, even if I am the only spectator in the bleachers and South Africa the only country in the stadium, the Games will still go on."[59]

A Premature Celebration: The Re-Banishment of South Africa

By the time the IOC members gathered in Lausanne, the prevailing sentiment within the body had discernibly shifted. Collectively, the pressure that African nations had applied; the support that they had attracted; the volume of African and other countries that had pledged to boycott the Olympics; and the attendant loss of elite athletes, including Kenya's Kip Keino and Ethiopia's Abebe Bikila, the defending Olympic marathon champion, had clearly become more compelling to the IOC delegates than their recent justification to re-include South Africa. On the occasion, Ganga also directed a stirring speech to the IOC's Executive Committee in an effort to convince its members that a serious mistake had been made in Grenoble:

> Olympism is not merely a word on paper. Neither is it a multicolored flag to be displayed only outside one's own country. Olympism is a state of mind, which is experienced every day and the Games mark the end of an Olympiad, i.e., a four year period of friendship in sport. If the South African Blacks wish to take part in the Olympic Games, as some of you affirm, they must fulfill the conditions which are laid down. Indeed, we have no desire to see Black South Africans neatly dressed up like

the monkeys which are displayed at fairs and sent back to their cages as soon as the celebrations are over. They would serve as an attraction and nothing else. We know full well that some of you here would be satisfied with this type of masquerade, this sort of exhibition. However, we want to reassert forcefully that this is not in conformity with the Olympic spirit. As for those of you who accused the Africans of introducing politics into sport, we shall have the opportunity of proving to you that politics were part of international sport long before our time.[60]

By a vote of forty-seven to sixteen, with eight abstentions, the IOC newly banned South Africa from the Mexico City Games, prompting the country's invitation to be withdrawn. Ganga visibly celebrated with Constantin Andrianov, the IOC representative from the Soviet Union, while also expressing his intent to contact the group of African American activists to ask them to reconsider their position regarding a boycott of the Games. Conversely, the IOC's revised decision hit South Africans particularly hard. As Harry Blutstein has contended, "The greatest impact was psychological. White South Africans now saw that its apartheid policies could see it excluded from international competitions. Sport was important for cohesion within the country . . . playing international matches against other countries helped forge a national identity and build solidarity among the white nationalities—Anglo and Afrikaner—which otherwise differed in many ways."[61]

Yet there were also non-White South Africans who openly bemoaned the decision, seemingly believing that the apartheid regime had genuinely intended to field a multiracial team in Mexico. For example, Joseph Leserwane, an elite Black South African sprinter, lamented, "I was the saddest man in Africa when I heard the news. All of the strength left my legs and my heart went out of me."[62] Fred Thabede, a Black boxing official, similarly condemned the IOC's decision and, in particular, the central role that African nations had played in exacting it: "The African states know as well as any that for the past seven years South Africa's committee has been struggling to have an integrated team at the Olympics. And now what do these African states do? They slap us in the face in the most blatant showing of discrimination against our whites and nonwhites that I have ever seen."[63]

Although Thabede's frustration is understandable, no reasonable person should have considered sincere the South African regime's stated intentions given its unwavering dedication to apartheid in all aspects of life in the country. Commenting on South Africa's alleged commitment to racial equality in sport, which had initially facilitated its readmission to the IOC, South African exile R. Hlongwane provided an example of how the regime's disingenuousness would manifest itself: "The South African Olympic trials will not be fair if the black and white men do not compete against one another. If you have two lightweight champions, one black and one white, do you sniff at them to decide who goes? If so, you know who will go."[64]

1969–70: The Process of Expulsion

The reestablishment of South Africa's suspension from the Olympic Games undoubtedly constituted a significant accomplishment for African activists, politicians, and sports officials. However, the increasingly isolated nation had still been able to evade the ultimate punishment: expulsion. In order to avoid that fate, South African officials periodically indicated—albeit almost surely insincerely—that the country was willing to offer sporting concessions similar to those it was reputedly amenable to making in 1968.[65] Dismissing this recognizable artifice, Africans from across the continent remained united in their commitment to eliminate racial discrimination in South African sport, with the ultimate aim of ridding the continent of apartheid altogether. To this end, the SCSA maintained pressure on the IOC, as did individual African governments. For example, when Pretoria coordinated the (all-White) "South African Games" in 1969 as part of an effort to reaffirm and showcase its athletic legitimacy, the government of Kenya declared that, following the event, its "much sought-after runners would refuse to compete against any British athletes who participated in the tournament."[66] In response, the British ultimately hedged, withdrawing their official team from the "Games," but permitting individual athletes to travel to South Africa if they desired to participate. Ultimately, the South African

84 AFRICA AND THE OLYMPICS

Games were widely considered to have been a sporting and political failure, further damaging, rather than enhancing, the country's already marred international image.

Although the South Africans had survived, still only suspended rather than expelled, they would not be as fortunate the following year. In 1970 the SCSA declared that its member nations were newly poised to boycott the upcoming 1972 Olympic Games in Munich if South Africa wasn't fully removed from the IOC, demanding that this issue be taken up at the IOC's sixty-ninth annual session in May 1970 in Amsterdam. During the meeting, SCSA officials strategically employed one of the IOC's most frequently invoked defenses of South Africa, namely that politics and sports should not mix. In pursuing their case, Ganga and the Nigerian president of the SCSA, Abraham Ordia, argued in Amsterdam that "sport in South Africa has come under the absolute control of the government, which decides and regulates the policy of the South African NOC." Thus, they implored the IOC to "follow the actions of international sports federations that have already expelled South African sport federations."[67] Frank Braun, the president of South Africa's NOC, could only offer bluster and vitriol in response, perhaps trying to please his supervisors back home, knowing that the outcome of the impending vote was all but certain.

Irrespective of the international condemnation of apartheid, within the IOC's membership the racial and geographical composition still favored the South Africans, thereby injecting some uncertainty into the proceedings. Indeed, although many newly independent African and Asian nations entered the Olympic Movement during the 1960s, eventually composing 61 percent of the non-White member nations, their IOC representatives only possessed 33 percent of the voting power within the body by the end of that decade.[68] In order to maintain this level of control, eleven of the White nations—those with "long athletic traditions" so favored by the IOC—had two or more voting members, while many Black nations had none. In fact, of the NOCs without an IOC representative in 1970, only 12.4 percent were from White nations, while 87.6 percent were from non-White nations.[69] These disparities notwithstanding, ultimately the IOC did vote, thirty-five to twenty-eight, to expel the

South Africans. But it is important to note that the power within the organization was disproportionately wielded by the "traditional" White nations, with the votes reflecting this imbalance: 68 percent of these delegations voted in favor of South Africa while 98 percent of the non-White nations voted against the embattled nation.

Although the leaders of the SCSA, along with anti-apartheid organizations and activists around the world, celebrated the outcome of the IOC vote, Ordia quickly dampened these triumphant spirits via a sobering statement following the decision: "It is nothing to be happy about. They are Africans—they are my brothers. I want to compete with them. I want to invite them to Nigeria. I want to invite them to the Pan-African Games. But for God's sake, let them change. If this were the medicine that will let them live, then this will not be in vain."[70] Elsewhere, the IOC representative from Egypt wrote Brundage to express similar sentiments in the wake of the decision: "The victory at the Amsterdam Session was not an African one, rather it was an IOC one. We Africans are sorry to keep away some of our people from the Olympic Games; we would rather have welcomed recognitions of a Non-Racial Olympic Committee for South Africa that believes in and applies rules and regulations of Equity and Non-Racial policy in sports."[71] Meanwhile, Brundage, nearing the end of his extremely long IOC career, seemed resigned to these transformed sporting and political realities, writing to Ordia in June to congratulate him and, by extension, the SCSA: "My compliments on the manner in which you and Mr. Ganga presented your case in Amsterdam. It impressed the members of the IOC—and undoubtedly helped win approval for your point of view. Under your competent leadership, I am sure the Supreme Council [SCSA] will progress rapidly and successfully."[72] For opponents of the presence of apartheid in Olympic sport, the war against South Africa had finally been won, but similar battles against racial discrimination in subsequent Olympic Games were already looming.

The End of Apartheid, the Return to the Olympic Games

Over the decades that followed the IOC's decision in Amsterdam, every four years the Olympic Games served as a reminder to South Africans

86   AFRICA AND THE OLYMPICS

that the door to the international community of sporting nations remained firmly closed. The 1992 Games in Barcelona, however, finally presented an opportunity for reentry to the Olympic Movement. This potential readmission was only even conceivable because two years earlier the South African government had commuted the life sentence of Nelson Mandela, the iconic leader of the African National Congress (ANC), which had led the struggle against apartheid. The country's reformist president, Frederik Willem de Klerk, also unbanned political parties and, more broadly, gradually suspended the state's array of apartheid policies in an attempt to shed South Africa's pariah status. Responding to these seismic developments, IOC president Juan Antonio Samaranch's comments reflected a sanguinity that had long been dormant: "We were the first sports organization to close the door on South Africa, and we shall be very happy if we are the first to open it."[73] In the midst of this period of cautious optimism regarding the reforms that would eventually lead to the complete dismantlement of apartheid—yet still some time before the country's first democratic elections, which were slated for 1994—the prospect of rejoining the Olympic Movement in time for the 1992 Games began to materialize and steadily gained support.

Although 1990 was undoubtedly a momentous year in the history of South Africa, 1991 was arguably the most transformative year in the nation's Olympic history. In July of that year, the IOC formally recognized South Africa's newly constituted nonracial NOC, which would in turn pave the way for the country to participate in the 1992 Games—its first in thirty-two years—contingent on the government continuing to reform society and rescind apartheid laws and policies. Additionally, the IOC initiated an assortment of evaluative measures and processes, most of which were overseen by African members, regarding sport in the country that had to be satisfied before the body would permit a South African Olympic squad to emerge onto the field of the Estadi Olímpic Lluís Companys as part of the opening ceremony in Barcelona.

To South Africa, Again: The Mbaye Mission

Central to the IOC's various assessment processes was the Apartheid and Olympism Commission (AOC), which the IOC had formed in the late 1980s. The AOC was charged with monitoring events in

Isolating Racism

South Africa and making recommendations to the IOC, which included identifying the conditions for the country's reintegration into the Olympic Movement, should those materialize. By the time of Mandela's release, the AOC director was the respected Senegalese jurist and IOC member Kéba Mbaye. Sam Ramsamy, who joined the IOC in 1989 and who had served as the SANROC chairman from 1976 to 1990, was another key member of the AOC. In March 1991 the Senegalese administrator led what became known as the "Mbaye Mission," which also included Jean-Claude Ganga, who was by then the President of the Association of the African NOCs, to assess the situation on the ground in South Africa. In his official report, Mbaye made it clear that the matter of political rights was not on the IOC's agenda, stating, "Democracy is desirable, but it is not our role to insist on a universal franchise. . . . The difference between South Africa and other countries which are not democratic is that there is racist legislation in South Africa. . . . If we remove all this legislation now, what is left? There is perhaps a country where not everyone has what they want, where democracy is not total. But there are a lot of countries like this in the world."[74] Mbaye's comments constituted a sober reminder that the IOC was focused on ending racial discrimination only in the sporting domain. If this development, in turn, precipitated positive social and political change more broadly, that would certainly be welcomed, but South Africa's return to the IOC was predicated solely on its government's sportive, rather than on its political or social, policies.

Irrespective of Mbaye's apolitical thrust, while in South Africa the members of the mission met with numerous political leaders, including de Klerk, Mandela, and other ANC officials, as well as with various representatives of Black sports organizations. And Ganga, for one, came away duly impressed. Writing later that year about his experience, he declared:

> My visit to South Africa gave me the opportunity to personally realize that there have been many changes in sports. These have been felt in the composition of the clubs, the utilization of the facilities by all racial groups, even if this is recent, as well as in the

88   AFRICA AND THE OLYMPICS

willingness of all South African sports leaders to work towards the [racial] unification of the sports movement as a whole, be it at the club level, in regional and national organizations, or in the Olympic Committee of South Africa. . . . Everything is not perfect yet, surely: the "one man, one vote" is to come and all the facilities are not used by all the racial groups in South Africa. What matters is that there are no more laws forbidding any South African to practice sport in such or such area.[75]

Ultimately, owing to the favorable impressions that the Mbaye Mission members formed during their time in South Africa, the AOC recommended to the IOC that the country be readmitted into the Olympic Movement. Regarding the importance of the AOC's visit and its resultant recommendation, Cornelissen has argued that "the mission really carried great foreign policy significance, for it constituted a diplomatic validation of the reform processes under way in the country. It also gave momentum to negotiations between SANROC and [the country's all-White] Olympic committee, which in turn led to the establishment of the new and ostensibly non-racial Interim National Olympic Committee of South Africa (INOCSA)," which would later drop the "interim" label.[76]

Misguided, or at Least Premature, Celebration?

Perhaps surprisingly, not all South Africans were excited about these developments, deeming them premature considering the array of significant political and social inequity issues in the country that remained unresolved. These critics included Dennis Brutus, who argued that these weightier concerns needed to be addressed first, while also correctly predicting that the country's Olympic squad would remain predominately White for the foreseeable future; the ninety-seven-member 1992 team, for example, featured eighty-five White athletes. Brutus further suggested that this imbalance would persist owing to the durable impact of apartheid. Citing the sport of marksmanship as an example, he famously declared that "under apartheid, blacks were not [even] allowed to own guns!"[77] Meanwhile, writing shortly after the IOC's decision, Douglas Booth also decried

Isolating Racism

South Africa's readmission, declaring that it was "a classic example of deflection theory that attempts to trivialize apartheid—but it fits neatly in the apologetic, authoritarian, undemocratic, parochial, and apolitical world of sport."[78] Other observers focused on the domestic sporting arena, pointing out that even sending a multiracial team to Barcelona would do little to redress the formidable challenges related to the racial integration of sport within the country, far removed from exuberant crowds gathered in Olympic stadiums. For example, Steve Tshwete, the ANC's chief sports liaison, cautioned, "It's all well for the people at the top to say South Africa is going to the Olympics, but the integration of sports must begin at the bottom, and this is not something that can be conveniently hurried."[79]

Sam Ramsamy: An Experienced Hand at the Helm of the New SANOC

Against the backdrop of this chorus of criticism, or at least concern, Sam Ramsamy was named the first president of the new, multiracial South African NOC. This appointment instilled confidence in fellow African activists who had long been at the center of the effort, working side by side with Ramsamy to remove apartheid from South African sport. For example, Ganga declared, "The fact that our brother and friend Sam Ramsamy . . . is now chairman of the South African NOC gives us every reason to think that the whole process will go along satisfactory lines."[80] Ganga also offered an identifiable moment for the verification of this success: "We will know we have succeeded when we see a Black South African win a race and watch the whites cry [in celebration] when they see their [new South African] flag raised and anthem played."[81]

Ramsamy didn't disappoint, pouring his efforts into ensuring that the country would not squander its invitation to Barcelona by pressing the South African government to continue to institute social and political reforms lest its readmission to the IOC be rescinded. Ramsamy's determination also prompted individuals who had earlier suggested that the country ought to proceed more slowly to adjust their stance. For example, Steve Tshwete, who had initially urged caution and called for a more gradual approach, articulated the ANC's shifting position regarding the possibility and, eventually the reality, that South Africa would participate in the 1992 Games. Citing the ability of multiracial sport to meaningfully, positively transform the nation, even if not immediately, he asserted,

> As for the Americans' militant opinion that no sanctions should be dropped before full civil rights are granted, no, that is not our position. We are seeing a coming together of sporting bodies in a mutual desire for nonracial sport in South Africa. The racists even realize where the future lies. This is not a small victory. It means not just two sports bodies are coming together, but two huge streams of humanity are coming together. This strengthens the whole cause for democracy in this country. It does not end on the cricket pitch or the running track, it goes far beyond.[82]

Barcelona's Impact on Race Relations in South Africa

Of course, no evidence exists that proves that South Africa's inclusion in the 1992 Olympic Games generated any lasting racial cohesion in the country. But it is instructive to consider both the contemporaneous and subsequent comments and actions of South African athletes, leaders, and other observers related to this worthy goal. For example, Jan Tau, a Black South African marathoner and the flag bearer for South Africa's 1992 Olympic squad, affirmed regarding the juxtaposition of Black and White athletes from the nation in Barcelona that "it felt incredible to be standing together."[83] Meanwhile, Edward Griffiths, the sports editor of the South African *National Sunday Times*, captured the significance of the opening ceremony and its potentially enduring impact on the nation via his dispatch from Spain: "Last night, on a balmy evening beside the Mediterranean, the glory overflowed for every South African. The world, in its most visible and emotional form, had welcomed South Africa back to the fold. . . . We will never stray again."[84] For others, participation in the Barcelona Olympics generated personal pride and dignity, which had been elusive targets for non-Whites during apartheid. In the buildup to the 1992 Games, for example, Tshakile Nzminade, a Black employee of a South African mining company who was, in 1990, the tenth-fastest runner in the world in the 200-meter dash, proclaimed, "I will be so proud to find myself lining up next to people I only hear about or see on TV. I think I can do well, but just running on the same track with those people will be like winning the race."[85] Ultimately, Nzminade did "win the race," qualifying for the team and participating in Barcelona, even if he did fail to medal.

South Africa's future leaders also recognized the momentousness of the country fielding its first multiracial Olympic squad. For example, just prior to the opening ceremony, Nelson Mandela visited with South Africa's team in a private gathering, expressing both his respect for the assembled athletes and his hope for the future of the nation: "Our presence here is of great significance to our country, a significance which goes beyond the boundaries of sport. Our country has been isolated for many years, not only in sports but in other fields as well. We are saying now, 'Let's forget the past. Let bygones be bygones.' I want to tell you that we respect you, we are proud of all of you, and, above all, we love you."[86]

If Mandela's comments were intended to heal the nation as it emerged from the dark shadows cast by apartheid, the words of Elana Meyers, who earned the silver medal in the women's 10,000-meter event, suggest that South Africa's inclusion in the 1992 Games not only had an immediate socio-racial impact on the nation but also an enduring one. Reflecting in 2016 on the powerful, and ultimately durable, moment she had shared with the gold-medal winner, Ethiopia's Derartu Tulu, she averred,

> I went to Barcelona with a vision of representing my country and competing. However, it did not take me long to realize that the Olympics is more than winning medals; it is a platform to drive social change and foster peace and understanding. It is where participants share sporting values and spread optimism and creativity to all. The 1992 Olympics in Barcelona . . . took place before South Africa's first democratic elections. When I think about it, I still remember the emotions I felt when I won the silver medal in the 10,000-meter event and the lap

of celebration with Derartu Tulu. We draped our national flags—South African and Ethiopian—around our shoulders and ran around the track together. At that moment, I suddenly understood that the Olympics are more than a competition of nations. It is celebration of what we can achieve collectively as human beings. After the 1992 Games, I was surprised by the warm reception I received back home in South Africa. I learned that the images of that celebration with Tulu helped to unite my country. It gave people courage and hope to rebuild and reconcile South African society. Even today, people in my home country stop me on the street to tell me where they were in the moment of the race and how much it still means to them.[87]

Far removed from the medal podiums in Tokyo and Mexico City, an international coalition of African activists, sports officials, and political leaders secured two important victories: the initial suspension of South Africa from the Olympic Movement and its eventual expulsion. Having recently shed European colonial domination, African nations were eager to isolate South Africa, the unyielding epitome of White minority overrule, and eventually eradicate apartheid from the continent altogether. As Cornelissen has argued regarding Africans' persistence and motivations to remove South Africa from the Olympics, "The extended campaign led by black African states was built on a collective identity of colonial dispossession and an appeal to a supposed universal ethic against the racism and injustices of the apartheid system."[88] Securing the Olympic ban constituted an important initial step in the protracted struggle against the apartheid regime.

Following the subsequent expulsion, Africans hardly relaxed, immediately and unreservedly turning their attention to the other remaining vestige of European colonialism: the White minority regime in Rhodesia (Zimbabwe). Employing many of the same tools and tactics, Africans sought to expel the Rhodesian NOC from the Olympic Movement but also took aim at countries that continued to maintain sporting links with South Africa, namely New Zealand.

3

Africa Protests

Combatting Racial Injustice via Olympic Boycotts

I'll be brokenhearted if I can't compete. I've been away from my wife and kids, training, for three months. But I cannot be the only Black African to run. If the others go [boycott], I must, too.

> —Motsapi Moorosi, the only athlete on the Lesotho Olympic team as the 1972 Munich Games approached and African delegations contemplated a boycott, August 1972

Whereas Kenya is aware that rugby is not an Olympic sport and the Kenyan Delegation is very appreciative of the friendship and hospitality accorded to it by the Organizing Committee of the Games and the people of Canada and Montreal, in particular, and is conscious of the effect that the withdrawal of Kenya and other African countries would have on the Games. We in Kenya, along with all other African nations who have already decided and announced their stand on this issue and all other African countries who will follow the example of Kenya and the other African countries, regret to announce that it will not take part in the games of the XXIst Olympiad, including the opening ceremony due to take place later today, until New Zealand is forced, or otherwise withdraws, from this competition.

> —John Kasyoka, the *chef de mission* from Kenya, July 17, 1976

Owing to the newfound political independence of dozens of African countries coupled with South Africa's suspension and eventual expulsion by the IOC (International Olympic Committee), the 1960s was a heady period for much of the continent. However, the ensuing chapter in the continent's Olympic history was considerably more fraught, with African countries not only threatening boycotts but also actively engaging in them.[1] For example, by announcing their intention to boycott the 1972 Olympic Games in Munich, African leaders effectively pressured the IOC to prohibit Rhodesian athletes from participating in the event. Although Rhodesia was poised to field a multiracial team in Munich, just as it had in the past, its White minority regime continued to bear a strong resemblance to the apartheid government in neighboring South Africa. Consequently, the IOC forbade Rhodesia from rejoining the Olympic Movement until after it formally gained its independence in 1980, reemerging as the sovereign nation of Zimbabwe.

Throughout the 1970s African sporting protests were, just as they had been during the preceding decade, directed at the apartheid regime, despite the ongoing IOC expulsion of South Africa. Indeed, just prior to the 1976 Olympic Games in Montreal, twenty-nine of the thirty-one African nations slated to compete opted to boycott the event because the IOC had declined to suspend New Zealand after its national rugby team had toured South Africa earlier that year in defiance of the United Nations' call for a sporting embargo of the country. In turn, the opportunity to compete in the Olympics that virtually all African athletes consequently lost drew worldwide attention to the ongoing racial injustice in South Africa, thereby expanding the international campaign against apartheid. Spurred on by the African boycott of the 1976 Games, the following year leaders of the British Commonwealth nations, including many from Africa, unanimously ratified the Gleneagles Agreement, which discouraged sporting engagement with South African athletes or squads as part of the broader effort to isolate the apartheid regime. Shortly thereafter, South Africa's national rugby team, the Springboks—a squad that was (and remains) central to Afrikaner culture and served as the sporting symbol of the regime—made its last foreign tour prior

Africa Protests

to the end of apartheid. Following that overseas engagement, the Springboks were no longer welcome anywhere in the world.

It wasn't until the Moscow Olympic Games in 1980 that the sporting solidarity that African nations had so impressively exhibited since independence finally ruptured. Although the Cold War had been raging for decades by then, the Moscow Games constituted the first instance of the US or the USSR hosting an Olympic Games during this contentious era. As a corollary of their broader conflict, the two superpowers relentlessly lobbied African nations to either participate or boycott, accordingly. Predictably, African leaders largely based their Olympics decisions on their respective political allegiances to either Washington or Moscow. And it was these divergent determinations that ultimately fractured the formerly united African front. As such, it's impossible to declare that, in 1980, a monolithic Africa had scored yet another victory associated with the Olympic Games, as has been contended in previous chapters. Rather, both the participating and boycotting countries need to be evaluated on their own merits and plights.

Mexico City 1968: The Origins of the 1972 Protest

Efforts to ban Rhodesia from the 1972 Olympics had actually started in 1968 at the Mexico City Games. But to fully understand Rhodesia's relationship with the IOC, this history must be traced much further back in time. The British colony of Rhodesia (originally known as Southern Rhodesia), located in Southern Africa, first participated in the Olympic Games in 1928 in Amsterdam. By the mid-1960s, though, the decolonization of most of the rest of the continent had greatly unsettled Rhodesia's White population. To forestall a similar outcome, on November 11, 1965, just as Britain was preparing to grant Rhodesia independence, the predominantly White government of the colony issued the Unilateral Declaration of Independence (UDI). Although colonial officials in London fumed over this perceived act of impudence, newly deeming Rhodesia a rogue state, they weren't sufficiently outraged to take up arms against their racial brethren. Great Britain did, however, seek to prevent Rhodesia from participating in various world bodies, including the IOC, so as to deny the UDI government any opportunity to cast itself as a legitimate, autonomous entity. As Blutstein has explained regarding Rhodesia and the Olympics, "Winning medals was a secondary objective. It was more important to attend the Olympic Games as a sovereign state, which would confer de facto recognition" in the eyes of the international community of nations.[2]

In fact, even before the UDI Rhodesia had been a problematic case for the IOC. For example, during the buildup to the 1964 Games in Tokyo, newly independent African states argued that, owing to its White minority regime, Rhodesia's National Olympic Committee (NOC) should not be permitted to send a squad to Japan. Ultimately, a compromise was reached that required the Rhodesian athletes in Tokyo to compete under Great Britain's Union Jack flag and to use the British anthem, "God Save the Queen," as its own. Although this arrangement momentarily defused the situation, in practice this "compromise satisfied no one and did not bode well for future Olympics," as Robert G. Weisbord has compellingly argued.[3]

By 1968 a similar bargain looked decreasingly achievable, though the Rhodesians themselves remained supremely confident that they'd be able to participate in the Mexico City Games. For example, at an Olympic fundraiser on January 12 of that year, Ian Smith, the UDI leader, declared that sending a team to Mexico would be a "wonderful breakthrough for Rhodesia, not only in the sporting world, but in general as far as Rhodesian acceptance throughout the world is concerned."[4] To this end, Rhodesia's NOC had selected a team of fifteen White and two Black athletes, while the IOC, minus the assortment of African nations, remained fully supportive of Rhodesia's participation.

At the end of May, though, the United Nations (UN) announced a series of wide-ranging sanctions, which included calls on all member states to refuse admittance to Rhodesian passport holders and to suspend all airline service into and out of the rebellious nation. Shortly thereafter, the Supreme Council for Sport in Africa (SCSA) demanded that Rhodesia be prevented from participating in Mexico City, citing the UN resolutions and, in general, the illegitimacy of the UDI. The possibility of an African boycott, which had been

Africa Protests

threatened previously in response to South Africa's possible readmittance, was once again openly discussed. In turn, despite pressure from an increasingly disgruntled Avery Brundage and like-minded IOC members, the Mexican Games Organizing Committee opted not to send the Rhodesians the entry visas and Olympic identity cards that could have helped its squad circumvent the UN sanctions. Brundage apparently only learned about the Mexicans' decision via the media and, in response, threatened—albeit absurdly, considering that it was the host nation—to ban the Mexican Olympic Committee from its own Games.[5] Mexican officials could safely ignore Brundage's fulmination, though, as the UN sanctions provided them with the requisite cover, while it quickly became clear that the Rhodesians would not be welcomed in Mexico City.

Although Africans across the continent once again rejoiced, many of the newly banned athletes were naturally devastated. For example, Bernard Dzoma, one of the two Black athletes who had been selected for Rhodesia's team, lamented, "I cannot understand why, as a Black man, I am made to suffer by people a long way off, who, for reasons I don't understand, don't like Ian Smith, and want to throw me out of the Olympics in the interests of Black people in my country."[6]

Munich 1972: Africa Stands Firm

Although African nations and the Mexican Organizing Committee had successfully conspired to keep Rhodesia out of the 1968 Games, the involvement of Rhodesian athletes in the ensuing Olympics, in Munich, was at least initially a distinct possibility. Indeed, well before the commencement of the Games in West Germany, the Rhodesians had been extended the standard invitation to participate, and more than a year "prior to the opening ceremonies, Rhodesian officials had traveled to Munich to pick up their written invitation, a somewhat less customary procedure."[7] Yet there were already signs that Rhodesian participation would meet with at least some resistance. Even the largely empathetic IOC agreed, at its 1969 meeting in Dubrovnik, to send an independent commission of inquiry to Rhodesia to investigate whether the segregationist policies of Ian Smith's UDI regime

98   AFRICA AND THE OLYMPICS

also affected sports. Ultimately, though, little came of this exploratory mission, and the West German Organizing Committee continued to look much more favorably on the Rhodesians than its Mexican counterpart had. Yet government officials still had to determine how to navigate the international sanctions imposed on the rogue state, as West Germany had formally recognized the UN resolutions, even though, at the time, it was not a member of the body.

Meanwhile, Brundage, who was preparing to preside over his last Olympic Games, remained adamant that the Rhodesians would be present in Munich. In a 1971 television interview, for example, the IOC president truculently declared, "Rhodesia observes the Olympic rules; there is no racial segregation in that country's sports. Anyone who is against the Rhodesian government would also have to put himself against every government in the world."[8] Sensing the IOC president's swelling obstinance, African nations decided that they had to act.

Once again, their preferred measure was a boycott. On March 31, 1971, Ethiopia and Zambia announced that they would withdraw from the Games if the Rhodesians were permitted to participate. Just a week later, Jean-Claude Ganga, speaking on behalf of the SCSA, suggested that other nations would follow if the Rhodesians were present. Some two months thereafter, Abraham Ordia wrote Brundage to remind him why the Africans were poised to withdraw:

> I wonder if you are aware that racialism and racial discrimination is now increasingly practiced in Rhodesia by a white minority against the black majority in that country? This is clearly evident in sport, particularly in regard to recent legislation that restricts parks (and the sports facilities in them) to white Rhodesians only, and in the strict racialist exclusion of non-white Rhodesians from public swimming pools, etc. . . . While I agree with you that *another long and rancorous debate* [Brundage used these exact words in a prior letter] will not serve the Olympic cause, I must also point out with respect that the fears and anxieties entertained in several quarters on the subject of racial discrimination in sport in Rhodesia cannot be brushed aside.[9]

An Unlikely Consent

The IOC meeting slated for mid-September 1971 in Luxembourg appeared to offer hope for some type of resolution that would satisfy all parties. And it seemingly did, at least initially. At the congress it was agreed that, pending consent from African officials, Rhodesia would again compete under the British flag, use the British national anthem at any medal ceremonies, participate under its colonial name, "Southern Rhodesia," and list the nationality of its athletes in the official record of the Games as "British subjects." As Ian Smith had been unwaveringly adamant that Rhodesia was an independent nation, it seemed certain that he would reject these conditions. To everyone's surprise, though, the UDI leader consented. Moreover, the president of the Rhodesian NOC, Ossie Plaskitt, declared that the Rhodesian athletes were prepared to march under the Boy Scout flag or even the Russian flag if that's what it would take to participate in the Munich Olympics, before adding, "Everyone knows very well that we are Rhodesians and will always be Rhodesians."[10]

Black African observers were naturally stunned. But rather than resign themselves to Rhodesia's inclusion, they refused to endorse this recycled compromise and ratcheted up their campaign against the rogue nation. In particular, officials from Zambia, Uganda, and Tanzania began calling for a boycott. And there was plenty of popular support for this measure. For example, in an editorial in Nigeria's *Daily Times* following the proposed compromise agreement, the authors declared, "We are opposed to the participation of the illegal regime at the Olympics under any guise. Granted that by participating under British canopy, the illegal regime would do no pride to its claim to sovereign independence, the fact remains it will participate at all. Compliance with the IOC's conditions should not be a ticket for its participation. What applies to South Africa for reasons of her apartheid policy should also apply to Rhodesia."[11] These and other exhortations notwithstanding, no African country was ready to take the first step and actually commit to a boycott. As such, on August 12, 1972, the Rhodesian team, consisting of thirty-seven White athletes, seven Black athletes, nine White officials, and one Black official, arrived in Munich.

Africa Finally, Forcefully Pushes Back

The SCSA once again spearheaded the African campaign to pressure the IOC to ban Rhodesia from the Games. The key figures within the organization who were directing these efforts included its Nigerian president, Abraham Ordia, and Jean-Claude Ganga, its Congolese Secretary General. But Sam Ramsamy, the South African anti-apartheid activist, was also heavily involved. He would later recall, "Hour by hour, with each telephone call and clandestine meeting, the seeds of African solidarity were being sown. 'Would you prepare to withdraw?' Ordia asked. 'Yes,' came the replies, one by one."[12] Owing to these labors, by August 17, 1972, some sixteen nations, mostly from Africa, had submitted official notifications of their intent to boycott. They were subsequently joined by other African countries and also received support from athletes hailing from the Bahamas, Jamaica, Trinidad, Barbados, the United States, and Venezuela who had all refused to compete against Rhodesian athletes in the last warm-up event in West Germany prior to the start of the Games. Ordia and Ganga also called on the Eastern Bloc countries to join the boycott, which they seemed inclined to do.

Later in August officials from the SCSA and the various African NOCs issued a joint statement, which contended that because the British government had not issued British passports to the members of Rhodesia's Olympic squad, as per the compromise agreement with the IOC, these athletes were in Munich and poised to participate in the Games in violation of that accord. The official announcement read as follows: "Until the evidence is produced to prove that the British Government has delivered passports to the members of the Southern Rhodesian team to enable them to participate in the Games of the XXth Olympiad in Munich, we consider that the issuance of the ID cards by the Organizing Committee of the XXth Olympiad, because it has no legal capacity, cannot confer citizenship or nationality, in so far as international law is concerned, on any participants in the Games of the XXth Olympiad."[13] The African IOC representatives further argued that since no country in the world had formally recognized the UDI government, the Rhodesian NOC had no official standing. Finally, Dennis Brutus was also on the ground in Munich, reminding IOC officials that South Africa was still a part of the broader conversation and arguing that Rhodesia's inclusion would only encourage Pretoria.

Boxed in by the terms laid out in the compromise agreement with Rhodesia, pressured by the UN, and deeply troubled by the looming boycott, the IOC convened in Munich days before the Games were set to commence in order to vote on Rhodesia's fate. In the end, the tally was thirty-six against Rhodesia and thirty-one for, with three abstentions. In the aftermath of the ballot, Brundage seethed bitterly in a letter directed to Ian Smith, writing, "If the African politicians think they won a victory, they are much mistaken. This action was denounced unanimously by the whole world of sport, and it will take them many years to recover from the hostility that has been aroused."[14] The following day, Brundage sent a similar missive to the head of the Rhodesian NOC, declaring, "I am still appalled by the action of the Committee [IOC] in the Rhodesia case, which I consider the most serious mistake it has ever made. I hope it will not be repeated. It was the first time in 20 years the Committee failed to follow my recommendation. If . . . the Black African countries feel they have won a victory, they are much mistaken because the whole world was outraged by this political intervention . . . and they have lost any sympathy they may have had. The action of the Rhodesian representatives at Munich was exemplary."[15] Yet the outgoing IOC president could do little more than issue these parting shots. African officials and activists had once again scored a major victory for racial justice on the continent, newly denying another White minority regime access to the prestigious Olympic forum.

The Backlash to and Repercussions of the Rhodesian Ban

Even as Africans across the continent rejoiced, the backlash that Brundage had foretold arrived both swiftly and harshly. Almost immediately, African officials became targets of the West German and, more broadly, Western media for supposedly marring the Games by injecting politics into the allegedly otherwise unsullied Olympic environment. Additionally, angry West German citizens and others from farther afield took to sending vitriolic, often anonymous letters to various African officials. For example, the Nigerian president of the SCSA, Abraham Ordia, received one such note authored by "Munich Inhabitants," which spewed: "Mr. Ordia, get out of Munich, you black criminal. We don't want you and your black dogs."[16] Another letter, whose author claimed to have been the former chief medical officer at the University of Nigeria (presumably during the colonial era), was even more severe. "So, you n—s have won! You picked on little Rhodesia. That is so typical for n—s. Especially the ones who go for their education from the whites (UK or USA). Congratulations you bastards. May your bones bleach among the black vultures."[17]

Certain African athletes also suffered, though in highly divergent ways, owing to Rhodesia's removal from Munich. For example, because the IOC had barred Rhodesia just prior to the start of the Games, some African teams, including Tanzania, had to scramble to get their athletes to West Germany. A member of the Tanzanian squad, Hamad S. Ndee, later recalled how disruptive the last-minute decision to allow the delegation to travel to Munich had been: "It took over 36 hours—Dar es Salaam–Nairobi–London–Dusseldorf by air; Dusseldorf–Cologne by train; Cologne–Munich by air; and this had a devastating effect on the performance of the Tanzanian athletes at the Games. For example, some of the boxers had to weigh in at 5:00 a.m., having only arrived in Munich at 1:00 a.m. that morning, for competition that evening." Ndee continued, explaining, "Although many of us had fasted throughout the journey, some failed to meet the weight requirements in their respective categories and thus were disqualified without ever reaching the ring. Those who did qualify to fight were so tired and weak that not one of them managed to progress to the second round."[18]

Arguably, though, the most lamentable development associated with the proposed African boycott was Brundage's response to the Palestinian terrorist assault on the Israeli Olympic team that tragically claimed the lives of fifteen people. In his remarks, Brundage declared that the Games had suffered from "two savage attacks," equating the Africans' efforts to ban Rhodesia with the assassination of the Israeli athletes. Although the retiring IOC president subsequently apologized, his contempt for Africa had, once again, been on full display. Irrespective of the racist vitriol directed at African sporting officials—by Brundage, Western media outlets, and anonymous letter writers—or perhaps in part because of this vitriol, three years after the Munich Games, the IOC fully expelled Rhodesia from the Olympic Movement by a vote of forty-one to twenty-six.

1976: The Complex Issue of New Zealand

With both the South Africans and Rhodesians banished, the 1976 Olympic Games in Montreal promised smoother sailing. But this event turned out to be even more tumultuous than either Mexico City or Munich had been. The issue for African nations in 1976 was the presence of New Zealand, which had maintained close sporting ties with South Africa. At the end of June the New Zealand rugby team, known as the All Blacks, had arrived in South Africa for a tour that would include a series of matches, with the Montreal Games set to begin in just a few short weeks. Exacerbating the situation was the Soweto Uprising on June 16, 1976, the day before the Games commenced, which left at least 175 Black South Africans dead, victims of police violence. It was in this politically charged climate that African politicians, activists, athletes, and sports officials reunited to remind the global community of the persistence of racial injustice in South Africa and, once again, used the Olympic Games to draw attention to their cause, with the threat of boycott again their weapon of choice.

As with the prior two Olympics, the most significant developments occurred in the weeks just prior to the commencement of the Games, with the final push to exclude New Zealand coming only days before the opening ceremony. Indeed, even though in April the SCSA had announced a selective boycott of events in which New Zealand athletes participated at the Olympics were the All Blacks to go to South Africa, as African delegations initially began arriving in Montreal, the New Zealand matter barely registered within these circles, even if most officials were aware of the All Blacks' rugby tour.[19] As then–IOC vice president and Tunisian NOC president Mohamed Mzali explained: "Three days before the opening of the Games, there was no concerted effort, strategy, or agreement on any attitude to take. But, 48 hours before the opening, 13 African countries sent IOC President Killanin a letter in which they demanded no more, no less than the exclusion of New Zealand from the Olympic Games if it did not withdraw its rugby team from South Africa.... The withdrawal of the Tunisian delegation had become ... compulsory [only] from the moment that the vast majority of African and Arab-Muslim countries withdrew."[20]

The SCSA Takes Up Its Position on the Frontlines, Again

Jean-Claude Ganga and the SCSA again assumed primary responsibility for uniting the various African delegations in opposition to New Zealand's participation, but Dennis Brutus and SANROC (South African Non-Racial Olympic Committee) were also present in Montreal and played an important role. Prior to organizing the mass withdrawal, both Ganga and Brutus had tried to work back channels in an effort to deescalate the situation, or at least to tender less severe measures before a boycott became the only remaining option. For example, meeting clandestinely with Lance Cross, an IOC member and president of the New Zealand NOC, Ganga indicated that he could guarantee African participation if the All Blacks would "cut short their tour of South Africa and fly home" immediately. He also appealed to Cross, saying, "I read yesterday that two of the All Blacks players got caught too close to some kind of demonstration and suffered the effects of tear gas. Use that as a starting point. Just say you are stopping the tour to guarantee the safety of your players and officials."[21] In response, Cross indicated, rather unenthusiastically, that he would discuss this proposal with his government, while also reiterating that New Zealand did not practice racial discrimination in sport. He further reminded Ganga that he had no jurisdiction over the New Zealand Rugby Union, that the organization was not affiliated in any way with the New Zealand NOC, and that rugby wasn't even an Olympic sport.

In his array of retorts, Cross was articulating sentiments held not only by the New Zealand government but also by most IOC members. Even the Tanzanian representative, Mohamed Mzali, questioned the targeting of New Zealand.

Africa Protests

Why attack New Zealand, in particular? Why not denounce the [other] 26 countries which . . . continue to have sports relations with South Africa? Without wishing to defend New Zealand, I must point out that two years ago the New Zealand Government refused the South African rugby team entry into New Zealand by not granting the Springboks visas. The New Zealand officials ask us how they can ban 30 of their citizens leaving the country to go on a world [rugby] tour. What has the IOC to do in all this, and why do certain people want to make it responsible for rugby?[22]

But the SCSA and, in particular, its president, Abraham Ordia, was unmoved by these and other arguments and repeatedly rebutted them, declaring at one point in the buildup to the Montreal Games that "New Zealand can have South Africa or it can have the Black African countries—it cannot have both."[23] In the following press statement, he delivered some of these ripostes, while also expressly calling out the New Zealand government, led by conservative prime minister Robert Muldoon, whose election platform had explicitly called for sporting engagement with the apartheid regime:

I am often asked the question: "why pick on New Zealand when some other countries still maintain sports relations with South Africa?" It seems to me that a government that makes an election manifesto out of permitting sporting exchanges with South Africa (reversing the policy of the previous government) and which has refused to make any effort to discourage tours, which only give support to South Africa's legally enforced policies of apartheid in sport, must condone those policies of apartheid in sport. Hiding under the flimsy excuse of "non-interference in sport" does not impress or inspire anyone, nor does it explain why the New Zealand government has refused to give leadership and taken a stand on such a vital issue. In Canada, Australia, and Great Britain, although a few sports associations and clubs still continue to compete with South Africa, the Governments of these countries are publicly opposed to such exchanges and make their views well known to the associations and clubs involved. The New Zealand Government, in contrast, defiantly and openly aids and supports such sporting exchanges. That is why we make a clear difference between New Zealand and other countries. That is why we shall continue to boycott all competitions, Championships, or Games in which New Zealand, individually or collectively, are also to feature. The present National Party of New Zealand campaigns on a policy of support for apartheid sport. Mr. Robert Muldoon said, "A National Government would welcome a Springbok Rugby team to New Zealand even if there were threats of violence and civil strife."[24]

Ordia's compelling contentions notwithstanding, the African organizers of the protest eventually realized that a path of reasoned persuasion to deny the participation of New Zealand was futile. Instead, buoyed by an Organization of African Unity (OAU) resolution issued in early July 1976 that called for African countries to "reconsider" their participation in the Olympic Games if New Zealand took part, Ganga, Ramsamy, and other African activists quickly transitioned to building a coalition of nations willing to withdraw from the Games. Less than two weeks later, the OAU announced that African nations should take the "appropriate measures"—namely, boycott—should the IOC ignore their request. According to Ramsamy, "We took no delight in this realization, but instead applied ourselves to our work, which had now changed from seeking a solution to coordinating the boycott."[25] Montreal's Elizabeth Hotel, especially Ganga's room there, became the epicenter of these efforts. With Ganga and his wife sharing the space with Ramsamy as they attempted to rapidly build the alliance, sleep became a luxury that none of them could afford. As Ramsamy explained:

> Ganga's hotel room became a makeshift office, and we worked hard to develop and pursue a strategy and also to ensure the free flow of info and debate between the stakeholders: government officials in capital cities around the [African] continent, sports administrators, and those teams who had already arrived and settled in the Athletes' Village. I barely slept for three days.

Africa Protests 107

African solidarity proved to be a complicated construction, and we took great care to put the right blocks in the right places.... So, it continued, hour after hour. The telephone rang almost relentlessly and, with a five-hour time difference between Canada and most African countries, our days merged blearily into nights. Yet, the jigsaw came together.[26]

The Painful Realization of a Lost Cause

As the opening ceremony approached, it became clear that the IOC was unwilling to exclude New Zealand. Simply put, the organization's leadership argued that the country hadn't violated any Olympic regulations, nor was rugby an Olympic sport and thus there was scant cause to remove them from the Games.[27] As always, minimal African representation within the IOC handicapped efforts by the continent's array of activists and officials to influence the body. At the time, for example, there were only eleven African IOC members and two of them, Reginald Honey (South Africa) and Reginald Alexander (Kenya), were White. Given the odds stacked against the African lobbyists and the anticipated, attendant failure of the boycott to effect change, the proposed withdrawal from the Games became a matter of principle—arguably, it always had been—rather than an instrument expected to achieve a desired outcome. This righteous approach was manifest in the statements of various African sports officials. Isaac Lugonzo, for example, the chairman of Kenya's National Sports Council, declared, "We will not align ourselves with a country that has sports ties with South Africa," while a Zambian official explained, "We're on the front line of the whole apartheid thing. Any nation that condones that [apartheid], we just can't take part with them."[28]

Other African officials even more forcefully articulated their rationalizations and the sentiments that undergirded them. For example, Kenya's chef de mission, John Kasyoka, denounced both the IOC and New Zealand in a statement issued on July 17, the day of the opening ceremony of the Games. "On 15th July 1976, at a meeting attended by Representatives of the National Olympic Committees of Africa present in Montreal, the Representatives of all National Olympic Committees present at the meeting, including Kenya, brought to the notice of the IOC the indignation of the entire sports men and women of Africa at the collaboration of the sporting authorities of New Zealand with racist South Africa despite worldwide condemnation of such sporting relationship."[29] Similarly, in a letter announcing the country's withdrawal from the Games on the day they began, the head of the Ethiopian Olympic Committee, Tsegaw Ayele, bluntly criticized New Zealand and South Africa in the strongest terms, while dismissing any justifications for the inclusion of New Zealand:

> Our protest was based on the fact that the New Zealand rugby team, in defiance of world condemnation of Apartheid and the consequent expulsion of South Africa from the Olympic Movement, has accepted an invitation to go and play in South Africa. . . . A large portion of the people of New Zealand has condemned the tour and tried by the means in their power for the cancellation of the tour. In the meantime, the South African Government has murdered more than 200 Black students in Soweto because they simply demonstrated in a peaceful way for the preservation of their rights. The world has been shocked by this act of savagery and the entire International Community has condemned it, except the Government and the sport authorities of New Zealand, which maintained the rugby team tour, giving the evidence by this decision of their unconditional support to Apartheid and to the Genocide of the Black people. The protest advanced that the rugby union is an independent body is a lie because we know that the previous governments of the countries in that zone have prevented their teams from visiting South Africa or receiving South African teams in their country. In such circumstances, we are convinced that the decision of New Zealand to send a rugby team to South Africa and to maintain this decision after the massacre of Soweto is a deliberate, premeditated move to reinforce the philosophy of Apartheid and to support the extermination of the Black race.

Whatever will be the interpretation which will be given to our decision, we believe that the participation of Africans in the Olympic Games with the representatives of New Zealand is intolerable and unacceptable.[30]

The president of the Algerian Olympic Committee, Mohamed Zerguini, echoed these sentiments in a letter to Lord Killanin explaining his country's decision to withdraw:

How can one participate in the Olympic Games with sports teams from a country that did not hesitate, during the Games, to send athletes to South Africa. . . . When one knows that all this took place at the time of the Soweto massacres and those carried out in other South African cities, New Zealand's attitude could only be described as an unacceptable provocation. . . . The majority of the leaders of the Olympic Movement showed their solidarity with New Zealand by listening more to their hearts than their heads. . . . It was clear that the condition of one continent [Africa] did not weigh very heavily in the eyes of the leaders of the Olympic Movement.[31]

This litany of powerful assertions notwithstanding, in the end New Zealand did participate in Montreal. And African nations did boycott the Games, as did a handful of other countries. Because of the eleventh-hour nature of the efforts, though, the boycott was staggered and fitful, with African states withdrawing their teams at different moments. For example, Tanzania never sent its Olympic squad, while Cameroon "agreed to take part in the opening ceremony, in deference to Canada, their alphabetical neighbors and allies at the U.N., but then withdrew."[32] Egypt and Morocco also participated in the opening ceremony, and even in the athletic events on the first day of the Games, before departing. And so on. When the boycott dust had finally settled, only two African countries—Senegal and the Ivory Coast—fully participated in the Montreal Games, which prompted speculation that they retained some form of covert diplomatic or political links with the apartheid regime in Pretoria, though these accusations quickly dissipated.

Lost Opportunities and Principled Stands:
The Impact of the Boycott on African Athletes

As always, the athletes and, to a lesser extent, the coaches and sports officials from the boycotting nations paid the most significant price, having trained for years with the goal of participating in the Olympic Games only to have that endeavor denied in the final hours of the protracted preparatory process. In total, some 440 African athletes lost the opportunity to compete in Montreal. Yet many of them echoed the principled stances that their respective governments had made. For example, just prior to the boycott deadline, Isaac Akioye, a Nigerian Olympic official, began waking athletes and coaches, telling them, "Start packing. We're going home today. We are going to show them they cannot push around Black Africans."[33] Even Lee Evans—two-time Olympian and, famously, one of the two African American athletes who had raised their gloved fists on the medal podium in Mexico City as a form of protest against racial injustice in America—similarly adopted this type of principled position. In 1976, while serving as the sprint coach for the Nigerian team, Evans remarked, "I knew the heavy stuff would come down at the Olympics. I was just waiting for it to happen. I'm glad we are making a stand, even though I'd like to see how my guys would have done. The Olympics aren't so big that we can't give them up. We feel that a sacrifice must be made."[34]

Others were seemingly less content—or in some cases, seemingly less principled—openly lamenting the timing of the New Zealand rugby tour to South Africa rather than the tour itself, aware that its proximity to the Games was probably the most influential factor in prompting the boycott. For example, the elite Kenyan half-miler Mike Boit vocally bemoaned, "Why didn't New Zealand just wait until after the Olympics for that tour?"[35] Even some of the New Zealand athletes empathized with the Africans, questioning their government's actions. For example, Dick Quax, a 5,000-meter contestant, declared, "I can't blame the Africans. I mean, knowing how they feel about the South Africans. I blame the rugby people and I blame our government for putting us in this position. If our government says sports and politics don't mix, they ought to come here."[36] Other African athletes similarly understood that politics and sports were deeply intertwined and, in this case, that this combination was responsible for their dejection. As Modupe Oshikoya, a Nigerian entered in the women's hurdles, long jump, and pentathlon, remarked, "We got a message today from the government. We have to go home. It's very difficult. All that hard work. I came to compete."[37] Other athletes were seemingly more bitter, including Nigerian long jumper Charlton Ehizuelen, a twenty-two-year-old student at the University of Illinois: "I don't like it. I have done really good. I won the NCAAs last year. I had a good chance of winning a medal."[38] Still others were simply resigned to their Olympic fates, obligated to respect their government's wishes, even if they still wanted to participate. For example, Joshua Kimeto, a Kenyan 5,000-meter runner, on the eve of the boycott, commented, "We haven't heard from our government, but if our chief says, 'go home,' we go home. But, we'd like to compete." Star Ugandan hurdler John Akii-Bua similarly remarked, "The government sent me here and the government can call me home. [But] I would not care to make history" (fig. 3.1).[39] Finally, in one especially ironic, arguably even cruel, twist, the absence in Montreal of the Tanzanian runner Filbert Bayi, then the world-record holder in the men's 1,500 meters, paved the way for John Walker of New Zealand to secure the gold medal in this event.

FIGURE 3.1. African Olympic delegation(s) leaving the 1976 Olympic Games. Photo by Reg Lancaster. Courtesy of Getty Images

The Aftereffects of the 1976 Boycott

Following the conclusion of the Montreal Games, the boycott continued to reverberate around the world, even many years later. For example, almost three decades removed, Ramsamy remarked that "such selfless gestures were made in support of the oppressed peoples of South Africa, and such sacrifices should not be forgotten."[40] Meanwhile, in the more immediate aftermath of the event, letters laced with vitriol—some proudly signed, others anonymously authored—regularly arrived in the mailboxes of the major African figures involved in the boycott, namely Ganga, Ordia, and Brutus. One such anonymous letter directed to Ordia, postmarked from South Africa, read as follows:

> We read that, to mark the International Year of Mobilisation of Sanctions against South Africa, the United Nations has presented you with a gold medal for "outstanding services" to the International Community in their "on-going and valiant struggle against apartheid!" In view of all your words and actions in this regard over the years, and the unforgivable disappointments visited by you on Black athletes whom you have prevented from competing in such major meetings as the Montreal Olympics, we call on you to make a public statement that you will return the medallion to the donors as it is made from South African gold. To do less than this would be to compound the destruction you have caused to the lives of many athletes, both black and white. . . . To put names to this letter would be superfluous for, as you well know, they stretch from Cape Town to Cairo.[41]

Although African activists and officials were forced to endure these bigoted missives in the wake of the Montreal Olympics, the boycott also bore important political and sporting fruit. The following year, with the threat of boycott again looming, this time surrounding the Commonwealth Games in Edmonton, the prime ministers and presidents of the Commonwealth of Nations, including the New Zealand premier, Robert Muldoon, unanimously approved the Gleneagles Agreement, which discouraged athletic

Africa Protests 113

contact and competition with South Africa. As Geoffrey Miller has argued regarding the causal relationship between the Montreal boycott and Gleneagles, "The African boycott, contrary to the Olympic spirit though it was, achieved its objective, for in the following year when threats of another boycott cast shadows over plans for the Commonwealth Games at Edmonton, Muldoon joined other Commonwealth prime ministers in endorsing the agreement . . . which was exactly what the Africans had demanded at Montreal and, thus, the SCSA could claim a victory."[42]

Perhaps less tangibly, the African nations' principled efforts at the Montreal Games further isolated the apartheid regime in the international sports world by drawing renewed attention to its racist domestic policies. For example, in a letter crafted by Ganga to the commissioner for Sports and Physical Culture in January 1977, he sanguinely opined, "With regard to the long term results of the attitude of Africans in Montreal . . . I am rather convinced that in spite of the incoherence by which it was characterized, the boycott of the Montreal Olympic Games by African countries will have a great influence on the attitude of those countries which continue to encourage South Africa and support its policy of racial discrimination in sports."[43] Although Ganga was expressing his optimism regarding the prospective, enduring effects of Montreal less than a year after the Games had concluded, other observers, possessing the advantage of the passage of time, have confirmed the SCSA president's prescience. For example, writing some decades removed from the event, Courtney Mason affirmed the boycott's far-reaching impact: "The high profile of the [Montreal] Olympic Games ensured that the word 'apartheid' appeared in many newspapers and on television broadcasts worldwide. This was significant in forming international consciousness regarding the anti-apartheid movement. As the world awakened to apartheid policy, opposition was the general response. Anti-apartheid campaigns began to evolve, and sport sanctions became an integral component. Most notably, South Africa's isolation from international rugby became a major catalyst of change. In essence, rugby was too important in the lives of too many white South Africans to be sacrificed completely."[44] Ultimately, the 1976 Montreal

114 AFRICA AND THE OLYMPICS

Olympic Games could reasonably be considered another "win away from the podium" for Africans, but this particular advance in the extended struggle against racial injustice took more time to materialize and, arguably, required more sacrifice than had previous victories.

1980: African Olympic Unity Cleaved by the Cold War

If African harmony had once again been on display in Montreal in 1976, that durable unity finally fractured under the weight of the Cold War as the 1980 Olympics approached. Slated for Moscow, these Games featured unprecedented Cold War dimensions and implications. Although many African nations invoked the policy of "non-alignment," attempting, often unsuccessfully, to remain neutral in this global conflict, most remained dependent on economic and political assistance from either the East or West and thus were vulnerable to Cold War pressures. The Western bloc of nations initially floated the prospect of boycotting the Moscow Games following the Soviet invasion of Afghanistan in December 1979. In response, many African leaders beholden to the West adhered to this appeal, similarly citing this unprovoked aggression against a sovereign nation as justification for withholding their athletes. Once again, Olympic sports and international politics were hopelessly intertwined. The boycott of Moscow would, in turn, have subsequent Olympic repercussions, as an assortment of nations, including many from Africa, retaliated by opting not to send squads to the 1984 Los Angeles Games.

Planted in Montreal: The Seeds of the 1980 Boycott

The seeds of potential trouble in 1980 had actually been planted in 1976, in Canada. At the Montreal Games the Soviet Union and its allies had openly voiced support for the African-led boycott, though they ultimately opted not to join it, mindful of how the ensuing Moscow Olympics might be affected. Although this diplomatic calculus seemingly satisfied the Western bloc of nations, the Soviet invasion of Afghanistan provided them with ample justification to rally support for a boycott. The ensuing lobbying and associated rationales offered by Western and African leaders, respectively, to either send athletes to Moscow or keep them home highlighted the hypocrisy, contradictions, and absurdities of the Cold War, during which political allegiances reliably outweighed all other considerations.

The Soviet Fortieth Army crossed the border into Afghanistan on December 24, 1979, reaching the capital, Kabul, shortly thereafter and subsequently installing a Soviet loyalist as the leader of the country. The outcry from the West was just as swift as it was predictable, and with the Olympics set to commence in fewer than seven months after the invasion, the Moscow Games quickly became an indirect target of the West's condemnation of the invasion. On January 20, 1980, US president Jimmy Carter issued an ultimatum: if Soviet troops failed to leave Afghanistan within a month, America would boycott the Moscow Games. Ultimately, though, Carter didn't formally commit the United States to this course of action until March 21. Meanwhile, as it became increasingly clear that the Soviets were not prepared to withdraw from Afghanistan (in fact, they wouldn't end up departing for another nine years), the Americans began lobbying other nations to join the proposed boycott, applying both diplomatic and economic pressure to compel as many countries as it could to withhold their Olympic delegations.

Continental Debate Regarding the Proposed Boycott

Across Africa there were widely varied responses to the Americans' entreaties. Many Africans objected to the Soviets' violation of state sovereignty, citing basic human rights and their own similar vulnerability to the military ambitions of a significantly more powerful, if unnamed, aggressor. For example, the editor of the *Nation*, a Kenyan daily, accused the Russians of "virtually colonizing Afghanistan while the rest of the world watched."[45] Conversely, a number of high-ranking African officials, as well as the influential SCSA leadership, pointed out that the Americans had spoken out against the 1976 Montreal boycott, remained supportive of, or at least engaged with, South Africa's apartheid regime, and only selectively cared about African nations. Moreover, the SCSA argued that Afghanistan was not an "African issue," whereas the 1976 issue regarding New Zealand had been.[46] Zambian Sports Minister, Nalumino Mundia, expressed similar sentiments in explaining why his country would reject the

American boycott: "The West cannot expect African support for politically inspired sports boycotts when it criticized Africa's use of sports as a weapon to fight apartheid. When we boycotted . . . the West accused us of politicizing sport. How can our critics expect any support now?"[47] Meanwhile, African leaders of all stripes, statuses, and ideological persuasions remained exceedingly mindful of their own Cold War allegiances, even as many of them publicly invoked non-alignment. They also realized that their boycott of the 1976 Games meant that a repeat decision regarding Moscow could see their athletes unable to participate in the Olympics for a full twelve years, from 1972 to 1984.[48] The stage was truly set for a vocal debate on the continent.

Adding to this state-level dialogue was input from countless African journalists, fans, and other observers. Many of these commentators were opposed to the boycott and, in general, held favorable opinions of the Soviet Union, which had aided a number of African independence movements, including in Angola, Mozambique, and Zimbabwe, during their respective liberation struggles. Yenyi Sakaba, for example, writing in the *Nigeria Standard* in February 1980, argued, "[The Soviet Union] gives us aid without conditions or strings attached . . . assists us in the liberation struggle against colonialism . . . and is a genuine friend of the oppressed peoples of the world."[49] Encouraged by this type of reciprocal support and eager to guarantee as many participants in the Games as possible, the Soviets actively courted—and even enticed—African states. In fact, the USSR had for some time been sending coaches and equipment to various friendly African nations and was now offering to subsidize the travel and accommodations of any African Olympic squad, enabling these delegations to travel to Moscow either at no charge or on significantly reduced fares and to stay for free while there.[50]

Many members of the African media similarly rejected the boycott, but rather than praising the Soviets, they focused instead on critiquing the West and, in particular, the United States. For example, an editorial in the Nigerian newspaper *Punch* from February 1980 argued, "When African nations decided to boycott the Olympics because of the presence of New Zealand—notorious for her sporting ties with the apartheid regime—the very same United States accused Africa of trying to distort the aims and spirit of the games by introducing politics into sport. Now it is Africa's turn to teach the United States a lesson in sport and politics."[51] Similarly, a piece from Tanzania's *Daily News,* also from February, opined, "If the Western countries had at least shown some understanding of the African argument in 1976—our use of the Olympics for peaceful protest against the barbarian Boers in the South—at least we would not be questioning their wisdom of involving the Olympics now in superpower politics."[52]

Still other African observers criticized the United States for focusing its attention on the peoples of occupied Afghanistan while ignoring the plight of Africans and, in particular, Blacks in Rhodesia and South Africa. For example, a letter addressed to the *Daily News* in February 1980 admonishing America's selective invocation of human rights abuses declared, "When a human being is oppressed, it does not matter where he is or the composition of his colour. The fact is that they suffer equally. Why would Carter fight for the rights of Afghans but ignore Black South Africans, is it just because Afghans are not Black?"[53] Similarly, Mohammed Hamza, writing in the *Nigeria Standard* in the ensuing month, contended that "the West's refusal to engage in Southern Africa, but to pursue policies in Central Asia [Afghanistan], meant that those [Southern] Africans were the only humans destined to have no rights."[54]

"The Greatest" Fails to Land a Knockout Punch: Ali's Return to Africa

Criticism of the US-led boycott was arguably most vocal during and after an ill-fated lobbying trip to the continent by Muhammad Ali at the request of President Carter. During a goodwill visit to India in February 1980, Carter contacted "The Greatest" and asked him to stop in a collection of African nations on his way back to the United States to gather support for the boycott of the Moscow Games. Carter later explained, "There was specific interest on my part in having Muhammad Ali explain our country's position on the Olympic boycott, and also in his pointing out what our nation is, what its basic policies are, our commitment to freedom and human rights, and the fact that we have black Americans who have been successful with a diversity of religious commitments."[55]

Carter's selection of Ali was both deliberate and strategic. The heavyweight boxing champion was widely revered across Africa, dating back to his first trip, in 1964, to the continent, which had included stops in Ghana, Nigeria, and Egypt. But it was his defeat in Zaire (Congo) of George Foreman a decade later, in what was billed as the "Rumble in the Jungle," that truly cemented Ali's legacy on the continent. Throughout this period Ali consciously linked his struggle for racial equality in America to the cause on the continent. As Yomi Kazeem explains regarding this efficacious approach,

> Ali's popularity was rooted in his personal struggles and beliefs. Unapologetic about championing his blackness and defiantly embracing his roots, his involvement in the civil rights movement of the 1960s made him a favorite among Africans who could identify with his causes and struggles.... As disappointment grew in post-colonial Africa, Ali was deified by Africans who felt they were being let down by former anti-colonial heroes turned presidents who had promised so much but given so little.... Ali was really the first "African" American ... and Ali went that step further and said himself: "I am an African."[56]

Despite Ali's popularity, Carter's hopes and vision for this diplomatic mission could not have been more divergent from what ultimately transpired. The string of disappointments began on the boxer's first stop, in Tanzania, with the country's president, Julius Nyerere, refusing to even meet with Ali. Going forward, the woefully unprepared Ali fielded innumerable questions by hostile journalists regarding American foreign policy and its neglect of Africa, while he himself was variously accused of being an "agent of American imperialism," a "Black traitor," and an "Uncle Tom." Ali quickly discerned that Africans were largely unconcerned with the events in Afghanistan and were, instead, much more concerned with the plight of their Black brothers and sisters in apartheid South Africa. For example, a Nigerian journalist rhetorically asked, "[Is it] Muhammad Ali's mission ... to convince us that Russian troops in Afghanistan should

Africa Protests

concern us more than racist troops in Zimbabwe?" Meanwhile in Ghana, a writer in the *Daily Graphic* implored Ali to "go home and tell the United States government [that] what is happening in South Africa and Zimbabwe bothers Africans more than events in Afghanistan, a country which most of us hadn't heard of before."[57] Prompted by this type of recurring reproach while in Nigeria, he vowed, "I will drive it home to Jimmy Carter that these people are not bothered in the least whether the Olympics Games are held. What they are concerned about is the total liberation of Africa."[58] And directing similar comments to a different Nigerian audience, he declared, "To me, South Africa is worse than Russia. They kill my brothers daily, trade in them and subject them to all sorts of inhuman torture. . . . America is guilty of taking sides with apartheid in South Africa and is, even still, maintaining trade ties with the enemies of humanity."[59]

Upon returning to the United States, Ali both met with Carter and filed a report that earnestly summarized his impressions. Ultimately, virtually all of Ali's efforts while on the promotional tour had been lost in a torrent of African denunciation of both the United States' ongoing support of the South African regime and its seeming indifference toward Black South Africans; as such, the legendary boxer failed to change the minds of any of the African leaders with whom he met regarding the boycott.

The 1980 Boycott: Mixed Results

By the time the Games finally arrived, a handful of African nations— nineteen in total—had opted not to send athletes to Moscow. Most of these states formally boycotted the Games, but others simply failed to dispatch delegations for either political or financial reasons, or both, but without making any official declarations. The publicly articulated justifications for withholding Olympic squads varied widely, though Cold War considerations were almost certainly the most decisive factor in each country's deliberations.

Among the African nations that formally joined the boycott was Zaire, a solid Cold War ally of the United States and a country highly dependent on American aid. Liberia, a West African nation that had been founded by the United States, similarly withdrew, as did Kenya, which also enjoyed close relations with Washington. The uneasiness of Kenya's president, Daniel Arap Moi, regarding Soviet actions in the Horn of Africa further served to deepen his country's support. Speaking in February 1980, Arap Moi alluded to these security concerns:

> Let there be no misunderstanding of our motives in this matter. We are not against the Soviet Union as a nation nor are we trying to harm the Olympic Movement. But we do not believe that the interests of our country and the peace of the world are going to be served by ignoring what is clearly a threat to the security of small nations and ultimately to world peace. Kenya has built up strong solidarity with other small nations, which, like us, believe that the world is safer for all mankind when the superpowers do not try to involve us in their quarrel. Sportsmen do not live in an ivory tower of their own.[60]

Elsewhere, David Kanin has suggested that there was an additional, strategic motive for the Kenyan president's support of the boycott: "Moi received the red-carpet treatment on his trip to Washington, D.C. in February 1980 and used the Olympic issue to pull his country closer to the United States than at any time under his predecessor, Jomo Kenyatta."[61]

Given its historic engagement with and participation in the Olympic Games, Egypt constituted another notable African nation that withheld its squad. In Egypt's case, religious concerns were primarily responsible for the country's withdrawal from the Games, with both citizens and leaders outraged that the Soviets were killing "our fellow Muslim brothers" in Afghanistan.[62] Anwar Sadat, the Egyptian president, cited this violence in an April 1980 speech in which he explained his country's determination to join the boycott: "This decision reflects the sentiment of Egyptian sportsmen and their unions, their belief that a boycott is necessary because the Soviet Union violates the sovereignty of member states of the United Nations and commits the ugliest crimes of genocide. The Soviet Union also violates the Olympic principles of brotherhood, love, and peace, and the hands of the Soviet leader are tainted with the blood of our brothers, the honorable and peaceful people of Afghanistan. . . . Sportsmen worldwide should speak out against the treacherous Soviet aggression upon a peace-loving nation."[63] The prime minister of Morocco, Maati Bouabid, offered similar political and religious justifications: "We are completely in agreement with a boycott of the Olympic Games in Moscow. We have taken this stand because of the unjustifiable Soviet intervention in Afghanistan, a Muslim and non-aligned country."[64]

After initially indicating it would not support a boycott, Ghana, too, eventually withheld its athletes but for much less solemn reasons. On May 27, the state-owned *Daily Graphic* ran an editorial that endorsed the country's decision not to participate in Moscow due to the contention that Ghanaian "athletes were below standard and there was a lack of money to send them. Nobody likes the idea of having athletes return home from international competitions with long faces and long stories to tell without any medals," while still trying to distance the country from the American-led boycott.[65] Ultimately, most of the African nations that were poised to send athletically competitive delegations to the Games rejected the boycott, with twenty-two squads from the continent eventually traveling to Moscow. Framing the boycott solely in terms of its athletic impact, although arguably in somewhat exaggerated fashion, Nicholas Evan Sarantakes points out that "although a number of African nations decided to boycott Moscow, their absence looked good only on a map. They were weak athletic powers and most people would not have noticed their presence had they been at the Olympics."[66]

Ultimately, it's difficult to assess how the various participating and boycotting African nations might have "won away from the podium," regarding the 1980 Moscow Olympic Games, and thus it's challenging to characterize their actions and associated outcomes utilizing this book's overarching framework. Of the twenty-two African countries that sent teams to Moscow, only four—Ethiopia, Zimbabwe, Tanzania, and Uganda—featured medal winners. Yet all of these NOCs could claim to be upholding the Olympic Movement's principles merely by participating in the Games, providing their athletes an opportunity to compete in an unrivaled sporting event for which they had trained so extensively. Another victory these nations could assert was their unyielding resistance to the United States—in this case the various forms of pressure that Washington applied in an attempt to enlist African states to join the boycott.

Conversely, those African countries that withheld their Olympic delegations from Moscow could avow victory by citing both their demonstrable championing of the oppressed citizens of Afghanistan and their virtuous insistence on the inviolable sovereignty of independent nations. African countries with sizable Muslim populations could also invoke religious affinity with the countless victims of the Soviets' aggression. Ultimately, regardless of their respective decisions, every African leader could claim some type of victory, even if only a qualified one, related to the 1980 Games. Indeed, by siding with the United States or the USSR they accordingly ensured that the flows of money, weapons, and other forms of Cold War assistance emanating from Washington, DC, and Moscow to their respective countries would continue, uninterrupted.

The 1984 Olympic Games: Africa (Largely) Present, Again

The American-led boycott of the Moscow Games all but guaranteed retaliation by the Soviet Union and its allies four years later, as the 1984 Games in Los Angeles approached.[67] In the end, a total of eighteen countries opted not to send squads to the United States, including the African nations of Angola, Upper Volta (Burkina Faso), Ethiopia, and Libya.[68] Predictably, many of the boycotting nations were situated in the Eastern Bloc and all were Soviet allies. Disappointingly for the Soviet Union, a series of African nations, including Benin, Mozambique, and Congo-Brazzaville, all of which featured Marxist-Leninist governments, ultimately decided to dispatch their athletes to Los Angeles. So, too, did Somalia disregard Soviet pressure to boycott, in this case owing to the USSR's support for Ethiopia during the Ogaden, or Ethio-Somali, War (1977–78). Ironically, as Alfred E. Senn has argued, "The Soviet success in persuading the African states to come to Moscow may actually have undermined possible support for their own boycott action in 1984; a number of African states quickly disassociated themselves from the Soviet action just as they had the American efforts in 1980."[69]

Even those Africans nations that sent squads to Los Angeles, though, had not abandoned the pursuit of racial justice in Olympic sport. In particular, African officials and activists were concerned that South African athletes were "sneaking into Olympic participation by acquiring passports of convenience," an accusation that, among others, Sam Ramsamy had made in a July 1984 letter to the IOC president, Juan Antonio Samaranch.[70] Although there were many examples of this alleged form of inventive naturalization, the case of Zola Budd, an elite distance runner born in South Africa, drew the most attention. Budd was able to avoid the ongoing IOC ban on South African athletes by controversially securing, in a highly expedited manner, British citizenship owing to the fact that her grandfather was British. Once in Los Angeles, she would become (in)famously entangled with the American runner Mary Decker-Slaney during the 3,000-meter race. (Budd's case is discussed in greater detail in chapter 5.)

Other African observers protested the persistent rugby connections between various nations and South Africa, an issue that had also received attention at the 1980 Moscow Games, having first burst onto the Olympic stage in 1976. Drawing particular ire ahead of the 1984 Games was a proposed tour of South Africa by England's Rugby Football Union in May of that year, just two months prior to the start of the Los Angeles Olympics.[71] Even though South Africa had long since been expelled from the Olympic Movement and rugby remained beyond the IOC's purview, Africans continued to fashion the view of any sporting engagement with the pariah nation an Olympic matter. A letter from Anani Matthia, the president of the Association of National Committees of Africa (ANOCA), to the chairman of the British Olympic Association in March 1984 showcases this ongoing strategy:

> I am compelled to write you in order to launch a strong protest with regards to the proposed tour of the Rugby Football Union to racist South Africa in May 1984. . . . What is particularly intriguing is the timing; why should the tour come up just when the Los Angeles Olympic Games are around the corner?

... The apartheid sports policy was instituted purposely to humiliate Africans in that country from enjoying their basic rights. And as long as the constitution is not amended, we in Africa will continue to view any sporting contacts with racist South Africa as a hostile act, and we shall reserve the right to act accordingly. We appeal to you to bring pressure to bear on the Rugby Football Union to cancel this tour, which you will agree with me does not serve the interest of international sports and, particularly, the Olympic Movement.[72]

When Ethiopia announced its boycott of the Los Angeles Games in early June, it also cited England's rugby tour of South Africa. Ethiopia took this measure because, as officially reported in the Soviet news service *Tass*, "the United States uses the games for purely political purposes against socialist and progressive states. Along with that, the NOC of Ethiopia expressed a resolute protest in connection with the British government's refusal to cancel the English rugby team's trip to the racist-ruled republic of South Africa."[73]

Naturally, Los Angeles Olympic Committee (LAOC) officials feared that the boycott could spread further, throughout Africa. In fact, when Angola announced, just weeks after Ethiopia's pronouncement, its intention to similarly withhold its athletes from the Games, the LAOC president, Peter Ueberroth, considered sending a team of officials to Africa to encourage the more than forty NOCs on the continent that had already committed to the Games to maintain their pledge. However, this measure ultimately proved unnecessary, as the number of African nations unwilling to send athletes to Los Angeles remained extremely small. Instead, the Los Angeles organizers turned their attention to Zola Budd, voicing concerns about her newfound British citizenship and stressing that the IOC should take "appropriate action." Meanwhile, Ueberroth declared that he was "anxious that the IOC permit nothing to be done that would even appear to cater to South African interests."[74] Whether these public statements sufficiently appeased the leaders of African nations or these statesmen simply didn't have the appetite for further boycotts remains unclear. Regardless, the impact of the boycott of the 1984

Africa Protests

Games was negligible, with African states abandoning the principled stances that had characterized their previous campaigns. Even the SCSA rejected a call to keep Africa's athletes away from Los Angeles. The era of Olympic boycotts was, seemingly, finally over.[75]

Boycotts, or even the threat thereof, were arguably the most powerful weapon in the African nations' Olympic Games arsenal during these turbulent years. For almost two decades African countries had remained virtually united in the pursuit of their shared Olympic goals, powerfully and unapologetically challenging the Brundage-driven notion that sports and politics do not, and should not, mix. Indeed, Africans repeatedly invoked boycott as a highly potent politico-sporting tactic to advance their mutual aim of liberating sport on the continent from racial discrimination. However, by the 1980 Olympic Games the solidarity that the continent had so steadfastly maintained finally cracked, with Cold War allegiances largely dictating which African athletes would be traveling to Moscow and which would be staying home. By 1984 Cold War considerations continued to shape these decisions but in a much less determinative fashion. African leaders had apparently concluded that boycotts no longer constituted an effective weapon and that the political outcome did not outweigh the athletic sacrifice. With the end of White minority rule in Zimbabwe in 1980, the conclusion of the Cold War in 1989, and the dismantlement of the apartheid regime in South Africa between 1990 and 1994, the impetuses for boycott by African states steadily evaporated, marking the conclusion of a tumultuous, if highly principled, era.

4

Parlaying Individual Olympic Success into Positive Change on the Continent

Twenty years ago, I ran for my life as I tried to escape the soldiers with guns. Today, I run for my life as I chase down the incredible opportunity God has laid out in front of me. . . . I ran in the [refugee] camp to survive. Now I run to help others not only survive, but to thrive.

> —South Sudanese Olympic distance runner Lopez Lomong, promoting his charitable foundation, 4 South Sudan

This school lunch program has helped many children to develop a focus in their lives. Without this food, they will lose focus and return to hopelessness. A meal a day really helps to keep that focus. In other parts of the world, people talk about three or four meals a day. We need to raise the awareness that there are kids out there who don't have anything to eat. Without education, there is no progress in any country. The future of this world is in these children we are trying to keep in school. In many rich countries, people don't know about this program. I am, therefore, a shining example of how one school meal a day can transform the life of a hungry child.

> —Paul Tergat, two-time Olympic silver medalist and World Food Programme (WFP) "Ambassador against Hunger" from Kenya, reflecting on the future of this WFP program and its importance in his life

Over the decades, African politicians, sports officials, and activists have used the Olympic Games to improve the plights of countless residents on the continent by advancing a broad range of social-development objectives. But individual African athletes have also utilized the Games as a vehicle to effect positive change, including by improving public health, fostering national unity, facilitating athletic development, increasing access to education, encouraging gender equity, and generating goodwill, both at home and abroad. Many of these individuals were elite competitors who have used their athletic celebrity to raise awareness and, often, funds for particular causes that resonate with them. In order to coordinate these efforts, many of these former Olympians have created charitable foundations, utilizing their high-profile athletic status to fundraise for their respective organizations. Other Olympic athletes, such as the members of the Refugee Team, have raised global awareness of evacuees and other disadvantaged peoples through their sheer perseverance and commitment. This chapter examines an array of Olympians who have engaged in these types of altruistic beneficence and the vital contributions they have made. Collectively, these selfless humanitarian and social-development efforts constitute yet another victory in Africa's overall advance.

National Athletic and Educational Development via Olympic Success

Following independence African countries had scant resources to allocate for sports programs and projects; however, their participation in and, eventually, their record of notable achievements at the Olympic Games ultimately helped them to achieve broader goals related to national development. As David B. Kanin has argued, for African states, "international [sporting] successes spurred the development of athletic programs and the near deification of sports heroes."[1] In turn, following their athletic careers many of these Olympic legends focused their efforts on sports-related educational initiatives and activities, thereby advancing various social-development objectives in their respective nations.

Mike Boit, a Kenyan middle-distance runner, was one of the first athletes who parlayed Olympic success into the delivery and enhancement of sports-related instruction in his home country. After winning bronze at the 1972 Munich Olympics in the 800 meters, he relocated to the United States to attend Eastern New Mexico University, earning a BA in 1976. Subsequently, Boit completed two MA degrees from Stanford University before earning his doctorate in physical education administration from the University of Oregon in 1986.[2] With this sheaf of American degrees in hand, he returned to Kenya to join the faculty of the Department of Physical Education at Kenyatta University and would eventually direct the institution's Exercise and Sports Science program.[3]

In addition to educating and mentoring countless Kenyan college students, Boit also served as Kenya's sports commissioner from 1990 to 1997 before returning to Kenyatta University. Accustomed to living abroad and thus beyond the reach of the highly controlling Kenyan Athletics Federation, he championed his country's athletes rather than its bureaucracy. For example, as sports commissioner he ensured that the state quickly returned Kenyan runners' passports to them, enabling them to travel abroad to compete, and invited agents into the country for the first time. In turn, these two seemingly simple initiatives had far-reaching beneficial results. As biographer John Manners has contended, "Mike is too honest to admit it, but he is responsible for the Kenyan dynasty in distance running." Meanwhile Boit humbly explained that "the idea was that everyone should benefit from his own talents. That's a basic human right."[4]

Boit and Manners also cofounded, in 2004, the Kenya Scholar Access Program (KenSAP), which helps "high-achieving, low-income Kenyan high school graduates gain admission to the most selective colleges and universities in North America, all with full financial aid." Since its inception, the organization has placed over 230 students at institutions such as Harvard (27 students), Yale (17), Princeton (14), Cornell (9), Dartmouth (9), and Stanford (7), in addition to some forty-five other elite colleges and universities. According to the organization, "While guiding its students through the admissions process, the program also prepares them for American campus life, both academically and culturally, and later provides counsel and support throughout the students' undergraduate careers and beyond."[5]

Generating National Unity via the Olympic Games

African Olympic athletes have also helped foster national unity, oftentimes simply by medaling in an event. These successful competitors naturally rouse citizens in their respective home countries, as African nations don't typically emerge from Olympic Games with large medal hauls. In practice, the comity that their achievements have helped to generate has cut across ethnic, religious, racial, regional, and other types of social divides. Although some critics argue that sports-inspired unity is often fleeting—quickly created following an athletic achievement but ultimately not very durable—even when the gulfs that are bridged are extremely wide, the impact is not entirely or inherently ephemeral.[6]

Generating National Unity in a Deeply Divided State: Josia Thugwane and South Africa

The example of Josia Thugwane, the first Black South African to win an individual gold medal (for the marathon at the 1996 Olympic Games in Atlanta), is illustrative of the potential for this type of enduring impact. Owing to apartheid, Thugwane, who both worked in and was sponsored by a South African mining company, had not even been legally permitted to vote in his own country until just two years prior to the Atlanta Games. But following the election of Nelson Mandela in 1994 he, like so many other Black South Africans, desired to make his new president proud. Indeed, when asked why he aspired to go to the Olympic Games, Thugwane declared, "In my mind, I understand just one thing: to go there [Atlanta] to represent Mandela."[7] In this endeavor Thugwane faced considerable pressure and, in some ways, the burden of his country's disturbing past as he prepared for the Atlanta Games (fig. 4.1). As American sports journalist Mike Wise explained, "Following apartheid, South Africa's first healing, unifying moment on the sporting stage had come the year before, when the Springboks stunningly won the Rugby World Cup. . . . [But] never had just one black man [Thugwane] faced the possibility of millions of white South Africans on the brink of euphoria if he could medal."[8] Ultimately, his gold-medal performance

FIGURE 4.1. A South African stamp issued in 2000 commemorating Josia Thugwane's victory in the marathon at the 1996 Olympic Games in Atlanta. Hipix / Alamy Stock Photo

in the marathon confirmed that he had done much more than simply "represent" his president, the singular objective he had earlier identified; he had also precipitated for millions of South Africans—Black and White—a victory-inspired ecstasy.

It was the durable consonance across racial lines that Thugwane's victory generated, though, that rendered it more than just an athletic accomplishment. Reconstructing the events of the race during which three Black South African runners took the lead in the marathon, Wise continued: "Three black men, unable to vote in their own country until two years ago, unable to compete internationally until five years ago, [were] together in the lead, on the last day of the Games. . . . In South Africa, cars on the freeway began pulling off at filling stations, crowding televisions around cashiers, to see whether Josia could win as the race concluded."[9] And once he won there was elation: "Bedlam—on two continents. Annalize [the White girlfriend of Josia's coach] hugged White and Black strangers in the streets, stating 'the whole country is so proud. Josia is like the lost child that's come home.' . . . They poured out of the Black townships, out of the gated White neighborhoods, out of malls and restaurants, off the motorways into filling stations. Hell, Shift B stopped production at the Koorfontein Mines, where Josia is employed—all celebrating the glory of one man, one flag."[10]

Following Thugwane's victory Mandela declared, "Josia is our 'Golden Boy,' and he has reinforced our pride and confidence as a nation." Perhaps even more tellingly, though, was the surprise that greeted fellow Olympian Penny Heyns, a White swimmer. Although she had earned two gold medals in breaststroke events at the Atlanta Games, Heyns wasn't sure how she and Thugwane would be received upon arriving back home in South Africa. She said, "There was this expectation when we got back that white people would be happy for me and black people would be happy for Josia. The big surprise for both of us was that the celebration was so united. It was quite overwhelming, actually."[11]

A letter to the editor that appeared in *Sports Illustrated* months after the conclusion of the Atlanta Games suggests the durable impact of Thugwane's victory on and its ongoing importance for the "New South Africa"—that is, post-apartheid South Africa—for

South Africans everywhere: "To me, as a South African–American and a sports fan, the most recent meaningful event involving South Africa took place in the U.S., on the last day of the Atlanta Olympics. As Josia Thugwane received his marathon gold medal, I was moved to see the flag of a new country raised in victory. Both national anthems were sung, representing the new South Africa under the pragmatic leadership of Nelson Mandela."[12]

Developing Unity Beyond the Nation

Although the International Olympic Committee (IOC) had effectively denied the participation of refugees in the Olympics since the birth of the Modern Games owing to the requirement that a participating athlete be formally associated with a recognized nation, in 2016 the IOC finally assembled the Refugee Olympic Athletes Team, which competed later that year at the Rio de Janeiro Games. Africans from three different countries—South Sudan, Ethiopia, and the Congo (DRC)—constituted eight of the ten members of the squad. Owing to their displacement and associated status, as well as to their disparate nationalities, these athletes' spirited participation in the Olympics fostered forms of solidarity and empowerment that inherently transcended individual nations. During the announcement of this initiative, IOC president Thomas Bach affirmed this boundless impact: "This team is a symbol of hope to all the refugees in our world. It is also a signal to the international community that refugees are our fellow human beings and are an enrichment to society. These refugees have no home, no team, no flag, no national anthem. We will offer them a home in the Olympic Village, together with all the athletes of the world."[13] Minky Worden of Human Rights Watch similarly praised the IOC for generating this opportunity for the refugee athletes as well as for the broader implications of this initiative: "In a year when refugees have found borders, camps, and minds closed, the International Olympic Committee did something remarkably open. The creation of a refugee team reframes the debate, to focus not on fear and pushing away, but on inclusion and celebrating the resilience and potential all refugees represent."[14]

Although these athletes weren't particularly competitive at the Olympic level and, predictably, none of them medaled at the Games, they fully realized the significance of their inclusion for the wider, international community of refugees. They also harbored hopes regarding what their participation might generate for others facing similar challenges. For example, Anjelina Nadai Lohalith, a 1,500-meter runner from South Sudan, declared:

> It is very challenging when you are chased away from your homeland. Nobody can feel happy when you are chased or [when] you stay in another country. But right now, I feel proud. I'm proud to be a refugee. We are representing the millions of refugees all over the world. Maybe, in years to come, I will represent myself. But, at this moment, we are their light. Wherever they are, at least they will now have some encouragement and know: we can do something. Wherever they are, they are human beings. They are not animals. That is why we have been given this chance. So, they should not be looked down on. Or treated unfairly.[15]

Other members of the Refugee Olympic Team similarly eyed the global community of refugees when considering the importance of their participation in the Rio Games. Yet they also retained domestic improvement objectives, aiming to eventually return to, and elevate the plights of people still residing in, their respective home countries. As South Sudanese runner Yiech Pur Biel explained:

> I know I have a message to tell the world. First, I feel a lot of pressure because millions of refugees are looking to us to tell [the world] what they are living. Secondly, it's about my nation: South Sudan. If I succeed and only go live abroad, there's no legacy that I give to other people. I want to come back and serve the nation, show them the way as a peacemaker, tell the world that we can challenge our leaders. Because the leaders make the problems. Thirdly, it's about my family. The background I come from; it's a terrible history, you see. I must change that. Maybe I can go back to that village now to help the young people. Because I know that it's not only my family that was suffering, and I can go serve them. I am going to rescue my people from that disaster.[16]

The Refugee Olympic Team competed again at the 2020 Games in Tokyo, with the roster expanding from ten to twenty-nine athletes. Owing primarily to the ongoing conflict in Syria, the proportion of African athletes on the squad dropped considerably, to just 34 percent (ten out of twenty-nine). Irrespective of the exact composition of the team, once again, none of the refugee participants medaled. But of course, that was never the point.

Building a Better Future: Olympians and Charitable Foundations

A number of African Olympic athletes have utilized the sports-celebrity status they earned via success at the Games to establish charitable foundations. The assistance that these organizations provide comes in many forms, some of which are related to sports and athletic development. Other foundations, however, offer support unrelated to athletics by, for example, improving access to healthcare, education, and clean water or by enhancing overall nutrition. In some cases, these foundations partner with domestic or international nongovernmental organizations (NGOs), while others forge ahead on their own.

Lopez Lomong: Giving Back from a New Nation to an Old One

Born in 1985 in Kimotong, in what is now South Sudan, Lopepe "Lopez" Lomong eventually became one of the countless victims of the Second Sudanese Civil War, which stretched from 1983 to 2005. After being abducted at age six, he escaped, surviving as one of the conflict's over twenty thousand "Lost Boys"—ethnic Nuer and Dinka boys displaced or orphaned during the fighting who undertook harrowing journeys to reach refugee camps in bordering Kenya or Ethiopia. After spending a decade in the Kakuma refugee camp in Northeastern Kenya, Lomong's passage to the United States was facilitated by the Unaccompanied Refugee Minor Program. At sixteen years old, Lomong relocated to upstate New York, where he starred in track during high school. From there Lomong went on to compete at Norfolk State University and, subsequently and much more extensively, at Northern Arizona University, where he became an NCAA champion. Even more personally transformative, though, was his attainment of US citizenship in 2007. In the ensuing year he earned a spot on the US

Olympic squad for the Beijing Games in the 1,500 meters, and owing to the formidable challenges Lomong had overcome in his life, the team captains elected him to serve as the flagbearer for the delegation.

With his athletic career secure, Lomong turned his gaze back toward Africa—to his former homeland. South Sudan had gained its independence from Sudan in 2011 following decades of fighting but still faced considerable impediments during its infancy as a sovereign nation. To assist with the fledgling country's development, he established the Lopez Lomong Foundation in 2012. Sharing his inspiration for this initiative, Lomong explained, "Over the past few years, I have made many trips back to Kimotong [South Sudan]. Every trip left me convinced that the problems the people face can be resolved.... Out of conversations with friends and other athletes, I came up with the idea to start my own foundation."[17] He then outlined the four core issues that the organization would seek to remedy:

There are four basic needs that must be addressed to improve the lives of the people in South Sudan. First, we need clean water. Today, women spend a large portion of their day walking to the river to fetch water. They carry large buckets of water back to the village. Even then, the water is not very clean.... Second, I want to open up access to education.... Sudanese boys and girls are just as eager to learn, but they do not have access to education. I want to change that by building a school in Kimotong. In addition, I want to provide vocational training for women in my village and the surrounding areas. Education is power, and I want to empower my sister and my mother and the other women of the village and give them a real future.... My third priority is to improve nutrition by opening up access to better farming tools and methods.... In Kakuma, my food came in bags from the U.S.A. I used to stare at the American flag on the bag of corn. That food kept me alive. However, one of the best days in Kakuma came when someone gave us seeds so that we could grow our own food. That's what I want to do for my people in South Sudan. Finally, I have never been able to erase the image of the poor mothers who brought their children to me, asking me to give their children medicine to make them well. I could not do anything to help them on that first trip. I came away not only frustrated but angry. . . . A hospital in Kimotong would be a godsend, but even a small clinic will save lives. I want to start with the latter.[18]

Lomong quickly identified World Vision, a long-standing international NGO, as a potential partner, as the organization was already active in the target area. Following a series of promising discussions, they collaboratively formed 4 South Sudan. Promotional material for the organization says, "[4 South Sudan] changes lives and brings healing to South Sudan . . . offering care, support, and a better future to families in South Sudan recovering from a legacy of warfare . . . bringing hope to families who face the realities of poverty and the lingering impact of daily violence. By providing access to clean water, health care, education, and nutrition, we are providing a brighter future for the South Sudanese."[19] For his efforts, in 2012 Lomong received the Visa Humanitarian of the Year Award, which recognizes "outstanding achievements by athletes in social activities and personal commitments outside the arena of competition."[20]

Peter Kipchumba Rono: Educational Success through Athletic Endeavor

Peter Kipchumba Rono, a Kenyan 1,500-meter runner who captured the gold medal at the 1988 Seoul Olympics, shares Lomong's drive to assist disadvantaged Africans. In the fall of 1988, just after the conclusion of the Games, he traveled around his home country, delivering a series of inspirational talks to students in an array of communities in the Rift Valley, where he had grown up. In particular, Rono wanted the members of his audiences to be aware of the possibility of earning athletics scholarships at American institutions of higher education, just as he had at Mount St. Mary's University in Maryland. Following this informal tour of over twenty schools, Rono explained, "I wanted them to have a knowledge of sport, but also to know that they did not have to go [to college] for athletics only. They should also have an education in something they could benefit from throughout life."[21]

Over time, Rono devised a more formal plan to facilitate these types of educational opportunities. In the regional capital, Kapsabet, by the early 1990s, he had opened the Nandi Education and Training Centre, which aims to help Kenyan students secure athletic scholarships in the United States.[22] The program began rather humbly, with just five students. Interestingly, even as it eventually grew, many of the enrolled students had never even visited Nairobi, Kenya's capital city, let alone traveled overseas. Despite this challenge, though, the program steadily expanded, and by 1996 it was "fully functional, with a full-fledged office and proper management." (Rono's wife, Mary, had previously run the center whenever Peter was abroad.)[23] Students at the Training Centre also benefitted from regular visits by other Kenyan Olympians, including Patrick Sang, Paul Tergat, and Tegla Loroupe, who interacted with them and, at times, even provided financial support for them to travel and compete abroad.

Abraham Cheruiyot is one of the many Nandi Centre attendees who has tangibly benefitted from this experience. Paying only a processing fee to attend, he trained there for roughly nine months before qualifying for a scholarship in the United States. Although he received multiple offers, he ultimately chose Iowa State University, where he would eventually earn two bachelor's degrees. When asked in 2009 about the opportunity that Rono's initiative had enabled him to secure, Cheruiyot was effusive:

> I don't have the right words to describe what sort of person Peter is. He is a great man. He has a good heart. . . . Peter is always giving, without thinking [about] what he can gain. That is how so many of us here in the U.S.A. got here. Peter has his mother and children here in the U.S.A., and yet he has athletes staying at his house. What Peter has given back to the Kenyan nation is that he had enough contacts here to be able to help over 200 Kenyans get scholarships. Peter has greatly inspired me. He has instilled in me the ability to work hard. At camp, he taught us that life was all about working hard. He emphasized education and the need to work hard.[24]

After helping hundreds of Nandi Centre enrollees secure scholarships at American colleges and universities, in 2000 Rono and his family moved permanently to the United States. Rono accepted a coaching job at Farleigh Dickinson University in New Jersey, before transitioning to a position at New Balance, a major sports footwear and apparel manufacturer headquartered in New Jersey. Meanwhile, the Nandi Centre persisted, with Rono continuing to support its student-athletes in any way he could, including by expanding scholarship opportunities to other countries, including Canada, Australia, and Germany. Owing to these seemingly endless, selfless efforts to assist his fellow Kenyans, Rono was appointed a United Nations Goodwill Ambassador in 2006, tasked with the specific objective of overcoming malnutrition in developing countries through the use of spirulina, a microalga rich in vitamins, proteins, and minerals. Collectively, the wide range and profound impact of Rono's post-Olympic altruistic endeavors prompted one of his former students, Jael Koch, who set multiple records in women's cross-country while at Florida Southern College from 2003 to 2007, to remark, "It is hard to describe Peter accurately. He is a kind and humble person who doesn't get tired of helping others. . . . He is a people person who goes out of his way to help."[25]

Maria Mutola: Relentlessly Assistive

Maria de Lurdes Mutola, who hails from Mozambique, is another Olympic athlete who has worked tirelessly to improve the plights of not only her compatriots but of communities throughout the continent. Mutola was born in the capital city, Maputo, in 1972 while Mozambique was still under Portuguese colonial control.[26] By the time she was fifteen years old, Mutola had taken up running and enjoyed almost immediate success. Indeed, after only a few months of training, she won the silver medal in the 800 meters at the 1988 African Championships in Algeria and less than two months later—while she was still only fifteen—was representing Mozambique at the 1988 Seoul Olympics, which ran from mid-September to early October. The Seoul Games were, remarkably, just the first of six Olympics in which she would compete, spanning all the way to the 2008 Games in Beijing (see fig 4.2). Along the way she earned two Olympic medals: bronze in 1996 (Atlanta) and gold in 2000 (Sydney).

FIGURE 4.2. Maria Mutola competing in the women's 800-meter event at the 2004 Athens Olympic Games. Allstar Picture Library Ltd. / Alamy Stock Photo

Similar to Lomong and Rono, Mutola, once she had established herself as an Olympic-level athlete, turned her attention to helping others. The most significant of her many assistive initiatives was the formation, in 2002, of the Lurdes Mutola Foundation, which primarily aims to help young Mozambicans achieve their sporting and educational potential. In practice, though, the organization's various activities and programs transcend this core mission. For example, the foundation has partnered with the Mozambican Ministry of Health and UNICEF on an immunization campaign against measles and polio. Other initiatives include the 2007 launch of the Mais Escola para Mim (More School for Me) program, which strives to "increase the numbers of girls and young women who graduate from secondary schools, particularly in rural parts of the country." Via this program, the foundation aims, more expansively, "to address broad gender disparities in education in Mozambique and to change the lives of the young women involved, as well as to provide a successful model for the educational empowerment of women in rural African communities."[27] The Mutola Foundation has also partnered with WaterAid, an international NGO that aims to provide clean water and toilets for underserviced communities.

More recently, the foundation has sought to empower girls through soccer programming. To this end, since 2012 it has been recruiting and training coaches so that the participants can "increase their self-esteem, increase their knowledge of their rights, and receive the tools they need to create a bright future." In this same vein, the foundation established Copa Mutola, which is "a platform to raise awareness among the general public about girls' rights, sexual and reproductive health, and ways to prevent domestic violence and sexual abuse."[28] For this undertaking, Mutola partnered with various government ministries and NGOs, as well as with the Mozambican Football Federation.

Following Mutola's retirement from competitive track, in addition to continuing her impressive assortment of aforementioned community-oriented activities, she also reengaged with her first sporting love: soccer. Astonishingly, Mutola went on to play professionally in South Africa, while also captaining the Mozambican Women's National Team at the 2011 All-Africa Games. And amidst these myriad endeavors, Mutola also found time to coach Caster Semenya, the aforementioned South African runner who earned a silver medal at the 2012 London Olympics.

Paul Tergat: Running against Hunger

Like many of Kenya's Olympic stars, marathoner Paul Tergat grew up poor, in his case in a dry, drought-stricken area of the country's Rift Valley region. Compounding this inherent hardship was the fact that he had an astounding sixteen siblings. These challenges notwithstanding, Tergat's father pushed *all* of them to go to school. As the Olympian recalled, "I grew up in a very humble background. It was very difficult for us to go to school. Life was very difficult. Poverty was rampant in our area. . . . My dad wasn't a rich man, and he was quite old, but the only thing he knew was that he wanted us to go to school."[29] Yet the paucity of food remained a major impediment to the children's education. "It was very difficult to go [to school] every day because there was nothing to eat. Most of the kids didn't want to go to school because they were more interested in trying to get food, so we used to stay behind to look after the animals."[30]

Thankfully for Tergat and his intermittent classmates, in 1979, when he was ten years old, the United Nations World Food Programme (WFP) commenced a meal distribution program in schools in the Rift Valley. Tergat stressed the importance of this initiative, recalling,

> We were really excited to get a free hot meal. It was one of the motivating factors that pushed up class attendance and enrollment. At school, we were served maize and beans. At the time, we could not find this kind of food at home. When the WFP came, it was a relief to most of the parents to know that the kids wouldn't be around hungry and crying all day. My Mum was so excited. And it was the best incentive for us to know that when we got to school we would get a meal of hot, steamy food. We didn't miss a single day.[31]

Indeed, Tergat emphasized that the food literally fueled and facilitated his life objectives: "Getting the food when I was in primary school really helped me a lot to go ahead and realize my dreams. I think that without this motivation to go to school, a lot of us would have dropped out. It is hard to concentrate on an empty stomach."[32] For Tergat, the demonstrable fulfillment of these dreams includes two silver medals, earned in the 10,000-meter events at the Atlanta and Sydney Olympic Games, in 1996 and 2000, respectively, and an array of other athletic accomplishments, including the establishment of multiple world records.

Owing to the food security issues that Tergat experienced as a child, in 2004 he was named a United Nations WFP Ambassador against Hunger, a role in which he strives to raise both awareness about global hunger and the requisite funds to sustain various nutritional programs in Kenya and beyond. James T. Morris, the executive director of the WFP at the time, praised Tergat's appointment: "Paul is a natural advocate for the WFP. Few people are better qualified to explain how food aid can transform the lives of the world's 300 million chronically hungry children. It is a wonderful thing when people like Paul dedicate a part of their lives to help give kids a chance." Remarking on this undertaking himself, Tergat stressed, "There is a lot of hunger in this world and a lot of children are dropping out of school. I feel I have an obligation to give something back to the community. . . . The main thing is raising awareness and funds for the school-feeding program. I am happy that many people around the world have been following what I am doing. And I think my contacts and image around the world will have a big impact in supporting this program . . . and sustaining it for a long time."[33]

Tegla Loroupe: Running for Peace

Although Kenyan distance runner Tegla Loroupe participated in three successive Olympic Games (1992, 1996, and 2000), unlike many of the other athletes profiled above, she never medaled.[34] Yet this diminutive runner—Loroupe stands at just five foot one—has made immense contributions to her fellow Kenyans as well as to communities across the continent. At the center of these efforts has been the Tegla Loroupe Peace Foundation (TLPF), launched in 2003. The organization's core mission is to "promote the peaceful coexistence and socioeconomic development of poor and marginalized individuals and communities in Northern Kenya and the Greater Horn of Africa Region."[35]

The same year that Loroupe established the TLPF, the foundation began organizing the inaugural Peace Race, intended to prompt, via dialogue and genial athletic competition, the end of hostilities in areas plagued by conflict. Some eight years later, the event was held in Kapenguria, Loroupe's home region in far western Kenya, and proved to be particularly efficacious. In Kapenguria, cattle rustling had long been inciting violent clashes between various groups who were either engaged in this illicit activity or defending their livestock against it. Yet the Peace Race inspired even these hardened combatants to cease hostilities. In turn, a local journalist, Osinde Obane, filed this upbeat account of the outcome of the event: "More than 700 warriors have reformed and surrendered 38 guns to the Kenyan Government following peace efforts by world marathon ace Tegla Loroupe."[36] Local politician Allan Macharia further confirmed the impact of the Peace Race: "We recognize the contributions by Loroupe to bring peace among warring communities. Incidents of rustling have dropped, and warriors have surrendered illegal guns to the Government. These efforts will definitely promote development in the region."[37] The Ugandan Energy and Mineral Exploitation Minister, Peter Lokeris, was also in attendance, as the regional conflict had spilled into this neighboring country. Afterward, he further praised Loroupe for initiating talks between the belligerents and similarly remarked on the significance of the détente that the Peace Race had engendered: "The presence of illegal weapons is a big challenge to the development of the region and the joint disarmament will ease conflicts and boost development."[38]

Meanwhile, between the first version of the Peace Race in 2003 and the highly successful 2010 iteration, Loroupe was exceedingly industrious. In addition to winning the Leipzig marathon in 2004, finishing second in the Venice marathon in 2006, and finishing third in the Las Vegas marathon the following year, Loroupe was named a United Nations Ambassador of Sport in 2006 and the Oxfam Ambassador of Sport and Peace to Darfur in 2007. Commenting on these appointments, Loroupe humbly remarked, "I always go where there are not good people. I want to help them [the victims]."[39] Back in Kapenguria she also opened the Tegla Loroupe Peace Academy for children from Northwest Kenya, Eastern Uganda, Southern Ethiopia, and Southern Sudan who had been orphaned owing to the regional conflict. Although the school started modestly, enrollment rapidly expanded to hundreds of students, underscoring the need for a facility of this nature.

By 2015 Loroupe had reengaged with the Olympics, having been selected to serve as the chef de mission for the inaugural Refugee Team at the 2016 Rio de Janeiro Games. In fact, Loroupe not only directed the squad; she also personally trained five of the athletes—all of whom were originally from South Sudan—chosen for inclusion on the ten-member team, as well as dozens of others who ultimately were not selected for the squad. Commenting on these contributions, Loroupe declared, "I think I have the strength to prove that even small people can do something big. People treat these refugees like criminals. We need to treat them with respect."[40] One of the refugee athletes, Yiech Pur Biel, confirmed that Loroupe did indeed demonstrate the utmost esteem toward them: "Tegla is our mother, not only our leader. Most of us run because of war. Madam Tegla gives us a chance for other people to know the history of our lives. And we can forget what happened before. We can celebrate. We can have hope, like everyone else."[41] During the 2016 Games, Loroupe was also inducted into the Olympians for Life project for her work in promoting peace and took the opportunity to comment on her role as an Olympian and what that meant to her: "I grew up in a conflict zone. I lost relatives. Becoming an Olympian meant overcoming difficulties, hard work and having respect. Without peace, the children don't have time for education; there is no hope for progress. Disarming one bad person saves many lives. As an Olympian, I have an obligation to speak out and to give back."[42]

Improving the Plight of African Women and Girls via Olympic Success: Nawal El Moutawakel, Lornah Kiplagat, and Meseret Defar

Many current or former African Olympic athletes, including Nawal El Moutawakel, Lornah Kiplagat, and Meseret Defar, have used their status as celebrity athletes to promote and advance, in a highly deliberate and focused manner, the quality of life for women and girls across the continent. El Moutawakel, hailing from Morocco, has become a symbol for women's liberation and empowerment in the Muslim world and has actively championed women's rights in several different capacities. Kiplagat, from Kenya, has focused on training women athletes in her native country and, more broadly, has vigorously advocated for increased gender equity in her highly patriarchal homeland. Finally, Defar has been energetically involved in an impressive array of women's causes in her native Ethiopia, including, inter alia, the prevention of HIV/AIDS, the abolishment of child marriage, and the provision of athletic equipment for aspiring runners. Irrespective of their respective foci, the efforts of these three women exemplify the selfless contributions that African Olympians have made, and continue to make, to enhance the plight of women and girls on the continent.

Nawal El Moutawakel: Racing for Women's Rights

By winning the inaugural women's 400-meter hurdles event at the 1984 Los Angeles Games, Nawal El Moutawakel, just twenty-two years old and the only woman in Morocco's thirty-four-athlete delegation, became both the first Moroccan and the first Muslim woman to capture an Olympic gold medal.[43] Afterward, the king of Morocco, Hassan II, telephoned her to congratulate her on this feat, while also declaring that any girl born that day should be named Nawal. Upon returning home, the fanfare continued unabated. As El Moutawakel recalled, "I received thousands of letters at home from women all over Africa, thanking me for my victory for all Arab women. . . . I went home and there were thousands of people at the airport to greet us. There were people at my house all the time; I never had any time with my family. It was incredible."[44] Regarding the letters, she would later add, "Women would write to me and thank me for what I did for them through sport. Ladies with and without the veil told me that I'd liberated them."[45]

El Moutawakel's Olympic accomplishment is even more remarkable if the cultural milieu in which she was raised is considered. In her native Morocco, a conservative Muslim nation, women were actively discouraged from participating in sports, especially in athletic activities that involved racing around a track in minimal attire—shorts, a light top, socks, and sneakers. Given this context, the Olympic champion fully comprehended and appreciated the transcendent impact of her victory. Speaking a few months removed from her triumph in Los Angeles, El Moutawakel declared, "My win was very important to all of my people. It is also very important for the women of my country and all of Africa."[46] Later, she would reflect, "From there, a wide door opened up for many young girls from Morocco and in many Arab and African countries to allow women to compete. Since then, we have seen a lot of Moroccan girls, and the same with Arab countries from whom women had never attended the Olympic Games. They weren't attending just to attend, but attending to win."[47]

Notwithstanding El Moutawakel's athletic acumen and commitment, she retired in 1987, just three years after her Olympic medal–winning performance. In addition to a knee injury and chronic back pain, she also experienced two significant tragedies that factored into this decision. The first was the death of her extremely influential, supportive, and progressive father during the buildup to the Los Angeles Games, and the second was a plane crash in 1985 that took the lives of some of her cross-country teammates at Iowa State University, where she was enrolled.

Following El Moutawakel's retirement, she committed herself to promoting and advocating for women in sport and society, including by serving as an IOC member and, eventually, as the body's vice president. Meanwhile, she was appointed Morocco's Minister of Youth and Sports and also served in an array of other national sports organizations. In these various roles Nawal tirelessly campaigned for women's rights, including inclusion in sports. To this end, she often "brandished the Koran and recited stories about how the prophet Muhammed competed against his wife in archery, swimming, and horseback riding," initially conveying this story as justification domestically, before subsequently projecting the message abroad, to other Muslim nations. In defending both this outlook and her associated persistence, she once remarked, "Nowhere in our religion is it stated that women should stay home and only men should practice sports. It is difficult to push these guys, but I kept pushing and pushing."[48]

In 1993 El Moutawakel made arguably her most tangible contribution to women's sports and social standing in Morocco with the launch of the 5K Courir pour le Plaisir, or Run for Fun, an event held exclusively for women. The competition has since blossomed into the largest race for women in any Muslim country, attracting over twenty thousand participants annually. To maximize participation and engagement, Nawal waived all entry fees by securing an assortment of sponsorships and also arranged for the race to be broadcast live. Tom Knight, a British journalist, has described the event as having "sparked a cultural revolution in Morocco, with Nawal as its architect."[49] Moreover, as Anneliese Goslin has contended, "A race for women is nothing new in the West, but in male-dominated Morocco, it marks a massive social change."[50] Nawal acknowledges that this outcome was, indeed, her intent, commenting in an interview, "I wanted to bring women outside to feel the power of sports together. It's like a mini revolution."[51] Amina Danin, a Moroccan civil servant, confirmed this impact: "This is like a great party for women from every corner of Morocco. It is an expression of freedom."[52] Taking a moment to reflect on her contributions to women's social and sporting liberation in her home country during a 2009 interview, Nawal proudly asserted, "I have the satisfaction of contributing to the liberation of Muslim women—or, rather, of Muslim men, who will have been forced to meditate on my ability."[53]

Lornah Kiplagat: Gender Equality in the Mecca for Distance Running

Born in Kenya in 1974, Lornah Kiplagat would eventually become a world-class runner in a variety of middle-distance events. Kiplagat competed in the 2004, 2008, and 2012 Olympic Games, but not for her native Kenya. Instead, she ran for the Netherlands, having moved there in 1999 and subsequently gaining Dutch citizenship. However, Kiplagat's interest in her country of birth never waned, and in 2000 she opened the Lornah Kiplagat High Altitude Training Centre (HATC) in Iten, Kenya, the global epicenter of long-distance

148   AFRICA AND THE OLYMPICS

running (figs. 4.3 and 4.4). Although the HATC welcomes men, including (paying) sports tourists from abroad, the focus is on providing gratis training and education for Kenyan women and girls. In a wide-ranging interview in 2004, Kiplagat cited gender norms and expectations in Kenya to explain why a facility of this nature was needed:

> Women have no place . . . to train in a normal way . . . where they do not have to deal with jobs at home. Because, in most families, the ladies have to take care of the things in the house and the men can do whatever they want. Women don't have a lot of choices. . . . The only thing they do is wake up, take care of the cooking, take care of the children. . . . They run the whole family. And if they are at home training, it's not possible because there are demands [on them]. They need a place where they can be away from home and can concentrate only on running.[54]

Although there are other camps in and around Iten that accept female athletes, the gender dynamics Kiplagat outlined above disproportionally burden the women who attend them. For example, once there, women are expected to cook for and wash the clothes of the male attendees. In particular, Kiplagat identified the cleaning of men's shoes by women athletes as the most objectionable chore:

> What I found upsetting was washing their shoes. Training shoes. Because if they train a lot in the mud, after two or three days they want women to wash their shoes. I found it really upsetting that I should wash their shoes or socks. And that's what the men ask for the most, because that's one of the jobs they hate doing because it's really difficult. So, they try to push that [task] onto women. . . . I never agreed to do that. But some women—I was with them [at other camps]—they still did that. And some are even still doing it. But not in my place, not in my camp.[55]

Indeed, at the HATC male attendees may be encountered mopping the floors or even washing clothes. These sights often initially shock many of the women athletes but also help them grow in confidence until they a feel a sense of equality with their male counterparts.

FIGURES 4.3 AND 4.4. Images of the High Altitude Training Centre, Iten, Kenya

150 AFRICA AND THE OLYMPICS

It is this type of empowerment that Kiplagat is hoping to generate through the HATC experience. Naturally, she wants the attendees to leave as stronger, better runners, but she also encourages them to demand the same type of gender equality that prevails at her camp in other settings. Kiplagat describes this change in attitude as follows:

> The girls who have stayed in the camp have really changed. . . . They don't fear. If somebody's coming who says, "Do this for me," they don't say, "Oh, yes, I will do that." They say, "Why? Give me the reasons." . . . Really, the change has to begin somewhere. . . . We really try to tell them that we have to bring this change into their families . . . into their generation, into other generations. You have to help us to bring this message across. . . . I've given them a lot of courage. I'm sure some of them will end up back in their [home] villages, but they'll never be the same.[56]

John Manners, an authority on Kenyan distance running going back to his days in the country as a Peace Corps volunteer in the 1970s, confirmed the impact Kiplagat is making via the HATC: "Lornah was the first to really put her money where her mouth was with her investment in the training center. There is a qualitative difference between her camp and others. Her work is contributing to a dawning consciousness among Kenyan women that they can be treated better."[57]

Meseret Defar: Empowering African Women and Girls

Born in Ethiopia in 1983, long-distance runner Meseret Defar medaled at the 2004, 2008, and 2012 Olympic Games. Unlike many of Ethiopia's elite distance runners, though, Defar was not raised in a rural area of the country, daily loping to and from a far-removed school, but rather in the nation's capital, Addis Ababa. Defar worked her way up through Ethiopia's club running system before capturing her first Olympic medal, the gold in the 5,000 meters at the 2004 Athens Games. In 2008 she followed that performance with a silver medal in Beijing in the same event and a second gold in the 5,000 meters in London at the 2012 Games, becoming the first woman to claim consecutive Olympic victories at that distance. Immediately after securing the second gold medal, Defar was naturally exuberant:

Parlaying Individual Olympic Success into Positive Change on the Continent 151

"Today, after eight years, I have won gold again. . . . I feel as if I have been born again."[58]

Following her return home from London, the United Nations Population Fund (UNFPA) appointed Defar as goodwill ambassador for Ethiopia, which effectively launched her humanitarian career. The executive director of the UNFPA at the time, Dr. Babtunde Osotimehin, declared to Defar upon her appointment, "The talent you showed during the competition proves that women can achieve great heights in any field. Your contributions and feats have lit a shining torch for others to follow. Thank you for being a role model and a source of inspiration to women in Africa and beyond."[59] Going forward, Defar continued down this benevolent path, "consistently using the celebrity she has earned winning medals and breaking world records to highlight the needs of malnourished and impoverished children in the developing world" while also championing women's and youth causes.[60] For example, upon the renewal of her ambassadorship agreement with the UNFPA, the organization's in-country representative, Benoit Kalasa, remarked, "Just like her shining athletics career, Meseret Defar has demonstrated a strong commitment to promoting issues of women's empowerment, adolescent and youth development, and the prevention of HIV/AIDS. I believe that she will continue to advocate for these causes and help to send a powerful message that will reach the hearts and minds of people throughout Ethiopia."[61]

Indeed, in the years following her reappointment, Defar's advocation efforts have been impressive owing to both their volume and variety. For example, she has maintained her focus on children by, among other endeavors, serving as a major contributor to the Abebe Bikila Project, a children's running program in Ethiopia named after the eponymous Olympic legend. In particular, Defar solicits and collects donations of new and used athletic equipment to support this initiative. She has also traveled internationally, using her athletic celebrity status to generate funds to facilitate educational opportunities for Ethiopian children. Defar has also been an active participant in the Stop Early Marriage Campaign, which the former first lady of Ethiopia, Woizero Azeb Mesfin, launched in order to protect girls from the fate of childhood marriage. Meseret has also been an avid proponent of, and a participant in, the Women First Run event, a five-kilometer race exclusively for women, which the UNFPA has been supporting to promote gender equality and women's empowerment.[62] Finally, Defar has used her status to support the Entoto Foundation, which strives to facilitate access to medical supplies and treatment for Ethiopians, even if that means funding procedures abroad for individuals in need.[63] Ultimately, although Defar's Olympic achievements are undeniably impressive, she's also been generating countless victories for marginalized Ethiopian citizens over the years, far removed from the various medal podiums she's ascended.

Caster Semenya: Fighting for More than Gender Injustice

Caster Semenya was born in South Africa in 1991, during the initial stages of the broader process of dismantling apartheid. Already an elite athlete by her late teens, she won gold in both the 2012 and 2016 Olympics in the women's 800 meters and was also the flagbearer for the South African team in the 2012 London Games. Beyond her athletic prowess, she is probably best known as an intersex woman, meaning that she was born with a combination of male and female biological traits, which in Semenya's case also included elevated testosterone levels. As such, her inclusion in women's sporting competitions has been marked by considerable controversy. Other athletes with so-called differences of sexual development, or DSD, have similarly been targeted.

Regardless, Semenya has consistently identified as a woman and doesn't believe that her intersex-ness bestows her with any sort of athletic advantage. During a 2019 interview, for example, she remarked, "I don't understand when you say I have an advantage because I am a woman. When I pee, I pee like a woman. I don't understand when you say I am a man or I have a deep voice."[64] The great American hurdler Edwin Moses, in preparing a statement in conjunction with the announcement of Semenya's inclusion on *Time* magazine's list of the Most Influential People of 2019, went further, outlining the significant impact that she had already made related to sex, gender, and society: "Caster Semenya has taught us that sex isn't always binary, and has caused us to question the justness of distributing societal benefits according to 'male' and 'female' classifications. . . . However this issue is ultimately addressed, Semenya will have already made a singular historical contribution to our understanding of biological sex."[65]

Semenya's case continues to play out in court. In the summer of 2023, for example, Semenya won her discrimination case in the European Court of Human Rights. However, even this victory was tempered by the fact that the ruling didn't pave the way for her to return to the track to compete. As Graeme Reid and Minky Worden wrote in the aftermath of the decision, "Semenya's victory is in some sense a technical one. It enables Semenya to [further] pursue her case, but without any immediate prospect of being able to compete again—which is the point of her case." Regardless, World Athletics, the international governing body for the sport of athletics, has encouraged an appeal of the ruling, while also refusing to reconsider its invasive medical requirement that DSD athletes reduce their testosterone levels under an arbitrary, selective standard of femininity in order to be eligible to compete. Given this administrative obstinance, Reid and Worden warned that "the future of Semenya's athletics career—and that of many other women athletes—continue[s] to hang in the balance."[66]

While Semenya continues to be the face of the fight for inclusion in women's sporting events for any athlete who identifies as female, irrespective of hormone or testosterone levels, she has also tirelessly supported a wider range of social causes in her homeland. One way that Semenya seeks to improve life for underprivileged South Africans is via the Caster Semenya Foundation, which she established with her wife, Violet, in 2016. The organization's core mission is as follows: "Through combining education and sport development, the Caster Semenya Foundation empowers youth and communities from disadvantaged societies to discover their athletic prowess, build leadership capabilities and be nurtured to their full potential."[67]

These goals are manifest in an array of Semenya Foundation initiatives and programs, including the distribution of menstrual cups to South African girls to encourage them to stay in school during

154   AFRICA AND THE OLYMPICS

their menstrual cycles. More recently, the foundation entered into a formal partnership with Boston City Campus, a multilocation institution of higher education in South Africa, to serve as its official education partner. As part of this agreement, Boston City Campus awards bursaries to selected individuals, while foundation staff monitor and coach the awardees as they matriculate. Upon announcing the motivations to pursue this collaborative affiliation, Semenya explained, "Education is an opportunity and our aim as the Caster Semenya Foundation is to improve the lives of beneficiaries while making a solid contribution to our community."[68]

Another way Semenya pursues social improvement objectives is via the Masai Athletics Club, which she also coestablished with her wife. The location for this initiative is Soweto, Johannesburg, at Shapa Soweto, Nike's recently constructed training center, at which aspiring young runners from the region receive high-quality coaching. Semenya described the motivation for the Masai Club's creation as follows: "When you're a kid, you want love. You want support. You want to be appreciated. Those are the fundamental skills for a human being. It's the little things. We want them to smile every day when they wake up. They know, 'Ah, today I'm going to training. Tomorrow I'm going to training.'"[69] Semenya further explained that the club's motto is both deliberately simple and linear: "First you build the human, then you build the athlete, and then you build the leader."[70] In an interview from 2021, the Semenya spoke extensively about the promise and importance of this initiative.

Access to sport is so important because it is the start of hope and belief. Those from disadvantaged backgrounds lack resources, but when they can access them they are able to fulfil their dreams and achieve what they know they can. Dreams become true and life becomes easier. This is the most important thing, and why we are putting back into the community—allowing more kids to access sport through facilities so they can live up to their dreams. Shapa [Soweto] will help change their lives, as it will take them away from the streets and allow them to focus on their future. Giving kids the opportunity to educate themselves through sport is about self-awareness and discipline. Sport can be where their future begins.[71]

As impactful as Semenya's work in South Africa has been, her fight for inclusion in sport has arguably constituted her most transcendent campaign, one that will continue to impact women and girls far beyond South Africa's borders. As part of these efforts, Semenya has pushed back against an array of restrictive policies, including mandatory medication, which she was required to take between 2010 and 2015 in order for the IOC and World Athletics to clear her to compete. These governing bodies have also imposed these same requirements on other female DSD athletes with high testosterone levels. To protest these dictates, Semenya, in conjunction with the beauty brand Lux, launched a public campaign entitled "Born This Way," which "urges women to express their beauty and femininity unapologetically."[72] Semenya explained the importance of this initiative, which goes well beyond her personal battles in the realm of international athletics: "Some kids I have come across tried to commit suicide, others are survivors. They can't accept who they are. When you give birth to a kid, you can't choose their path. Life is not an act. . . . I can just [recognize] others with my same condition when I see them." She also acknowledges that these individuals don't possess the same type of social platform from which to voice their discontent.[73] Semenya has also linked this campaign to much broader, universal rights, remarking, "We are talking about human rights. We are talking about people being freed. People living their lives for who they are. . . . It's wrong to discriminate and also divide people. . . . At the end of the day, sport unites people and it speaks to the youth in a language they understand. . . . What I can do best is just go back there, fight for those who cannot fight for themselves, and fight for their rights."[74]

All the athletes considered in this chapter have used the status afforded them via participation in the Olympic Games to pursue a range of social-justice and equity objectives. Their corresponding, selfless actions feature the same levels of commitment and drive that these elite competitors demonstrated when engaged in their respective athletic activities. Many of these former Olympians have created foundations to organize and deliver a range of programming directed at marginalized and vulnerable communities in their home countries or, at times, beyond national borders. Buoyed by the fundraising abilities of these athletic celebrities and strengthened by a series of strategic partnerships, these charitable organizations have proven to be durable, reliable contributors to innumerable social causes.

5

The Olympic Games and Personal Improvement Strategies

Young Kenyans on track scholarships in the U.S. gain immeasurably through competition with the best American runners. If they were at home, they would stagnate for lack of competition. Besides, there is a lot of untapped athletic talent all around the country, which our team selectors and talent scouts would do well to discover.

—Kenyan sportswriter Norman de Costa,
responding to criticism regarding Kenyan runners
relocating to the United States on track scholarships, 1974

When I began running again last year, I had no idea I could ever run internationally again and certainly not in the inspiring atmosphere of a South African Olympic team! I can never forgive the people who hounded me or what they did to me, but now we South Africans might go back as heroes!

—Zola Pieterse (née Budd), the controversial White South
African distance runner, 1991, ahead of the 1992 Barcelona
Olympic Games

Across the decades that Africans have been participating in the Olympics, many of these athletes have strategically used the Games to improve their own political, financial, sportive, or educational interests. Some of these competitors have changed nationalities to enhance their Olympic prospects, while many others have similarly opted to compete at the Games for other countries but have parlayed their athletic acumen primarily to achieve financial, rather than sporting, success. Still other African Olympians have opportunistically utilized the Games as an occasion to defect, fleeing a variety of objectionable conditions in their home countries. Meanwhile, for roughly two decades starting in the late 1960s, many African athletes capitalized on their accomplishments, or at least experiences, at the Games to garner athletic scholarships to American colleges and universities.

This assortment of African Olympians who have utilized the Games primarily to derive personal benefit have largely been overshadowed by those who have more publicly embraced benevolent causes. Regardless, their individual victories—even if less conspicuous—have enhanced the lives of innumerable Africans across the continent. Beyond improving their own quality of life and, often, if only indirectly, the quality of living conditions for their families, their strategic actions have also illuminated, and at times prompted, corresponding actions to redress issues surrounding various political, sportive, social, and financial inequities.

Changing Nationalities: Insufficient Domestic Support

In recent decades many African athletes have used the Olympic Games as a vehicle for social mobility by permissibly changing nationalities. In these scenarios, wealthy countries that aren't particularly competitive in specific Olympic events naturalize foreign athletes, primarily from developing nations, and provide them with educational and financial rewards in their newly adopted states. For example, Ethiopian-born Maryam Jusuf Jamal won the first ever Olympic medal (a bronze) for the oil-rich country of Bahrain in the 1,500-meter race at the 2012 London Games, while Kenyan-born Ruth Jebet won Bahrain's first gold medal in the 3,000-meter steeplechase at the 2016 Games in Rio de Janeiro.

In fact, at the Rio Games more than thirty Kenyan-born runners competed for nations—primarily Bahrain and Turkey—other than Kenya; unlike Jebet, though, the vast majority of them failed to medal. Although she couldn't speak to the motivations or fates of

The Olympic Games and Personal Improvement Strategies   159

her fellow Kenyan runners, Jebet explained her decision to compete for Bahrain: "There was no support in Kenya. We talked with the Bahrain federation, and they said, 'You can come, and we will pay for everything.'"[1] Money earned in Bahrain is currently funding the education of Jebet's siblings in Kenya and has also afforded her family a modest home.

Certain Olympic observers and more than a few scholars have bemoaned this exodus of African talent as a perpetuation of the sporting "brawn drain" that began decades earlier when talented soccer players began leaving the continent to play elsewhere, signed by "predatory" clubs around the world.[2] Yet if we consider these African Olympians as laborers strategically offering their services to employers—in this case to foreign National Olympic Committees (NOCs)—who provide superior working and remunerative conditions, their decisions can instead be interpreted as both highly pragmatic and calculated, thereby challenging a victimization narrative.

Another African Olympian who switched nationalities due to a lack of domestic support is Nigerian-born sprinter Francis Obiorah Obikwelu. Born in 1978, Obikwelu was a promising athlete in both soccer and track. He relocated to Lisbon at the age of sixteen to try to forge an athletic career, even though historically Portugal hadn't been particularly competitive in any of the assortment of sprinting events. Unable to gain any athletic traction in the Portuguese capital, he resorted to working as a construction laborer in the heavily touristed Algarve region in the southern part of the country. Obikwelu remained determined, though. To this end, he learned Portuguese and eventually moved back to Lisbon, where he started to garner attention for his running prowess and where he was adopted by a Portuguese woman he still refers to as "Mother." His adopted home notwithstanding, Obikwelu remained a Nigerian citizen throughout these formative years, and as such, sporting officials from his homeland were closely monitoring his development. Owing to Obikwelu's numerous athletic accomplishments, the Nigerian Olympic Committee eventually selected him to represent his native country at the 2000 Sydney Games. Obikwelu's athletic dreams had finally come to fruition.

Following an injury incurred while at the Australian Olympics, Obikwelu traveled to Canada to undergo a knee operation, the costs of which the Nigerian Olympic Committee was supposed to cover. However, due to either neglect by Nigerian Olympic officials or the possible diversion of the funds (if they had, in fact, even been disbursed), Obikwelu was forced to spend his own money for both the airfare and the medical procedure, without any possibility for reimbursement. And it was this disagreeable experience that prompted him to switch his nationality, formally, to Portuguese. In 2001 Obikwelu approached Fernando Mota, the head of the Portuguese Athletics Federation, to inform him that he had decided to seek Portuguese citizenship. Just three short years later, Obikwelu was suiting up for his newly adopted nation at the Athens Olympic Games (fig. 5.1).

While in Greece, Obikwelu declared, "What matters now is Portugal. It's for the Portuguese that I want to win medals, to thank them for what they did for me."[3] And he delivered. In Athens he won the 100-meter dash and, in the process, set a European record that stood for over seventeen years. Owing to his Olympic success, numerous other athletic achievements, "his life story, and his personality, Obikwelu quickly became a popular figure in Portugal, endearingly earning the nickname 'Chico,' the shortened form of the Portuguese version of his first name [Francis]."[4]

Changing Nationalities: Athletic. and Long-Term Financial, Upgrades

In other scenarios, African athletes have assumed new national identities in pursuit of initial or further Olympic success by representing countries already competitive in their sport, with an eye toward longer-term financial security. Perhaps the most famous case of this type is of distance runner Bernard Lagat, who was born in Kenya and won Olympic medals for his country at both the 2000 and 2004 Games, before becoming an American citizen and competing for the US Olympic squad in 2008, 2012, and 2016.

Lagat's first meaningful taste of the United States began in 1996, when he enrolled at Washington State University (WSU), following in the footsteps of past Kenyan runners who had also attended

FIGURE 5.1. Francis Obikwelu competing for Portugal at the 2004 Athens Games. PA Images / Alamy Stock Photo

WSU. Just prior to earning his undergraduate degree, Lagat qualified for the Kenyan Olympic team for the 2000 Games in Sydney, where he would win the bronze medal in the 1,500 meters. Four years later Lagat again represented his native Kenya at the Games in Athens. However, the Olympian arrived in Greece carrying a closely guarded secret: some three months earlier he had become an American citizen. Lagat later explained why he switched nationalities: "I wanted to become an American, not for running, but for life after running. I did not want to be a farmer in Kenya like my father. I did not want to be a teacher there for $200 or $300 a month. I was ready to start a family. The United States presented opportunities that Kenya did not. . . . I love Kenya [but] how many thousands of Kenyans get out of school and there are no jobs? Or one job for 50 people? I wanted to be able to support my family here [in the US]."[5]

These reasonable justifications notwithstanding, Lagat could not have openly shared his decision to become a US citizen ahead of the 2004 Olympics, as any official awareness of this transition would have precluded his participation in Athens. As Jeré Longman explains, "Under international track and field rules, Lagat would not yet have been eligible to compete in Athens for the United States. Athletes who switch nationalities must wait three years before competing under a new flag, unless granted a waiver. Moreover, Kenya also does not allow dual citizenship."[6] As Lagat was technically no longer a Kenyan citizen, he should not have been permitted to compete, either for the United States or for Kenya. But as long as he maintained his secret, he could proceed, unconstrained by International Olympic Committee (IOC) restrictions. Lagat later defended his deceitfulness: "I wanted to run in the Olympics. I didn't want to be stopped. I just wanted to run."[7] And run he did, all the way to the bronze medal in the 1,500 meters. Once his secret was finally revealed, though, Lagat became embroiled in considerable controversy, and there were even calls for him to surrender his medal, but ultimately, no action was taken. Remarkably, Lagat would go on to compete for the United States in three successive Olympics, finishing fifth in the finals of the 5,000 meters at the Rio de Janeiro Games in 2016—his last—at the age of forty-one.

The Olympic Games and Personal Improvement Strategies

Becoming a Target of International Wrath: The Nationality Case of Zola Budd

Much more internationally sensational than any of the aforementioned examples of altered nationality related to the Olympic Games is the case of Zola Budd Pieterse. Although White South African athletes have only rarely been featured in this book, Pieterse's situation is particularly insightful as it's situated at the intersection of apartheid and the Olympics. Her case is also germane to the focus of this chapter, which considers the myriad ways that African athletes have attempted to improve their lives, athletically or otherwise, via the Games.

Readers of a certain age will almost certainly remember the controversy that the bare-footed South African runner generated when she accidentally tripped her American rival, Mary Decker-Slaney, during the women's 3,000 meters at the 1984 Los Angeles Olympics. In turn, Budd became the international personification of racial injustice in South Africa, while in America she was reviled for ruining the chances of fan favorite Decker-Slaney. But her story began long before the chaos on the track in Los Angeles.

Born in 1966 in South Africa, Budd was already an elite runner in the 3,000 meters by the age of seventeen, having broken the world record early in 1984. Unfortunately for her, the International Amateur Athletic Federation (IAAF), the international track-and-field governing body, refused to ratify the record-setting result due to apartheid South Africa's pariah status; nor was Budd going to be permitted to participate in the upcoming Los Angeles Games due to her home country's expulsion from the Olympic Movement.[8]

Consequently, in March of that year Zola traveled with her parents to England via Amsterdam under an assumed name. Sensing a bombshell, the London-based tabloid the *Daily Mail* had paid £100,000 for the exclusive rights to the story and had also underwritten the family's airfare, which included transport on a private plane between Amsterdam and London. Even more importantly, the newspaper had arranged for Zola and her father, Frank Budd, to receive British passports, to which they were entitled because Frank had been born in England. However, the expedited nature

164   AFRICA AND THE OLYMPICS

with which she received British citizenship—just ten days after applying—suggested that powerful figures had intervened on her behalf. Reflecting on these suspect developments, Budd Pieterse would later write, "It should have been the greatest moment of my life. . . . Instead, the [British] passport thrust me into the world spotlight as a symbol of abuse. . . . Daddy recognized my commercial value. . . . Together with the *Daily Mail*, which arranged the cloak-and-dagger operation to get me to England in what was, for it, a massive and highly successful publicity stunt, they turned me into some kind of circus animal. . . . I was plucked away from everything I loved and put in an environment where I, as a person, no longer counted."[9]

As Pieterse's words suggest, virtually incessant tumult marked her transition to England. In her first days there, she tried to deflect media attention by declaring to the press, in a barely audible, heavily Afrikaans-accented voice, "I am just a runner. I am not a politician."[10] But, obliged to live in England for at least six months each year to maintain her British citizenship, she was unable to hide behind this apolitical banner. Instead, she became the target of relentless anti-apartheid protests, led by Sam Ramsamy, then the chairman of the South African Non-Racial Olympic Committee (SANROC), who had been living in exile in London since the early 1970s. Budd was also variously labeled a "racist, opportunist, traitor, and moneygrubber."[11] Reflecting on this unpleasant treatment, she opined, "My quarrel with them [anti-apartheid activists] was not over apartheid, but over the way they attacked me, and I did not believe they had any right to use me as a target in their bid to dismantle apartheid."[12] In practice, Budd brought much of this unwanted attention on herself, as she repeatedly refused to publicly condemn the South African system of institutionalized racism.

In the buildup to the 1984 Olympics, Budd's parents divorced, and she subsequently forbade her father from attending the Games. Once in Los Angeles matters, of course, only worsened. Following the collision with Mary Decker-Slaney, the American was unable to complete the race, while Zola, who was bleeding from her rival's cleat, faded to a seventh-place finish. Budd was immediately, vociferously condemned by American observers, even after Decker-Slaney

The Olympic Games and Personal Improvement Strategies   165

admitted that her own inexperience in running in a pack had led to the entanglement. Upon the conclusion of the Games, Budd returned to a much more empathetic environment in England, as the British media had taken her side in the matter regarding Decker-Slaney. Reflecting on her turbulent first year in England, Pieterse later stated,

> If I had it to do over, I would do it quite the same, except I would not have tried to compete in Los Angeles. Not because of what happened with Mary. That was fate, and if it had been anyone else, it would have been nothing. But the Games were too soon for me. I needed more time to make the adjustment to the world outside South Africa. Maybe I could have done it if my family had given me support, but there was none. When I most needed help, the most important people in my life were not there at all.[13]

During the two years that followed the Los Angeles Games, Budd remained an elite runner but was injured in 1987 and suspended in 1988 for either attending or participating in—it remains unclear—an athletics event in South Africa. Ultimately, she decided to move back to her native country, depressed, exhausted from the constant scrutiny, emotionally drained, and on the verge of a breakdown, all at the age of just twenty-one.[14] Regardless, throughout this period, Budd largely remained a polarizing, rather than sympathetic, figure. For many White South Africans, she was a symbol of the nation's persistence in the face of global condemnation, while for most other observers around the world, her ongoing refusal to decry apartheid, even in its waning days, justified the contempt. Only in 1989, the year she married Mike Pieterse, would she finally denounce the racialized system.

Although Pieterse was not actively running that year, her book, *Zola: The Autobiography of Zola Budd*, was released then. For many critics, the most important, redemptive passage in the volume was as follows: "The Bible says men are born equal before God. I can't reconcile segregation along racial lines with the words of the Bible. As a Christian, I find apartheid intolerable."[15] Yet for most observers,

166   AFRICA AND THE OLYMPICS

Budd's attempt to atone for her previous silence arrived years too late. As William Oscar Johnson has compellingly argued, "Had she made that statement in 1984, it would have saved her years of emotional anguish and allowed her to compete trouble-free, at least politically. But she waited—perversely, it seems—until she had been drummed out of her sport and was stuck in exile before revealing publicly what she says she had always believed privately."[16]

With the denouement of apartheid commencing in 1990 and Budd Pieterse's successful return to the track the following year, the runner was both qualified and prepared to participate as a member of South Africa's Olympic squad for the 1992 Games in Barcelona. Interviewed in 1991, when the country's return to the Olympic Movement was still in question, Zola declared,

> This time, I will wait until there is some final word that we are truly welcomed back. I shan't go near an airplane leaving South Africa until the official stamp is on the invitation. But, oh, when the time comes, it will be wonderful—especially when we are allowed into the Olympics. There we will be, a true South African Olympic team, and many of us will be Black, of course, and we will be marching into the stadium in Barcelona, all together. There will be lots of tears and very full throats on that day. I look forward to it very much.[17]

As we learned earlier, the IOC did ultimately welcome South Africa back into the Olympic fold. And Budd did join her country's racially diverse squad in Spain, having finally revived her athletic career and restored, even if not fully, her reputation.

The Olympic Games as a Vehicle for Defection

In recent years, various African athletes have utilized the Olympic Games to improve their personal well-being not by temporarily switching nationalities in pursuit of political, financial, or sportive benefits but by permanently defecting and advocating for change in their home countries. For example, at the 2012 Summer Games in London, several African Olympians sought asylum. Among them were seven of Cameroon's thirty-seven-strong squad, including a

The Olympic Games and Personal Improvement Strategies 167

goalkeeper from the women's soccer team, a swimmer, and five boxers; four members of the Congolese delegation, including a technical director and a coach; and an array of Sudanese runners. But the highest-profile defection that year was undoubtedly that of Eritrean steeplechaser Weynay Ghebresilasie. Although he had borne the flag for his country's delegation during the opening ceremony in London, he cited "worsening conditions at home" as the impetus for his defection; three other Eritrean Olympians joined Ghebresilasie.

Yet not all the defections at the Games have been attributable to repressive domestic political climates. In some cases, African Olympians have simply desired to improve their athletic prospects. For example, Amuam Joseph, a Cameroonian Karate Federation member, referencing his compatriots' decision to defect during the 2012 Games, explained, "Back home, they aren't given the proper training. They know that if they are well trained, they could beat the person from another country. It pains them to be here and see people beat them who they could have beaten if they were well taken care of.... I am positively convinced that if the government did more in this field, we'd have little of this disturbance."[18] Regardless of why these African athletes chose to seek citizenship beyond the continent's borders, the Olympic Games presented each of them an opportunity to escape domestic grievances and, ideally, improve their overall well-being.

Parlaying Olympic Success into an Education in America:
African Athletes and the NCAA

In the early decades of Africa's running dominance, many athletes parlayed their successes at the Olympic Games to earn admission to American colleges and universities, receiving an education superior to what would have been available back on the continent, while also continuing to hone their athletic skills as members of NCAA track teams. Prior to 1982, turning professional disqualified athletes from competing in the Olympics, so pursuing educational goals while retaining their eligibility to participate in the Games was quite appealing to these African athletes. Over time, though, the NCAA enacted policies to curb this practice, predicated in part by complaints that these elite, seasoned African Olympians, were conferring the track-and-field programs that relied on them with an unfair advantage. In more recent years, the inverse of this arrangement has become common, with NCAA schools recruiting African athletes *prior* to any Olympic success, predicated on their potential, rather than on demonstrated results at the highest levels. But for roughly two decades, beginning in the late 1960s, innumerable African athletes, a plurality of whom were Kenyan, pursued higher education in the United States facilitated by their performances at the Olympic Games. While pursuing these more visible goals, they also faced the inherent challenges of living far removed from family and friends in a foreign environment, where racism was seemingly unavoidable.

Immediate Impacts: The Recruitment and Arrival of Julius Sang and Robert Ouko

Although NCAA institutions started recruiting talented runners from abroad beginning in the 1950s, these athletes mostly hailed from Canada and a series of European countries.[19] Elite African athletes did begin to trickle in during the late 1960s, but the first notable influx of Olympians from the continent arriving in the United States to enroll in college occurred in 1971 with Julius Sang and Robert Ouko. Both Kenyan runners had competed at the 1968 Olympic Games in Mexico City and had also performed well at the 1970 Commonwealth Games in Edinburgh, and thus they arrived as experienced, mature athletes. Indeed, both turned twenty-three years old during their first fall on campus in the United States.

Their initial recruitment was coordinated by Dr. Leroy Walker, who would go on to become the first Black president of the United States Olympic Committee. In 1971, though, Walker was still the head coach of the track-and-field team at North Carolina Central University (NCCU), an HBCU (historically Black college or university). In fact, Walker had already met Sang and Ouko in Mexico City in 1968, but at the time he hadn't been able to make the necessary arrangements to facilitate their relocation to North Carolina. These requisite measures included securing leaves of absence—which Walker wasn't able to organize until he visited Sang and Ouko at their homes in Kenya in 1971—from their shared employer, the Kenyan Prisons Service.

The Olympic Games and Personal Improvement Strategies 169

In practice American coaches didn't always have to travel to Africa to recruit athletes, though many did. Instead, a phone call, either directly to the athlete or to a key contact, would suffice; in some cases the arrangements were even made via fax. Regarding the financial appeal of recruiting foreign athletes in this manner, Brigham Young University track coach Clarence Robinson remarked in 1984, "It is less expensive and involves less traveling time, and the athletes are very appreciative. The American recruiting system is simply too complicated and expensive, and I can get a quality foreign student athlete for the price of a few phone calls and a stamp."[20]

Impediments and Conduits: The NCAA's Overage Policy

During their first outdoor season in the United States, in fall 1971, the two Kenyans performed superbly, delivering both world and collegiate record-breaking performances. But their advance would be quickly stymied by the enforcement of the NCAA's "overage-foreigner rule." Passed in 1961, the policy dictated that athletes would lose one year of eligibility to compete for an NCAA championship for every year they had competed abroad after turning nineteen. Given that these African athletes had already established themselves as world-class competitors *before* being offered scholarships at NCAA institutions, this rule adversely affected virtually every African who came to the United States via this type of sporting migration. Thankfully for this array of athletes and their respective American host institutions, in December 1973 Howard University successfully challenged the overage rule, which a federal court ruled violated the equal protection clause of the Fourteenth Amendment.

Even while the overage policy was in place, the performances of Sang and Ouko at NCCU prior to their NCAA ban and, subsequently, at the 1972 Olympic Games had prompted college coaches across the United States to scramble to establish "African connections."[21] Meanwhile, during the brief period while the overage policy was in effect, coaches at institutions of higher education administered by the National Association of Intercollegiate Athletics (NAIA) had enjoyed an advantage over their larger and more powerful NCAA counterparts. Indeed, although the NAIA is an athletic association composed of smaller American colleges and universities that are dwarfed by the NCAA's member institutions, it crucially did not feature any overage restrictions. Arguably, the NAIA's highest-profile recruit during this period was the Kenyan runner Mike Boit, who enrolled in Eastern New Mexico University (ENMU) in 1973, following a bronze-medal finish in the 800 meters at the 1972 Munich Games. Fellow Kenyan Mike Murei, who had also competed in Munich, joined Boit at ENMU but subsequently transferred to the University of Wisconsin, attracted by its superior athletic facilities and resources, as well as its more prestigious academic reputation. By 1974, a year after the NCAA's overage policy was overturned, over fifty African athletes were on track scholarships at American institutions of all sizes, in both the NAIA and the NCAA, with that number poised to grow.

Backlash: Disapproval at Home and Abroad

Following the 1972 Games in Munich, at which Julius Sang and Robert Ouko were members of the gold-medal 400-meter relay team (with Sang also adding a bronze in the individual 400-meter event), and the repeal of the overage rule the following year, the two Olympians were finally cleared to participate in the 1974 NCAA championships. However, not everyone was as excited about their re-inclusion. For example, Jim Bush, the track coach at UCLA, bemoaned that his relay squad "would [now] have to beat the Kenyan Olympic team in order to win their *own* national championship."[22]

Other Americans bitterly argued that these African athletes were receiving elite training and coaching—especially in the long-distance events—that should have been reserved for American collegiate runners. Moreover, these critics contended, this preparation improved the prospects of foreign athletes while undermining Americans' chances at international competitions, including the Olympics. In many respects, these objections constituted racial resentment toward Africans' mere inclusion on collegiate track teams, which was supposedly reducing opportunities for White American athletes. But even when American runners did figure on opposing squads, they and their coaches begrudged their African rivals' recurring success. This criticism was especially directed at African distance runners, as Washington State

The Olympic Games and Personal Improvement Strategies   171

track coach John Chaplin, who actively courted elite African athletes, explained in the mid-1970s: "Not until Black men started beating White men in the long distances was there any controversy. . . . Blacks are supposed to be sprinters. The foreign athletes, especially African distance men, are upsetting the prejudices that some of these guys who have complained about the presence of foreign athletes at U.S. colleges have been carrying around. They don't look up when a foreign black wins the 100-meters, but when he wins the 10,000 meters they notice, and they holler."[23] Regardless of when and to where these African Olympians arrived, their abilities—and at times their mere presence—thrust them face-to-face with racial prejudice in America.

The advanced age of these African athletes also seemed to factor into these grievances. For example, in 1977 a *Track and Field News* correspondent rhetorically asked whether "an overage foreign distance runner attending an American university using a free-ride scholarship honestly expect[ed] to endear himself to the crowd while beating a younger native American?"[24] Dr. Walker and others composedly rebutted this medley of thinly veiled racial criticism, compellingly contending, "The NCAA's are the *collegiate* championships. Any bona fide student in the university ought to be able to participate. Robert Ouko and Julius Sang are honors students at North Carolina Central [University]. They're an important part of our student body, and they qualify for every activity a student is allowed to engage in."[25]

Irrespective of Walker's efforts to allay these domestic critics' concerns, resentful Americans were not the only ones criticizing these African athletes. Indeed, as African athletes continued pursuing the educational and athletic opportunities on offer in the United States, they increasingly endured admonishment from their countrymen. Of particular and repeating disquiet was the aforementioned "brawn drain," or in this case "track drain," especially as the performance of some customarily dominant long-distance nations, notably Kenya, began to dip. For example, the Kenyan 1972-Olympic-medal winner Ben Jipcho decried this sportive connection with America, contending, "United States-based Kenyans are putting money before patriotism."[26] In response, the Kenyan NOC periodically denied these foreign-based athletes spots on national squads. Other local observers denounced the zeal with which foreign recruiters pursued African athletes. For example, the assistant secretary of the Kenyan Amateur Athletics Association criticized American recruiters for "wanting... anyone who can run." Further, the secretary said, "Agents come over here and try to take schoolboys away from their homes before they are ready."[27] Ultimately, although these migrant student-athletes enrolled in American colleges and universities were certainly aware of these various forms of rebuke, even this targeted censure did little to stem their outflow from Africa.

Opportunity and Perspective: African Athletes' Sentiments

The African Olympians themselves naturally harbored opinions regarding the sporting migration system into which they had willfully entered as well. Their comments reveal an understanding of the unrivaled educational and sporting opportunities available in America and the importance of intercollegiate sports in the United States, but also of the ways that host institutions benefitted from their success. For example, Ouko candidly stated, "It wouldn't be going too far to say that in many cases African athletes are being exploited by American colleges and receive precious little in return. . . . I had to fight to find time to study given the American system of college education, which puts sports on an absurdly high plane. . . . [But] don't get me wrong. I'm grateful for the chance to go to the States and to get a higher education."[28] Meanwhile, Julius Sang's appreciation for his opportunity abroad was made clear in a statement directed at Kenyan governmental and sporting officials, including the national track team coach, Jim Wambua, who regularly bemoaned the "track drain" from Africa: "If African athletes could get the same educational and training opportunities at home, they'd stay home, but since there are no track scholarships in Africa, the athletes should take the opportunity to use their running talents to further their education."[29] Seizing on these seemingly boundless educational opportunities, both Sang and Ouko were admitted to American institutions to pursue graduate degrees after graduating from NCCU.

Other elite African athletes were similarly unequivocal about their educational endeavors in the United States, stressing that these

The Olympic Games and Personal Improvement Strategies   173

invaluable studies would benefit them for the rest of their lives. For example, Suleiman Nyambui, an Olympic medalist from Tanzania who attended the University of Texas at El Paso (UTEP) from 1978 to 1982, declared in a 1982 interview, "Many foreigners, like from Tanzania, and other countries in Africa, come to America through the government. So, the first thing we come for is school. Running is second. I can stop running, but I can't stop learning. Actually, it makes me mad when I hear a foreigner, any foreigner, say 'he came here for running.' Education comes first. The U.S. is a big country and mine is a small one in many ways, so this is one way we can catch up, by learning."[30]

Into the mid- and late-1970s, American colleges and universities continued to extend scholarship offers to African Olympians, helping to put schools like Iowa State, Washington State, and UTEP squarely on the track-and-field map. Arguably, UTEP benefitted the most from these African athletes' participation. *New York Times* journalist Robert Reinhold described the institution's sporting ascension in a piece in the mid-1980s: "Small and remote, without any great claim to academic distinction, except in geology, the school . . . found a source of pride and joy in the track team since it rose to prominence in the 1970s."[31] In practice, this athletic success was attributable to the contributions of large numbers of African (and other foreign) "imports." Indeed, on UTEP's 1976 track squad, there were a dozen Kenyans.

Unfortunately for many of these African athletes at UTEP and elsewhere, they would have starred at the 1976 Olympics had their home countries not withdrawn from the Montreal Games in protest of New Zealand's inclusion. Consequently, during what was an Olympic hiatus for most African nations, American recruiters were forced to pore over the results from other international competitions, including the Commonwealth Games and the All-Africa Games, to identify the most talented runners.

The Arrival of African Female Athletes in America

Into the 1980s, elite African athletes continued to arrive to take advantage of the opportunities on offer at American colleges and universities. Joining these male sporting and educational migrants was the first notable influx of African female athletes. Although Title IX of the Education Amendments Act of 1972 was intended to create equal numbers of scholarships for male and female athletes at US institutions of higher education, the mandate was largely disregarded until enforcement of the legislation began in earnest in the early 1980s. Finally, these opportunities began materializing for African female athletes, enabling them to follow along the migratory trails that their male counterparts had blazed. Although these women were faced with many of the same challenges as their male predecessors, they also faced gendered issues, including the very act of leaving the continent. For example, as El Moutawakel explained in 1985, a year after she won gold in Los Angeles, "It is very unusual that a father lets go of his daughter in our society [Moroccan]. He knew I had a skill and with a little bit of coaching I could improve it.... I was the first one in our family to leave Morocco, and a girl. My brothers had never been out of Morocco. On the plane, I was scared. I was crying the whole way. I wished the plane would turn and take me back to Morocco."[32]

The End: The Inversion of the System

Among the last of the African athletes who parlayed Olympic glory into an American educational and sporting opportunity was Tanzanian distance runner Filbert Bayi, who had won silver in the 3,000-meter steeplechase at the 1980 Moscow Games. Bayi enrolled at the University of Oklahoma in 1982, but he transferred to UTEP for the 1983 season at his government's request, in an effort to improve his results. In El Paso he joined an array of fellow Tanzanians with whom he would train ahead of the 1984 Los Angeles Games. Interestingly, Bayi was thirty years old by the time he enrolled at UTEP but was able to avoid the overage rule due to a novel provision in a revised version of the policy. Although the rule had been reinstituted in 1980—newly applying to all athletes, not just foreigners, to ensure its constitutionality—it now contained an exemption for time spent in the military. Bayi qualified for the exemption, since he had served in the Tanzanian army since the age of eighteen.[33]

Regardless of this good fortune for Bayi, he would be one of the last Africans to seek higher education in the United States *after*

The Olympic Games and Personal Improvement Strategies   175

having achieved Olympic glory. By the mid-1980s, even the allure of an athletic scholarship in in the United States couldn't compete with the prize money suddenly available to elite athletes who turned professional, a status forbidden in American college sports but newly permissible for participants in the Olympic Games and similar competitions. For decades, the IOC, and in particular Avery Brundage, had obstinately and relentlessly championed amateurism, with the former IOC president once declaring, "We can only rely on the support of those [athletes] who believe in the principles of fair play and sportsmanship embodied in the amateur code in our efforts to prevent the [Olympic] games from being used by individuals, organizations, or nations for ulterior motives."[34] Eventually, though, even the IOC abandoned this principled position, permitting professional athletes to compete at the Games.

Consequently, the model that initially provided elite African athletes sporting and educational opportunities at colleges and universities in the United States following international success gradually inverted. Newly, American coaches were progressively extending scholarships to Africans with significant athletic potential but who had not yet secured a signature accomplishment. Indeed, by the 1984 Olympics, the next Games at which most African countries competed following the 1976 and 1980 boycotts, it was increasingly common for athletes from the continent to participate in and, at times win, Olympic events *while enrolled* at American institutions of higher education. Examples from the 1984 Los Angeles Games include the aforementioned Moroccan hurdler Nawal El Moutawakel, who was attending Iowa State University when she won gold; Kenyan runner Julius Korir, a student athlete at Washington State University who won the 3,000-meter steeplechase; and Somalian runner Abdi Bile, who participated in the 800 meters and 1,500 meters in Los Angeles, though without medaling, while enrolled at George Mason University.

This pattern of promising African athletes relocating to the United States seeking to benefit from high-quality education and training but without any Olympic medals already packed in their bags, continues to this day. In practice, many of these athletes have applied the instruction they received in the United States to achieve Olympic glory, either during or after their enrollment at an American college or university, though many others never make it to the medal podium or even qualify to participate on this grandest of sporting stages.

Regardless of exactly when you're reading this book, athletes from around the world are currently preparing for an upcoming Olympic Games. Given most African nations' lack of resources and the fact that many of these countries don't have sporting traditions in a wide array of Olympic sports, it's unlikely that African squads will be dominating the proceedings at future Games any more than they have in the past. These limiting factors will also continue to combine to restrict the number of athletes that any particular African country will send to the Games. For example, although the United States. has a population roughly 50 percent larger than Nigeria's, for the 2020 Games in Tokyo, America sent 613 athletes to compete in 35 sports, whereas Nigeria, Africa's most populous nation, sent only 55 athletes to compete in 10 sports.[35] Owing to their sheer number of participants at Olympic contests and facilitated by both national wealth and the IOC's ongoing emphasis on sports conceived and played primarily in the Global North, teams from beyond Africa's borders will continue to finish the Games with the largest medal hauls. Yet as this book has attempted to establish, African Olympic "victories" are typically realized far from the medal podium—often prior to, occasionally during, and with increasing frequency in the aftermath of, the Games themselves. And there's no reason to believe that this long-standing pattern of African individual and communal triumph associated with the Olympics won't continue. Every four years, and every year in between.

Notes

Introduction

Epigraph: Nelson Mandela, quoted in Kéba Mbaye, *The International Olympic Committee and South Africa: Analysis and Illustration of a Humanist Sports Policy* (Lausanne, Switzerland: IOC, 1995).

1. As of 2022, European athletes had earned over 12,300 medals; North American athletes, over 3,100; Asian athletes, over 2,100; Oceanic athletes, almost 700; African athletes, over 400; and South American athletes, over 300. See "All-Time Medal Count at the Summer Olympics by Country and Color from 1896 to 2020," Statista Accounts, released August 2021, https://www.statista.com/statistics/1101719/summer-olympics-all-time-medal-list-since-1892/.

2. These two marathon participants were unlikely initial representatives, as they were present in Missouri not for the Olympic Games but for the World's Fair (which celebrated the one hundredth anniversary of the Louisiana Purchase) as performers in the "Anglo-Boer War Historical Libretto" revue. With interest in the Games relatively minimal, in part owing to the Russo-Japanese War (1904–5), Olympic officials started inviting World's Fair participants to also partake in the array of sporting events. Somewhat surprisingly, Taunyne and Masiana performed fairly, finishing ninth and twelfth, respectively, out of thirty-one contenders, though they had both served as messengers for the Boers during the conflict. Both the Paris Olympic Games of 1900 and the St. Louis Games were staged as part of the World's Fair, though the IOC subsequently abandoned this practice, thereby decoupling the events. For more information regarding this unusual sequence of events, see M. R. Werner, "More Fun Than Games at the Games," *Sports Illustrated*, August 15, 1960, EM5–EM8; and Floris J. G. van der Merwe, "Africa's First Encounter with the Olympic Games in . . . 1904," *Journal of Olympic History* 7, no. 3 (1999): 29–34.

3. Days later Walter's teammate Charles Hefferon would win the silver medal in the marathon.

178   Notes to 5–12

4. Only FIFA's ban of South Africa in 1963 preceded the 1964 Olympic ban.

5. Afrikaners are South Africans who trace their lineage back to the original Dutch settlers, who arrived in the 1650s, differentiating them from other White subpopulations in the country.

6. Luke Tress, "The Mom Who Beat the Odds, and the Bureaucrats, to Become Israel's Top Runner," *Times of Israel,* January 16, 2019.

7. See, for example, Joseph Muiruri Njoroge, Lucy Atieno, and Daniele Vieira Do Nascimento, "Sports Tourism and Perceived Socio-Economic Impact in Kenya: The Case of Machakos County," *Tourism and Hospitality Management* 23, no. 2 (2017): 195–217.

8. Chris Mark, "Running for Economic Development in Kenya," *Stanford Social Innovation Review,* August 3, 2012.

9. The fifteen African nations eligible for the 1966 World Cup did, however, boycott that tournament in protest of FIFA's unwillingness to reserve a spot for an African country (eleven spots in the sixteen-team tournament were reserved for European nations). Instead, FIFA required the top African squad to compete against the top team from Asia and the best squad from Oceania in a playoff to determine which one of the three would earn a spot in the World Cup. By 1970 FIFA had allotted an automatic spot for the top African squad and another for the best Asian team.

10. The ancient Olympic Games appear to have been discontinued by around AD 400.

11. "Olympic Movement," International Olympic Committee, accessed March 28, 2024, https://olympics.com/ioc/olympic-movement.

12. Pascal Charitas, "The Birth of an African Olympic Movement between French and English Imperialisms (1910–1965)," in *Historical and Contemporary Issues in Olympic Studies: Proceedings of the Conference Held by the University of Johannesburg and the Olympic Studies Centre of the German Sport University Cologne in Johannesburg, November 30–December 2, 2015,* ed. Cora Burnett (Johannesburg: University of Johannesburg, 2015), 174.

13. The African cities identified as viable host sites included Tunis, Rabat, Casablanca, Dakar, Tripoli, Benghazi, Asmara, Libreville, Luanda, Cape Town, and Nairobi.

14. Conrado Durántez, "Africa and Olympism," *Olympic Review* 26, no. 20 (April–May 1998): 72.

15. Dikaia Chatziefstathiou et al., "Cultural Imperialism and the Diffusion of Olympic Sport in Africa: A Comparison of Pre and Post Second World War Contexts," *Olympic Studies Reader* 1 (2008): 105.

16. Chatziefstathiou et al., 105.

17. Dikaia Chatziefstathiou, "The Diffusion of Olympic Sport through Regional Games: A Comparison of Pre and Post Second World War Contexts" (unpublished research report, Olympic Studies Centre, 2008), 23.

Notes to 13–18

18. Owing to this durable reasoning, the first African Games would have to wait until 1965, almost three decades after Baron de Coubertin passed away.

19. In 1929 France, Italy, Belgium, and Great Britain refused to send athletes to Alexandria. At the time of the cancelation of the Games, the only registered participants included 4 from Morocco, 20 from Ethiopia, and 50 from Tunisia, though the organizers had been expecting some 1,300 from Egypt. Over three decades later, in the early 1960s, a competition that resembled the African Games—the Friendship Games—materialized, but these were organized by the French. The first African Games organized by Africans were the 1965 Games in Brazzaville.

20. John M. Hoberman, "Olympic Universalism and the Apartheid Issue," in *Sport, the Third Millennium: Proceedings of the International Symposium, Quebec City, Canada, May 21–25, 1990*, ed. F. Landry, M. Landry, and M. Yerlès (Sainte-Foy: Les Presses de L'Université Laval, 1991), 523.

21. David B. Kanin, *A Political History of the Olympic Games* (Boulder, CO: Westview Press, 1981), 5.

22. Hoberman, "Olympic Universalism," 528.

23. Chatziefstathiou et al., "Cultural Imperialism," 109.

24. Chatziefstathiou, "Diffusion of Olympic Sport," 41.

25. International Olympic Committee Archive (IOCA), Minutes of the Meeting between the Executive Board of the IOC and the Representatives of the National Olympic Committees, Munich, Germany (September 10–11, 1971), 4.

26. "IOC Members," International Olympic Committee, accessed March 28, 2024, https://olympics.com/ioc/members.

27. Kanin, *Political History*, 27.

28. With only a few exceptions, including the recently formed Olympic Refugee Team, this requirement has been unwavering.

29. Kanin, *Political History*, 27.

30. Pascal Charitas and David-Claude Kemo-Keimbou, "The United States of America and the Francophone African Countries at the International Olympic Committee: Sports Aid, a Barometer of American Imperialism? (1952–1963)," *Journal of Sport History* 40, no. 1 (Spring 2013): 73.

31. IOCA: E-RE02-CSSA/001, Supreme Council for Sport in Africa (SCSA): Correspondence, letter from Avery Brundage to Mr. J. C. Ganga, February 9, 1966.

32. IOCA: E-RE02-CSSA/001, Supreme Council for Sport in Africa (SCSA): Correspondence, letter from J. C. Ganga to Avery Brundage, October 5, 1970.

33. IOCA: E-RE02-CSSA/001, Supreme Council for Sport in Africa (SCSA): Correspondence, letter from J. C. Ganga to Avery Brundage, October 5, 1970.

34. William J. Baker, "Political Games: The Meaning of International Sport for Independent Africa," in *Sport in Africa: Essays in Social History*, ed. William J. Baker and James A. Mangan (New York: Africana, 1987), 288.

35. Ramadhan Ali, *Africa at the Olympics* (London: Africa Books, 1976), 49.

36. Alfred E. Senn, *Power, Politics, and the Olympic Games* (Champaign, IL: Human Kinetics, 1999), 10.

37. Kéba Mbaye, *Proceedings of the International Scientific Symposium to Open the African Centre for Olympic Studies (ACOS)* (Yaoundé, Cameroon: Eclosion, 2019), 102.

38. A small sample of this sizable corpus includes Douglas Booth, *The Race Game: Sport and Politics in South Africa* (London: Frank Cass, 1998); Jörg Krieger, "'We Don't Want to Be Pushed by Outsiders': The International Association of Athletics Federation's Attempts to Re-Admit South Africa to the Global Athletics Stage," *South African Journal for Research in Sport, Physical Education and Recreation* 39, nos. 1–2 (2017): 171–88; Michelle Sikes, "Ousting South Africa: Olympic Clashes of 1968," *Acta Academica* 50, no. 2 (2018): 12–33; and Matthew P. Llewellyn and Toby C. Rider, "Dennis Brutus and the South African Non-Racial Olympic Committee in Exile, 1966–1970," *South African Historical Journal* 72, no. 2 (2020): 246–71.

39. For examples of the former, see David Goldblatt, *The Games: A Global History of the Olympics* (New York: W. W. Norton, 2016); and Jules Boykoff, *Power Games: A Political History of the Olympics* (London: Verso, 2016). And for an example of the latter, see Gerald P. Schaus and Stephen R. Wenn, *Onward to the Olympics: Historical Perspectives on the Olympic Games* (Waterloo, Ontario: Wilfrid Laurier University Press, 2007).

40. Ali, *Africa at the Olympics.* The book contains over forty full-page photos and reads like an extended encyclopedia entry but retains utility given its singularity and its excellent coverage of the political events that shaped the Olympics in the 1960s and early 1970s.

41. The volume *Olimpismo: The Olympic Movement in the Making of Latin America and the Caribbean*, edited by Antonio Sotomayor and Cesar R. Torres, considers some of the ways that a handful of the populations of these regions have engaged with the Olympism, but the only analytical connection linking the nine chapters that compose the volume is geographical, while the book offers only minimal framing. See Antonio Sotomayor and Cesar R. Torres, eds., *Olimpismo: The Olympic Movement in the Making of Latin America and the Caribbean* (Fayetteville: University of Arkansas Press, 2020).

42. I had originally intended to conduct a significant number of interviews with many of the individuals who appear in the book. However, I ultimately abandoned this intention because so many of them have granted

Notes to 25–30 181

innumerable interviews over the years that examine a wide range of experiences. The volume of this testimony and its easy accessibility via various forms of popular media, including newspapers, magazines, and various internet sites, obviated the need to traverse the continent in search of audiences with these individuals. Moreover, their contemporaneous commentary is immune from the complications related to memory and the passage of time inherent to oral history.

Chapter 1: African Colonies and
Newly Independent Countries at the Olympic Games

Epigraph: B. A. A. Goubadia, *Our Olympic Adventure* (Lagos, Nigeria: Crownbird, 1953), 4.

1. In addition to Great Britain's colonies in Africa that featured independent NOCs, the British had previously permitted the formation of NOCs elsewhere in the empire, including Bermuda (1936), Jamaica (1936), Trinidad and Tobago (1948), and Barbados (1955). Conversely, the French insisted that no new NOCs could be formed in an imperial territory until it had achieved political sovereignty.

2. Pascal Charitas, "The Birth of an African Olympic Movement between French and English Imperialisms (1910–1965)," in *Historical and Contemporary Issues in Olympic Studies: Proceedings of the Conference Held by the University of Johannesburg and the Olympic Studies Centre of the German Sport University Cologne in Johannesburg, November 30–December 2, 2015*, ed. Cora Burnett (Johannesburg: University of Johannesburg, 2015), 178.

3. David Maraniss, *Rome 1960: The Olympics That Changed the World* (New York: Simon and Schuster, 2008), 55.

4. Although the IOC imposed a mandatory retirement age in the 1980s, which fluctuated between seventy and eighty, Alexander was grandfathered in under the previous policy, which afforded members lifetime appointments.

5. Maureen Margaret Smith, "Revisiting South Africa and the Olympic Movement: The Correspondence of Reginald S. Alexander and the International Olympic Committee, 1961–86," *International Journal of the History of Sport* 23, no. 7 (November 2006): 1193.

6. Sendeu Titus M. Tenga, "Globalisation and Olympic Sport in Tanzania" (PhD diss., Norwegian University of Sport and Physical Education, 2000), 109.

7. Robert Skinner, "Antidiscrimination: Racism and the Case of South Africa," in *The Ideals of Global Sport: From Peace to Human Rights*, ed. Barbara J. Keys (Philadelphia: University of Pennsylvania Press, 2019), 47.

8. As mentioned in the previous chapter, it remains unclear if Egypt sent an athlete to the 1912 Games, but its participation in the ensuing Games

182   Notes to 30–36

in 1920 (the 1916 Games were canceled owing to the First World War) is certain.

9. Shaun Lopez, "Football as National Allegory: *Al-Ahram* and the Olympics in 1920s Egypt," *History Compass* 7, no. 1 (2009): 284.

10. Wilson Jacob, "Working out Egypt: Masculinity and Subject Formation between Colonial Modernity and Nationalism, 1870–1940" (PhD diss., New York University, 2005), 171.

11. Christian Wacker, "Egypt Goes Olympic: 1914 to 1932," *South African Journal for Research in Sport, Physical Education and Recreation* 39, nos. 1 and 2 (2017): 167.

12. Wacker, 166.

13. Lopez, "Football as National Allegory," 282, 284.

14. The soccer team did, however, defeat Hungary 3–0 in the opening round, which prompted a number of European media outlets to praise the Egyptians and declare that they had "arrived." Subsequently, a 5–0 defeat to Sweden in an ensuing round, which crashed the team out of the tournament, served to temper some of the earlier acclaim.

15. Jacob, "Working Out Egypt," 233.

16. Jacob, 235.

17. The soccer team defeated Turkey 7–0 in the opening round and Portugal 2–1 in the quarterfinals before being drubbed by Argentina 6–0 in the semifinals. They then lost the third-place game to the Italians by a whopping 11–3 score, again dampening the initial excitement regarding the squad's performance.

18. Jacob, "Working Out Egypt," 250.

19. Pascal Charitas, "Anglophone Africa in the Olympic Movement: The Confirmation of a British Wager? (1948–1962)," *African Research and Documentation* 116 (2011): 36.

20. There were two exceptions to this policy: if the athlete was born in the United Kingdom or if they had been residing there for the five years immediately prior to the date for entries for the Games. Neither helped the prospects of inclusion for African athletes.

21. Charitas, "Anglophone Africa," 39.

22. *Daily Times* (Nigeria), May 28, 1952.

23. France's colonial policy aimed to "assimilate" Africans, culturally and otherwise, so that they would effectively become Black French men and women.

24. IOCA, Correspondence 1951–1966, letter from François Piétri to Otto Mayer, January 6, 1951.

25. IOCA, A. Brundage correspondence, 1952–1956, note 0061524, letter from Otto Mayer to Avery Brundage, December 17, 1955.

26. IOCA, Minutes of the 50th Session of the IOC, Paris, France (June 13–17, 1955), 50.

Notes to 36–45   183

27. Avery Brundage Collection (ABC) 296,19, box 296, item 19, *Programa Cultural de le XIX Olympiada*, African Ballet (1956).
28. Denis Echard et al., "From Olympic Competitors to IOC Members," *Olympic Review* 25, no. 7 (February–March 1996): 26.
29. Echard et al., 26.
30. Sir John MacPherson, "Letter of Appeal," *Daily Times* (Nigeria), November 10, 1951, 10.
31. Amos Tinuayo Oduvale, Kanayo Onyiliogwu, and Olutola Oduyale, *History of Olympic Movement in Nigeria* (Lagos: Nigerian Olympic Committee, 2009), 17.
32. This population included descendants of the over thirty-two indentured servants that Britain arranged to travel from India to its East African protectorate from 1896 to 1901 to construct the Uganda Railway, though other Indian migrants had preceded this influx.
33. ABC 53,10, box 53, folder 10—Alexander, Reginald S. (Kenya), 1955–1963, letter from Reginald Alexander to Avery Brundage, August 21, 1963.
34. Lord Killanin, *My Olympic Years* (New York: William Morrow, 1983), 36.
35. B. A. A. Goubadia, *Our Olympic Adventure* (Lagos, Nigeria: Crownbird, 1953), 1.
36. For example, see Barbara Keys, ed., *The Ideals of Sport: From Peace to Human Rights* (Philadelphia: University of Pennsylvania Press, 2019).
37. Alfred E. Senn, *Power, Politics, and the Olympic Games* (Champaign, IL: Human Kinetics, 1999), 118.
38. IOCA: Correspondence 1957, Note: 0061525, Brundage Fund, letter from Avery Brundage to Otto Mayer, May 11, 1957. Emphasis mine.
39. Maha Zaoui and Emmanuel Bayle, "The Central Role of the State in the Governance of Sport and the Olympic Movement in Tunisia, from 1956 to the Present Day," in *The Olympic Movement and the Middle East and North Africa Region*, ed. Mahfoud Amara (London: Routledge, 2019), 39, 40, 46.
40. Zaoui and Bayle, 39.
41. Zaoui and Bayle, 39.
42. Over time, Nyerere softened his stance and associated rhetoric regarding tourism owing to the much-needed revenue it provided the country.
43. Tenga, "Globalisation and Olympic Sport," 110.
44. During the colonial period, mainland Tanzania was known as Tanganyika. In April 1964 Tanganyika merged with the Zanzibar archipelago, which had only achieved independence in January of that year, to form Tanzania.
45. Tenga, "Globalisation and Olympic Sport," 114.
46. Charitas, "Birth of an African Olympic Movement," 172.
47. Charitas, 183.
48. ABC 161,1, box 161, folder 1—Tunisia, Comité Olympique Tunisien, 1956–67, letter from Otto Mayer to Avery Brundage, July 24, 1957.
49. Maraniss, *Rome 1960*, 99.

50. IOCA, note 0061526, correspondence 1960–1961, International Olympic Committee/Avery Brundage Fund, letter from Avery Brundage to Marquess of Exeter, April 15, 1960.

51. IOCA, Brundage Collection, box 7598, Brundage correspondence to Otto Mayer, January 5, 1963.

52. IOCA, Correspondence 1962–63, note 0061527, Brundage Fund, letter from Otto Mayer to Avery Brundage, June 28, 1963.

53. ABC 53,10RA, box 53, folder 10—Alexander, Reginald S. (Kenya), 1955–1963, letter from Reginald Alexander to Avery Brundage, March 15, 1963.

54. David B. Kanin, *A Political History of the Olympic Games* (Boulder, CO: Westview Press, 1981), 95.

55. William J. Baker, "Political Games: The Meaning of International Sport for Independent Africa," in *Sport in Africa: Essays in Social History*, ed. William J. Baker and James A. Mangan (New York: Africana, 1987), 273.

56. Tsige Abebe, *Triumph and Tragedy: A History of Abebe Bikila and His Marathon Career* (self-published, 1996), 46.

57. Tim Judah, *Bikila: Ethiopia's Barefoot Olympian* (London: Reportage Press, 2008), 86.

58. Paul Rambali, a biographer of Bikila, claims that the Olympian was also beaten and tortured while detained, though that contention is not universal. See Paul Rambali, *Barefoot Runner: The Life of Marathon Champion Abebe Bikila* (London: Serpent's Tail, 2007), 177–90.

59. Rambali, 196.

60. John Underwood, "The Number Two Lion in the Land of Sheba," *Sports Illustrated*, April 12, 1965, 92.

61. Baker, "Political Games," 275.

62. Maraniss, *Rome 1960*, 401.

63. Rambali, *Barefoot Runner*, 283.

64. Francis Noronha, *Kipchoge of Kenya* (Nakuru, Kenya: Elimu, 1970), 47.

65. Martin Kane, "A Very Welcome Redcoat," *Sports Illustrated*, December 19, 1966, 80, 82.

66. John Underwood, "Lost Laughter," *Sports Illustrated*, September 30, 1968, 92.

67. Kanin, *Political History*, 95.

68. Ramadhan Ali, *Africa at the Olympics* (London: Africa Books, 1976), 100.

69. Richard Demak, "Nowhere to Run," *Sports Illustrated*, February 4, 2008, 18.

70. Demak, 19.

71. Demak, 19.

72. Skinner, "Antidiscrimination," 48.

Chapter 2: Isolating Racism

Epigraphs: Dennis Brutus, quoted in Michelle Sikes, "The Enemy of My Enemy Is My Friend? A Clash of Anti-Apartheid Tactics and Targets in

Notes to 59–66

the Olympic Movement of the Early 1960s," *International Journal of the History of Sport* 37, no. 7 (2020): 524; African National Congress, quoted in Richard Edward Lapchick, *The Politics of Race and International Sport: The Case of South Africa* (Westport, CT: Greenwood Press, 1975), 107.

1. Scarlett Cornelissen, "Resolving the 'South Africa Problem': Transnational Activism, Ideology and Race in the Olympic Movement, 1960–91," *International Journal of the History of Sport* 28, no. 1 (2011): 154.

2. Barbara J. Keys, "Introduction: The Ideals of International Sport," in *The Ideals of Global Sport: From Peace to Human Rights*, ed. Barbara J. Keys (Philadelphia: University of Pennsylvania Press, 2019), 10.

3. Harry Blutstein, *Games of Discontent: Protests, Boycotts, and Politics at the 1968 Mexico Olympics* (Montreal: McGill-Queen's University Press, 2021), 25.

4. Joan Brickhill, *Race against Race: South Africa's Multinational Fraud* (London: International Defense Aid Fund, 1976), 8.

5. IOCA, Minutes of the 55th Session of the IOC. Munich, Germany, May 25, 1959.

6. IOCA, Minutes of the 55th Session of the IOC. Munich, Germany, May 25, 1959.

7. IOCA, CIO CNO-AFRIS-APART Apartheid: dossier documentaire, box 7769, Alan Paton, "Opening Address, Conference of National Sports Bodies Convened by the Steering Committee of the South African Sports Association, Durban, 10–11 Jan. 1959."

8. Cheryl Roberts, *South Africa's Struggle for Olympic Legitimacy: From Apartheid Sport to International Recognition* (Cape Town: Township Publishing Co-operative, 1991), 3.

9. Roberts, 3.

10. Roberts, 3.

11. Roberts, 4.

12. Roberts, 4.

13. Cornelissen, "Resolving the 'South Africa Problem,'" 158.

14. IOCA, Brundage Collection, box 7596, Brundage correspondence to Mayer, February 24, 1959.

15. Robert G. Weisbord, *Racism and the Olympics* (New Brunswick, NJ: Transaction, 2015), 116.

16. Douglas Booth, *The Race Game: Sport and Politics in South Africa* (London: Frank Cass, 1998), 78.

17. Roberts, *South Africa's Struggle*, 5.

18. ABC, box 144, "SAN-ROC Constitution and Articles of Association."

19. Michelle Sikes, "From Nairobi to Baden-Baden: African Politics, the International Olympic Committee, and Early Efforts to Censure Apartheid South Africa," *International Journal of the History of Sport* 36, no. 1 (2019): 11.

186   Notes to 66–72

20. Portugal's empire in Africa included Angola, Mozambique, São Tomé and Príncipe, Guinea-Bissau, and Cape Verde.

21. Oginga Odinga, *Not yet Uhuru: The Autobiography of Oginga Odinga* (London: Heinemann, 1967), 237; Sikes, "From Nairobi," 15. Sikes explains, "The OAU's founding charter sealed the delegates' commitment to dislodging the colonial powers. Signatories pledged to carry out a number of anti-colonial and anti-apartheid resolutions, such as closing their ports to Portuguese and South African ships and forbidding planes from these countries to land or fly over. They also pledged to sever all relations between their governments and those of South Africa and Portugal, mobilizing the tools of soft power to challenge white minority rule." Sikes, "From Nairobi," 15.

22. Richard Espy, *The Politics of the Olympic Games* (Berkeley: University of California Press, 1979), 86.

23. Sikes, "From Nairobi," 8, 17.

24. Simon Stevens, "Why South Africa? The Politics of Anti-Apartheid Activism in Britain in the Long 1970s," in *The Breakthrough: Human Rights in the 1970s,* ed. Jan Eckel and Samuel Moyn (Philadelphia: University of Pennsylvania Press, 2014), 207.

25. "Ban on IOC Delegates Confirmed," *East African Standard,* August 3, 1963, 1.

26. Connie Field, dir., *Fair Play* (Minneapolis, MN: Clarity Films Production, 2010), 96 minutes. Later, Brutus would claim that the guards had encouraged him to try to escape so that they could justify shooting him.

27. "Echoes of a Pistol Shot," *Rand Daily Mail,* September 20, 1963.

28. Matthew Llewellyn and Toby Rider, "Dennis Brutus and the South African Non-Racial Olympic Committee in Exile, 1966–1970," *South African Historical Journal* 72, no. 2 (2020): 257.

29. Blutstein, *Games of Discontent,* 28.

30. Richard Edward Lapchick, *The Politics of Race and International Sport: The Case of South Africa* (Westport, CT: Greenwood Press, 1975), 63.

31. IOCA: Minutes of the 61st session of the IOC, Innsbruck, Austria (January 26–28, 1964), 6.

32. IOCA: Minutes of the 61st session of the IOC, Innsbruck, Austria (January 26–28, 1964), 6.

33. Alfred E. Senn, *Power, Politics, and the Olympic Games* (Champaign, IL: Human Kinetics, 1999), 133.

34. Cornelissen, "Resolving the South Africa Problem," 157.

35. Although SANROC was able to rally some support at the meeting, most IOC members were unsympathetic toward the organization, objecting to SANROC's usage of the word *Olympic* in its name and ultimately passing a rather petty resolution saying, "Neither the IOC nor any of its officials shall have any communication or dealings with it." That was unless it removed the word *Olympic,* which it never did. Weisbord, *Racism and the Olympics,* 122.

Notes to 72–80 187

36. Mihir Bose, *Sporting Colours: Sport and Politics in South Africa* (London: Robson Books, 1994), 71.

37. ABC 107,4LSA, box 107, folder 4—Commission on South Africa, 1967, letter from Avery Brundage to Sir Ade (May 19, 1967), 1.

38. ABC 107,4CSA: box 107, folder 4—Commission on South Africa, 1967, letter from Adetokunbo Ademola to Avery Brundage (June 5, 1967), 1. Given the role that the IOC report played in enabling South Africa to gain readmission, albeit only temporarily, to the Olympic Movement, Frank Braun, the head of the SANOC, declared, following the decision, "Ademola fought for us like a hero. He must rate as one of the people who have most helped South Africa to get back into the Olympics." That statement, though, surely mischaracterized Ademola's sentiments and intentions. See Bose, *Sporting Colours*, 72.

39. ABC 107,4AB, box 107, folder 4—Commission on South Africa, 1967, letter to the three members of the Special Commission to South Africa from Avery Brundage, August 31, 1967, 1.

40. Booth, *Race Game*, 96.

41. Cornelissen, "Resolving the South Africa Problem," 159.

42. Lapchick, *Politics of Race*, 104.

43. Michelle Sikes, "Ousting South Africa: Olympic Clashes of 1968," *Acta Academica* 50, no. 2 (2018): 19; Sendeu Titus M. Tenga, "Globalisation and Olympic Sport in Tanzania" (PhD diss., Norwegian University of Sport and Physical Education, 2000), 189.

44. Lapchick, *Politics of Race*, 104.

45. Lapchick, 92.

46. Lapchick, 92.

47. Weisbord, *Racism and the Olympics*, 123.

48. Ramadhan Ali, *Africa at the Olympics* (London: Africa Books, 1976), 42.

49. Llewellyn and Rider, "Dennis Brutus," 254, 264.

50. The thirty-six votes were cast by IOC members representing only twenty-three countries, underscoring the overrepresentation of "traditional" Western nations in the body. Moreover, seventy countries with IOC-recognized NOCs were not permitted to vote on the resolution.

51. Ali, *Africa at the Olympics*, 46. During apartheid the South African government assigned every citizen to one of four racial categories, which also dictated their social and economic status: White, Coloured, Asian, and Native (Black).

52. "Aftermath of the Boycott," *Daily Nation*, February 21, 1968, 23.

53. Ali, *Africa at the Olympics*, 46.

54. Ali, 44.

55. Ali, 47.

56. Ali, 47.

188 Notes to 80–88

57. Kéba Mbaye, *The International Olympic Committee and South Africa: Analysis and Illustration of a Humanist Sports Policy* (Lausanne, Switzerland: IOC, 1995), 111.

58. Ali, *Africa at the Olympics*, 48. An alternative version of this declaration indicates that these athletes would be "shown at the fair" and would "go back to the forest once the party was over." It's possible that the differences are matters of translation.

59. Blutstein, *Games of Discontent*, 30.

60. Mbaye, *International Olympic Committee*, 113.

61. Blutstein, *Games of Discontent*, 33. Within South Africa there are many White subpopulations, but the main two are "Anglo," made up of people of British descent who primarily speak English, and "Afrikaner," composed of people of Dutch descent who primarily speak Afrikaans, a combination of Dutch and indigenous languages and grammatical formations.

62. Tex Maule, "A Flare in the Dark," *Sports Illustrated*, June 3, 1968, 62.

63. Kevin B. Witherspoon, "Protest at the Pyramid: The 1968 Mexico City Olympics and the Politicization of the Olympic Games" (PhD diss., Florida State University, 2003), 61.

64. Tex Maule, "Switcheroo from Yes to Nyet," *Sports Illustrated*, April 29, 1968, 29.

65. Ali, *Africa at the Olympics*, 52.

66. David B. Kanin, *A Political History of the Olympic Games* (Boulder, CO: Westview Press, 1981), 100.

67. Cornelissen, "Resolving the South African Problem," 160.

68. Lapchick, *Politics of Race*, 196; Bose, *Sporting Colours*, 91.

69. Lapchick, *Politics of Race*, 196.

70. Lapchick, 195. Ordia even requested that Brundage try to convince Reginald Honey, the White representative from South Africa, to remain on the IOC, apparently as a gesture of goodwill and perhaps also to keep lines of communication open with the regime in Pretoria.

71. ABC 134,3, box 134, Folder 3—Comité Olimpique, 1971–1973, letter from A.D. Touny to Avery Brundage, May 3, 1971, 1.

72. ABC 358,4, box 358, folder 4—Important Letters—President, IOC, letter from Avery Brundage to A. A. Ordia, June 27, 1970, 1.

73. Christopher R. Hill, *Olympic Politics* (Manchester: Manchester University Press, 1992), 246.

74. Maureen Margaret Smith, "Revisiting South Africa and the Olympic Movement: The Correspondence of Reginald S. Alexander and the International Olympic Committee, 1961–86," *International Journal of the History of Sport* 23, no. 7 (November 2006): 1207.

75. IOCA, D-RM01-AAACNOA/032, Correspondence, 1991, "Letter from Jean Claude Ganga, President of ACNOA, to Mr. Ibrahim A. Gambari,

Notes to 88–97   189

Chairman of the Special Committee Against Apartheid at the United Nations," July 26, 1991, 1–2.

76. Cornelissen, "Resolving the South Africa Problem," 163.

77. Lee Sustar and Aisha Karim, eds., *Poetry and Protest: A Dennis Brutus Reader* (Chicago: Haymarket Books, 2006), 144.

78. Douglas Booth, "Accommodating Race to Play the Game: South Africa's Readmission to International Sport," *Sporting Traditions* 8 (1990): 195.

79. William Oscar Johnson, "It Is Time. It Is Time," *Sports Illustrated*, April 29, 1991, 40.

80. "Letter from Jean Claude Ganga," 2.

81. Rone Tempest, "S. Africa, after 21 Years, Is Readmitted to Olympics," *Baltimore Sun*, July 9, 1991.

82. Johnson, "It Is Time," 40.

83. William Oscar Johnson, "Welcome Back: The Presence of Nelson Mandela Marked the Momentous Return of a Former Pariah," *Sports Illustrated*, August 3, 1992, 27.

84. Johnson, 27.

85. Johnson, "It Is Time," 38.

86. Johnson, "Welcome Back," 26.

87. Elana Meyer, "Olympics: Breeding Ground for Transformative Action," Peace and Sport. August 14, 2016, https://www.peace-sport.org/.

88. Cornelissen, "Resolving the South Africa Problem," 164.

Chapter 3: Africa Protests

Epigraphs: Motsapi Moorosi, quoted in Jerry Kirshenbaum, "Buzz before the Curtain," *Sports Illustrated*, August 28, 1972, 35; John Kasyoka, quoted in IOCA, CIO JO-1976S-BOYCO, Boycott of the 1976 Olympic Summer Games in Montreal: Correspondence between the IOC and NOCs and Announcement of Withdrawal, 204884, "Statement Issued by Chef de Mission Kenya, Mr. John Kasyoka, July 17, 1976."

1. In fact, the first African nation to boycott an Olympic Games was Egypt, which refused to send athletes to Melbourne in 1956 owing to the Suez Crisis. However, this was an isolated incident and, of course, few African countries even had NOCs at that time.

2. Harry Blutstein, *Games of Discontent: Protests, Boycotts, and Politics at the 1968 Mexico Olympics* (Montreal: McGill-Queen's University Press, 2021), 37.

3. Robert G. Weisbord, *Racism and the Olympics* (New Brunswick, NJ: Transaction Publishers, 2015), 143.

4. Blutstein, *Games of Discontent*, 37.

5. ABC 196,5, box 196, folder 5—Rhodesian Problem, 1968–69, letter from Avery Brundage to Pedro Ramírez Vázquez, Chairman of the Organizing Committee of the Mexico City Games, July 31, 1968.

190 Notes to 97–106

6. Blutstein, *Games of Discontent*, 50.

7. Ramadhan Ali, *Africa at the Olympics* (London: Africa Books, 1976), 57.

8. Ali, 60.

9. ABC 151,20, box 151, folder 20—Nigeria Olympic Committee, 1970–72, letter from A. A. Ordia to Avery Brundage, May 22, 1971, 2. Emphasis added.

10. Weisbord, *Racism and the Olympics*, 147.

11. Amos Tinuayo Oduvale, Kanayo Onyiliogwu, and Olutola Oduyale, *History of Olympic Movement in Nigeria* (Lagos: Nigerian Olympic Committee, 2009), 129.

12. Sam Ramsamy with Edward Griffiths, *Reflections on a Life in Sport* (Cape Town: Greenhouse, 2004), 4.

13. Ali, *Africa at the Olympics*, 63.

14. ABC, box 184, letter from Avery Brundage to Prime Minister Ian Smith, November 19, 1972.

15. ABC 154,6, box 154, folder 6—Rhodesia, National Olympic Committee of Rhodesia, 1970–73, letter from Avery Brundage to Secretary General G. O. Plaskitt of the National Olympic Committee of Rhodesia, November 20, 1972, 1. Brundage personally responded to everyone who wrote him a letter criticizing the banning of Rhodesia, recurringly utilizing various versions of this language: "If African politicians think they won a victory, they are much mistaken."

16. Oduvale, Onyiliogwu, and Oduyale, *History of Olympic Movement*, 132.

17. Weisbord, *Racism and the Olympics*, 152. The original letters featured the pejorative N-word.

18. Hamad S. Ndee, "Sport as a Political Tool: Tanzania and the Liberation of Africa," *International Journal of the History of Sport* 22, no. 4 (2005): 680.

19. In response, the prime minister of New Zealand, Robert Muldoon, labeled the SCSA president "a liar and troublemaker" and suggested he could "stew in his own juice." Trevor Richards, *Dancing on Their Bones: New Zealand, South Africa, Rugby and Racism* (Wellington, New Zealand: Bridget Williams Books, 1999), 134.

20. Mohamed Mzali, "I Am Sorry about the Boycott of the Montreal Olympic Games," *Olympic Review* 100 (1976): 463. In the days leading up to the opening ceremony, only Tanzania (on July 10), Somalia (on July 14), and Congo (on July 15) had announced that they would boycott the Games.

21. Sam Ramsamy with Edward Griffiths, *Reflections on a Life in Sport* (Cape Town: Greenhouse, 2004), 63.

22. Mzali, "I Am Sorry," 464.

23. Richards, *Dancing on Their Bones*, 142.

24. IOCA, E-REo2-CSSA/004, Supreme Council for Sport in Africa (SCSA): Correspondence concerning Sport in South Africa and

Notes to 106–110

Apartheid, press statement by Abraham Ordia, president of the Supreme Council for Sport in Africa, London, November 17, 1976, 2.

25. Ramsamy, *Reflections on a Life*, 64.

26. Ramsamy, 64.

27. Moreover, under pressure from China, Taiwan had just been banned from the Games for refusing to compete under that name. Instead, Taiwan preferred *the Republic of China*. As Richards argues, "Having just told Taiwan it can't compete in the Games, the IOC was not about to bow to further 'political demands.'" Richards, *Dancing on Their Bones*, 155.

28. Steve Cady, "Taiwan, Nigeria Quit Olympics," *New York Times*, July 17, 1976, 1; Steve Cady, "Opening Ceremony of the Olympic Games," *New York Times*, July 18, 1976, 7.

29. IOCA, CIO JO-1976S-BOYCO, Boycott of the 1976 Olympic Summer Games in Montreal: Correspondence between the IOC and NOCs and Announcement of Withdrawal, 204884, "Statement Issued by Chef de Mission Kenya, Mr. John Kasyoka, July 17, 1976." In a subsequent letter sent to the IOC, Kasyoka also cited the Israeli commando raid to free the Israeli hostages being held at Entebbe International Airport in Uganda as another contributing factor to Kenya's decision to withdraw from the 1976 Olympics, presumably because forty-five Ugandan soldiers were killed in the raid and eleven Ugandan Air Force planes were destroyed. However, Kenya openly supported Israel, such that the Ugandan dictator Idi Amin issued orders to retaliate against Kenyans living in Uganda. Consequently, hundreds of Kenyans were killed, and thousands fled Uganda. See IOCA, CIO JO-1976S-BOYCO, Boycott of the 1976 Olympic Summer Games in Montreal: Correspondence between the IOC and NOCs and Announcement of Withdrawal, 204884, "Letter from Mr. John Kasyoka to the IOC, July 17, 1976."

30. IOCA, CIO JO-1976S-BOYCO, Boycott of the 1976 Olympic Summer Games in Montreal: Correspondence between the IOC and NOCs and Announcement of Withdrawal, 204884, "Letter from Tsegaw Ayele, Head of the Ethiopian Olympic Committee, to Lord Killanin," July 17, 1976, 1.

31. IOCA, CIO JO-1976S-BOYCO, Boycott of the 1976 Olympic Summer Games in Montreal: Correspondence between the IOC and NOCs and Announcement of Withdrawal, 204884, "Letter from Mohamed Zerguini, President of the Algerian Olympic Committee to Lord Killanin," September 15, 1976, 1, 2.

32. Ramsamy, *Reflections on a Life*, 65.

33. Pat Putnam, "It Was a Call to Colors," *Sports Illustrated*, July 26, 1976, 16.

34. Putnam, "It Was a Call," 14.

35. Cady, "Taiwan, Nigeria Quit Olympics," 1.

36. Putnam, "It Was a Call," 15.

37. Putnam, 17.
38. Putnam, 17; the NCAA is an initialism for the National Collegiate Athletic Association, an organization composed of member institutions of higher education, which administers and oversees intercollegiate athletics in the United States.
39. Putnam, 17, 19.
40. Ramsamy, *Reflections on a Life*, 65.
41. IOCA, E-RE02-CSSA/004, anonymous letter to Mr. Ordia, November 15, 1982, 1. (Although unsigned, the letter bears an RSA postal stamp.)
42. Geoffrey Miller, *Behind the Olympic Rings* (Lynn, MA: H. O. Zimman, 1979), 93. It didn't take long for Muldoon to backtrack, however, eventually allowing a controversial and ultimately violent South African rugby tour to New Zealand in 1981, before finally adhering to the Gleneagles Agreement.
43. IOCA, E-RE02-CSSA/001, Supreme Council for Sport in Africa (SCSA): Correspondence, 1976–1977, letter from J. C. Ganga to the Honourable Commissioner for Sports and Physical Culture of Ethiopia, January 14, 1977, 7.
44. Courtney W. Mason, "The Bridge to Change: The 1976 Montreal Olympic Games, South African Apartheid Policy, and the Olympic Boycott Paradigm," in *Onward to the Olympics: Historical Perspectives on the Olympic Games*, ed. Gerald P. Schaus and Stephen R. Wenn (Waterloo, ON: Wilfrid Laurier University Press, 2007), 292.
45. "Editorial: Let Us All Boycott Moscow Olympics," *Nation* (Kenya), February 4, 1980, 6.
46. Newly elected SCSA secretary general Lamine Ba, from Senegal, further articulated the SCSA's stance regarding the Moscow Games based on what had transpired during the organization's General Assembly in Yaoundé, Cameroon, in December 1979. "The Council expressed its wholehearted support for the Olympic Games in Moscow, declaring that it is ready to do everything in its power to ensure the success of the Games of the XXII Olympiad, inviting all countries belonging to the SCSA to ensure the widest and most representative participation of their athletes in these Games." Lamine Ba, "Wholehearted Support for the 1980 Olympic Games in Moscow," *Olympic Review* 150 (April 1980): 161.
47. IOCA, CIO JO-1980S-BOYCO, Boycott of the 1980 Olympic Summer Games in Moscow: Press Cuttings and Telexes—Reaction by Country (T-Z), January 1, 1980–May 31, 1980, "UPI Telex, February 10, 1980."
48. Zimbabwe had similar concerns, though for slightly different reasons. In May 1980, less than a month after receiving independence from Great Britain, Zimbabwe (formerly Rhodesia) announced it would not be joining the boycott. Dennis Hardman, secretary general of the Zimbabwean

Notes to 116–120

Olympic committee, said "No way" when asked if Zimbabwe would boycott the Moscow Games in response to a US call. "We've been out of international sports for 12 years and we're not waiting another four years until the Los Angeles Olympics." Given the new left-leaning government in the country under Robert Mugabe, it's highly doubtful that Zimbabwe would have joined the boycott, anyway. See IOC Archives, CIO JO-1980S-BOYCO, Boycott of the 1980 Olympic Summer Games in Moscow: Press Cuttings and Telexes—Reaction by Country (T-Z), January 1, 1980–May 31, 1980, "UPI Telex, no date."

49. Amos Yenyi Sakaba, "Ali and the Moscow Boycott," *Nigeria Standard*, February 12, 1980, 6.

50. The Soviet government also offered African fans reduced-price tickets to the events.

51. "1980 Olympics: The Soviets are Confident," *Punch* (Nigeria), February 7, 1980, 5.

52. "Muhammad Ali Punches In," *Daily News* (Tanzania), February 4, 1980, 12.

53. Abbe Richard, "Carter Can't Fool Us," *Daily News* (Tanzania), February 9, 1980, 9.

54. Mohammed Hamza, "Why Africa Should Go to Moscow '80," *Nigeria Standard*, March 7, 1980, 14.

55. Nicholas Evan Sarantakes, *Dropping the Torch: Jimmy Carter, the Olympic Boycott, and the Cold War* (Cambridge, UK: Cambridge University Press, 2011), 115.

56. Yomi Kazeem, "Africa Meant a Lot to Muhammad Ali—He Meant Even More to Africa," Quartz, June 5, 2016, https://qz.com/.

57. "I've Taken No Money: Ali," *Daily Graphic* (Ghana), February 11, 1980, 15.

58. "Ali Defends Africa's Interests," *Sunday Standard* (Nigeria), February 10, 1980, 2.

59. Iyiola Afolabi and Taiwo Hassan, ". . . And He Blasts America," *Punch* (Nigeria), February 8, 1980, 1.

60. IOCA, CIO JO-1980S-BOYCO, Boycott of the 1980 Olympic Summer Games in Moscow: Press Cuttings and Telexes—Reactions by Country (J-S), 206279, "UPI telex," 1.

61. David B. Kanin, *A Political History of the Olympic Games* (Boulder, CO: Westview Press, 1981), 142. Kenya was especially keen to participate in an alternative Games to be held just before the Moscow Olympics, in part so that its athletes would not entirely miss out on an opportunity to compete against some of the world's best. Ultimately, this alternative tournament, which became known as the Liberty Bell Classic, was held on July 16 and 17, 1980, for track-and-field athletes at Franklin Field on the campus of the University of Pennsylvania. Athletes from twenty-nine countries, including Kenya and eight others from Africa, participated in the event. But

many elite US athletes declined to participate, and even though a handful of records were broken and some race times were superior to those in Moscow, there was little fanfare, and it remains nothing more than a historical footnote, just as it appears here.

62. Leila Sfeir, "Policymaking in the Egyptian Olympic Committee" (PhD diss., University of Illinois, 1982), 112.

63. IOCA, CIO JO-1980S-BOYCO, Boycott of the 1980 Olympic Summer Games in Moscow: Press Cuttings and Telexes—Reactions by Country (D-F), 206278, "UPI telex, April 13, 1980."

64. IOCA, CIO JO-1980S-BOYCO, Boycott of the 1980 Olympic Summer Games in Moscow: Press Cuttings and Telexes—Reactions by Country (J-S), 206279, "UPI telex, January 28, 1980."

65. IOCA, CIO JO-1980S-BOYCO, Boycott of the 1980 Olympic Summer Games in Moscow: Memos and Press Reviews of the White House on Other Countries' Positions, 205735, "Foreign Media Reaction to Olympic Participation Issue—XX, Summary," June 4, 1980, 6.

66. Sarantakes, *Dropping the Torch*, 213.

67. In fact, back in 1980, not only had the head of the Ethiopian NOC, Ydnekatchev Tessema, criticized the United States for adopting an "attitude contrary to the Olympic Charter" by calling for a boycott of the Moscow Games, but he also implored the IOC to reconsider the location of the 1984 Games slated for Los Angeles. See IOCA, CIO JO-1980S-BOYCO, Boycott of the 1980 Olympic Summer Games in Moscow: Articles and Telex—Position of Killanin, Replies from IOC's Members to President's Letter of March 4, 1980, 206285, telegram from Ydnekatchev Tessema (Ethiopian NOC official) to the IOC, April 18, 1980.

68. In fact, Libya chose to boycott not because it had joined the Soviet-led coalition but because the United States had denied entry to two Libyan journalists allegedly linked to terrorist activities.

69. Alfred E. Senn, *Power, Politics, and the Olympic Games* (Champaign, IL: Human Kinetics, 1999), 198. Ultimately, as the Americans had done four years earlier, the Soviets organized an alternative sporting event spread across nine countries known as the Friendship Games. Some fifty countries participated, including many African nations, some of whom had boycotted Los Angeles and some of whom had not. Some African countries even sent athletes who hadn't qualified for the Los Angeles Olympics.

70. IOCA, IOC Correspondence, SAN-ROC file, 1976–1988, letter from Sam Ramsamy to Juan Antonio Samaranch, July 4, 1984.

71. In fact, the South African rugby squad had controversially toured the United States in 1981, which generated great consternation within the Los Angeles Games Organizing Committee, as officials feared that this

Notes to 123–129   195

sporting engagement with the apartheid regime would provide the Soviets with a legitimate reason to boycott the upcoming Los Angeles Games. For further information, see Derek Charles Catsum, *Flashpoint: How a Little-Known Sporting Event Fueled America's Anti-Apartheid Protest* (Lanham, MD: Rowman & Littlefield, 2021).

72. IOCA: D-RM01-AAACNOA/005, ANOCA, correspondence, January–April 1984, letter from Anani Matthia, the President of the Association of National Olympic Committees of Africa (ANOCA), to the Chairman of the British Olympic Association, March 17, 1984.

73. "Ethiopia has Joined the Soviet-Led Boycott of the Los Angeles Olympic Games," United Press International, UPI Archives, June 1, 1984, https://www.upi.com/.

74. Kenneth Reich, "Angola Becomes 15th Nation to Join Olympic Boycott," *Los Angeles Times*, June 27, 1984, B3, 18.

75. In support of North Korea, Ethiopia and the Seychelles did boycott the 1988 Olympics, held in Seoul, South Korea, though only Egypt seemed to do so for political reasons. Madagascar had been expected to participate but ultimately withdrew for financial reasons.

Chapter 4: Parlaying Individual Olympic Success into Positive Change on the Continent

Epigraphs: Lopez Lomong with Mark Tabb, *Running for My Life: One Lost Boy's Journey from the Killing Fields of Sudan to the Olympic Games* (Nashville, TN: Thomas Nelson, 2012), 226; "Paul Tergat: Ambassador against Hunger," World Athletics, April 9, 2004, https://www.worldathletics.org/.

1. David B. Kanin, *A Political History of the Olympic Games* (Boulder, CO: Westview Press, 1981), 95.

2. He was denied the opportunity to defend his medal-winning performance at subsequent Olympics, as Kenya boycotted both the 1972 and 1976 Games.

3. Boit had originally earned a BA from the same institution in 1972, when it was known as Kenyatta College.

4. Merrill Noden, "Catching up with Runners Mike Boit and Alberto Juantorena," *Sports Illustrated*, December 23, 2002, 17.

5. "Kenya Scholar Access Program," KenSAP, accessed March 28, 2024, https://www.kensap.org/.

6. This debate, in this case as it related to the 2010 Men's World Cup in South Africa, can be accessed in the following article: Dean Allen, "The Successes and Challenges of Hosting the 2010 FIFA World Cup: The Case of Cape Town, South Africa," *Soccer and Society* 14, no. 3 (2013): 404–15. More recently, Andrew M. Guest also has superbly traced and summarized this

debate in his book *Soccer in Mind*. See Andrew M. Guest, *Soccer in Mind: A Thinking Fan's Guide to the Global Game* (New Brunswick, NJ: Rutgers University Press, 2022), 124–31.

7. Mike Wise, "The Man South Africa Forgot," ESPN, August 5, 2015, http://www.espn.com/.

8. Wise.

9. Wise.

10. Wise.

11. Wise.

12. "Letters to the Editor," *Sports Illustrated*, November 18, 1996, 12.

13. S. L. Price, "The Longest Run," *Sports Illustrated*, July 25, 2016, 103.

14. Jeré Longman, "Groundbreaking Marathoner Now Fights for Rights," *New York Times*, August 5, 2016, 7.

15. Price, "Longest Run," 105.

16. Price, 109.

17. Lopez Lomong with Mark Tabb, *Running for My Life: One Lost Boy's Journey from the Killing Fields of Sudan to the Olympic Games* (Nashville, TN: Thomas Nelson, 2012), 223.

18. Lomong, 223.

19. Lomong, 228.

20. "Lomong Named Visa Humanitarian of the Year," Bring Back the Mile, November 15, 2012, https://bringbackthemile.com/.

21. Kibny'aanko Seroney, *From Strength to Strength: The Story of Ambassador Peter Kipchumba Rono* (Nairobi: Mvule Africa, 2009), 84.

22. The Nandi are a Kenyan ethnic group, of which Rono was a member, primarily centered around what is now known as Nandi County.

23. Seroney, *From Strength to Strength*, 111.

24. Seroney, 113.

25. Seroney, 115.

26. Mozambique attained independence from Portugal on June 25, 1975.

27. "Lurdes Mutola Foundation," Cultures of Resistance Network, accessed March 28, 2024, https://culturesofresistance.org/.

28. Fundação Lurdes Mutola, accessed March 28, 2024, https://www.flmutola.org.mz/.

29. "Paul Tergat: Ambassador against Hunger."

30. "Paul Tergat: Ambassador against Hunger."

31. "Paul Tergat: Ambassador against Hunger."

32. "Paul Tergat: Ambassador against Hunger."

33. "Paul Tergat: Ambassador against Hunger."

34. In 1992 she finished in seventeenth place in the 10,000 meters. In 1996 she finished in sixth place in the 10,000 meters. And in 2000, she finished in fifth place in the 10,000 meters and in thirteenth place in the marathon.

35. "Tegla Loroupe Peace Foundation," Wikipedia, https://en.wikipedia.org/ (page discontinued).
36. Osinde Obare, "Loroupe Seduces 700 Pokot Warriors to Give up Guns for Peace," *The Standard*, November 15, 2010.
37. Obare.
38. Obare.
39. Longman, "Groundbreaking Marathoner," 7.
40. Longman, 7.
41. Longman, 7.
42. "Olympics for Life Project Proves Popular at Olympians Reunion Centre by EY," International Olympics Committee, August 20, 2106, https://olympians.org/.
43. Her teammate Saïd Aouita won the men's 5,000-meter race at the same Games shortly thereafter.
44. Jon Hendershott, "Olympic Hurdle Champions: Benita Fitzgerald and Nawal El Moutawakel," *Track and Field News* 37, no. 9 (October 1984): 42.
45. Sarah Duguid, "Nawal El-Moutawakel, Morocco," *Financial Times*, June 8, 2012.
46. Hendershott, "Olympic Hurdle Champions," 42.
47. Christel Saneh, "Nawal El Moutawakel: The 54 Seconds That Changed Her Life," World Athletics, April 8, 2021, https://worldathletics.org/.
48. David Wharton, "Women, Minorities Fight for a Place at IOC's Table," *Los Angeles Times*, August 6, 2000, A4.
49. Anneliese Goslin, ed., *Inspirational Women in Africa: Making a Difference in Physical Education, Sport and Dance* (Juiz de Fora, Brazil: Universidade Federal de Juiz de Fora, 2016), 119.
50. Goslin, *Inspirational Women in Africa*, 119.
51. Duguid, "Nawal El-Moutawakel."
52. Goslin, *Inspirational Women in Africa*, 120.
53. Goslin, 120.
54. "Interview with Lorna Kiplagat: Training for Change," PBS, March 2004, https://www.pbs.org/.
55. "Interview with Lorna Kiplagat."
56. "Interview with Lorna Kiplagat."
57. Jonathan Beverly, "Lornah Kiplagat: Inventing Herself and a Better World," *Runner's World*, May 2, 2006.
58. "UNFPA National Honorary Ambassador Wins Gold at London 2012," United Nations Population Fund, August 17, 2012, https://www.unfpa.org/.
59. "UNFPA National Honorary Ambassador Wins Gold at London 2012."
60. "Meseret Defar," Global Athletics, accessed March 28, 2024, http://www.globalathletics.com/users/63/65/meseret-defar.php.

61. "Meseret Defar Renewed Agreement with UNFPA," United Nations Population Fund, March 10, 2011, https://ethiopia.unfpa.org/en/.

62. Goslin, *Inspirational Women in Africa*, 109.

63. "Entoto Foundation: Athletes for Africa," accessed March 28, 2024, https://www.entoto.org/.

64. Evelyn Watta, "Caster Semenya: Seven Things You Should Know about the Double Olympic Champion," International Olympic Committee, February 11, 2021, https://olympics.com/en/.

65. Edwin Moses, "Caster Semenya," *Time*, March 28, 2024.

66. Graeme Reid and Minky Worden, "Caster Semenya Won Her Case, But Not the Right to Compete: Court Ruling Is a Human Rights Victory," Human Rights Watch, July 18, 2023, https://www.hrw.org/.

67. Caster Semenya Foundation, accessed March 28, 2024, https://castersemenyafoundation.org.za/index.html.

68. Koketso Kgogome, "Caster Semenya Foundation Works for Education," GSport, February 19, 2021, https://gsport.co.za/.

69. Watta, "Caster Semenya."

70. Niellah Arboine, "Caster Semenya Talks Her Vision for Uplifting Youth in Soweto through Sport," Dazed, November 23, 2021, https://www.dazeddigital.com/.

71. Arboine.

72. Steve Brenner: "Caster Semenya: 'They're Killing Sport. People Want Extraordinary Performances,'" *The Guardian*, April 23, 2021. The IOC first instituted chromosome-based gender testing that was administered via a cheek swab. Women were declared ineligible if they did not have two X chromosomes.

73. Brenner.

74. "Caster Semenya Says Testosterone Case against IAAF Has 'Destroyed' Her 'Mentally and Physically,'" BBC, July 1, 2019, https://www.bbc.com/.

Chapter 5: The Olympic Games and Personal Improvement Strategies

Epigraphs: Norman de Costa, quoted in John Manners, "African Recruiting Boom," in *The African Running Revolution*, ed. Dave Prokop (Mountain View, CA: World Publications, 1975), 69; Zola Pieterse (née Budd), quoted in William Oscar Johnson, "Endurance Test," *Sports Illustrated*, June 24, 1991, 70.

1. Drazen Jorgic and Isaack Omulo, "Bahraini Overtures to Kenyan-born Runners Attract Medals, Controversy," *Reuters*, August 17, 2016.

2. See, for example, Paul Darby, "Out of Africa: The Exodus of Elite African Football Talent to Europe," *Working USA: The Journal of Labor and Society*, 10 (December 2007): 443–56.

Notes to 160–171   199

3. Rui Tavares Guedes, "Francis Obikwelu: Nascido para Voar," *Visão*, no. 599 (August 26–September 1, 2004): 80. Translation mine.

4. "Francis Obikwelu," Wikipedia, accessed March 28, 2024, https://en.wikipedia.org/.

5. Jeré Longman, "A Runner Dreams of Gold under a New Flag," *New York Times*, March 25, 2008. Lagat's family includes his wife Gladys Tom, whom he met at Washington State, and their two children.

6. Longman.

7. Longman.

8. The IAAF is an acronym for the International Amateur Athletic Federation. The governing body is now known simply as World Athletics.

9. William Oscar Johnson, "Endurance Test," *Sports Illustrated*, June 24, 1991, 74.

10. Craig Neff, "A Runner Runs Home," *Sports Illustrated*, May 23, 1988, 26.

11. Johnson, "Endurance Test," 74.

12. Johnson, 75.

13. Johnson, 75.

14. Neff, "A Runner Runs Home," 26.

15. Zola Budd with Hugh Eley, *Zola: The Autobiography of Zola Budd* (London: Partridge, 1989), 14.

16. Johnson, "Endurance Test," 71.

17. Johnson, 80.

18. Claire Parker and Sammy Westfall, "For Some Athletes, the Olympics Aren't Just to Compete but an Opportunity to Defect," *Washington Post*, August 3, 2021.

19. Aggrey Awori of Uganda was a notable exception. He represented Uganda in the 1960 Olympics, competing in the 110-meter hurdles, though he failed to medal. He attended Harvard University from 1961 to 1965 and excelled on the institution's track team. By the time he graduated, he held three outdoor and five indoor school records.

20. H. Stidwill and A. Flatah, "The Internationalization of Track and Field at American Universities," *Journal of Comparative Physical Education and Sport* 7, no. 2 (1985): 32.

21. John Manners, "African Recruiting Boom," in *The African Running Revolution*, ed. Dave Prokop (Mountain View, CA: World Publications, 1975), 64.

22. Manners, "African Recruiting Boom," 63. Emphasis mine.

23. John Bale, *The Brawn Drain: Foreign Student-Athletes in American Universities* (Urbana: University of Illinois Press, 1991), 137.

24. Bale, *Brawn Drain*, 137.

25. Manners, "African Recruiting Boom," 63.

26. Bale, *Brawn Drain*, 79.

27. Bale, 78.

28. Manners, "African Recruiting Boom," 68.

29. Manners, 68.

30. Jon Hendershott, "T & FN Interview: Suleiman Nyambui," *Track and Field News* 35, no. 6 (July 1982): 13.

31. Robert Reinhold, "Has a Big-Time Track Program Gone Too Big?," *New York Times*, April 29, 1984, 5.

32. Julie Cart, "Gold Medalist Nawal El Moutawakel Is a Symbol of Hope for Moroccans," *Los Angeles Times*, November 6, 1985, C1, C11.

33. It also offered exemptions for church missions and foreign service. Going forward, the rule was regularly amended, but the impact it had already made, coupled with the ability to earn a living running track while still competing in the Olympics and other international events, effectively ended the era of established, seasoned African athletes migrating to the United States for educational opportunities.

34. Ross Andrews, "Push to Allow Professional Athletes Took Hold in 1968 Olympic Games," Global Sport Matters, October 15, 2018, https://globalsportmatters.com/.

35. Collectively, the fifty-four African delegations sent roughly only 970 athletes to the 2020 Tokyo Olympics.

Bibliography

Archives
(ABC) Avery Brundage Collection, University of Illinois, Champaign, Illinois
(IOCA) International Olympic Committee Archive, Olympic Studies Centre, Lausanne, Switzerland

Films
Field, Connie, dir. *Fair Play*. Minneapolis, MN: Clarity Films Production, 2010. 96 minutes.
Greenspan, Bud. *The Olympiad's Greatest Moments: The African Runners*. 98 minutes. New York: Cappy Productions / Dreamworks, 1996.

Newspapers and Wire Services
Baltimore Sun
Cameroon Tribune
Daily Graphic (Ghana)
Daily News (Tanzania)
Daily Telegraph (England)
Daily Times (Nigeria)
Financial Times (England)
Irish Times
La Soleil (Senegal)
Los Angeles Times
Nation (Kenya)
New Nigerian
New York Times
Nigerian Chronicle
Nigeria Standard
Punch (Nigeria)
Rand Daily Mail (South Africa)
Reuters
Sunday Sketch (Nigeria)

Sunday Standard (Nigeria)
The Guardian (England)
The Guardian (Tanzania)
The Standard (Kenya)
The Times (England)
Times of Israel
Times of Zambia
UPI
Washington Post

Unpublished Materials

Chatziefstathiou, Dikaia. "The Diffusion of Olympic Sport through regional Games: A Comparison of Pre and Post Second World War Contexts." Unpublished research report, Olympic Studies Centre, 2008.

Jacob, Wilson. "Working out Egypt: Masculinity and Subject Formation between Colonial Modernity and Nationalism, 1870–1940." PhD diss., New York University, 2005.

Ogungbenjo, Daniel. "The Development of Nigeria's Participation in International Sport Competition and its Effects on the Nation." PhD diss., Ohio State University, 1978.

Sfeir, Leila. "Policymaking in the Egyptian Olympic Committee." PhD diss., University of Illinois Urbana-Champaign, 1982.

Tenga, Sendeu Titus M. "Globalisation and Olympic Sport in Tanzania." PhD diss., Norwegian University of Sport and Physical Education, 2000.

Tinuayo, Amos. "Twenty-Five Years History of Olympic Movement in Nigeria, 1951–1976." PhD diss., Pennsylvania State University, 1979.

Witherspoon, Kevin B. "Protest at the Pyramid: The 1968 Mexico City Olympics and the Politicization of the Olympic Games." PhD diss., Florida State University, 2003.

Published Sources

Abebe, Tsige. *Triumph and Tragedy: A History of Abebe Bikila and his Marathon Career*. Self-published, 1996.

Ali, Ramadhan. *Africa at the Olympics*. London: Africa Books, 1976.

Allen, Dean. "'The Successes and Challenges of Hosting the 2010 FIFA World Cup': The Case of Cape Town, South Africa." *Soccer & Society* 14, no. 3 (2013): 404–15.

Amara, Mahfoud, ed. *The Olympic Movement and the Middle East and North Africa Region*. London: Routledge, 2019.

Andrews, Ross. "Push to Allow Professional Athletes Took Hold in 1968 Olympic Games." Global Sport Matters, October 15, 2018. https:// globalsportmatters.com/.

Bibliography

Arboine, Niellah. "Caster Semenya Talks Her Vision for Uplifting Youth in Soweto through Sport." International Olympic Committee, November 23, 2021. https://olympics.com/en/.

Archer, Robert. "An Exceptional Case: Politics and Sport in South Africa's Townships." In *Sport in Africa: Essays in Social History*, edited by William J. Baker and James A. Mangan, 229–49. New York: Africana, 1987.

Ba, Lamine. "Wholehearted support for the 1980 Olympic Games in Moscow." *Olympic Review* 150 (April 1980): 159–61.

Baker, William J. "Political Games: The Meaning of International Sport for Independent Africa." In *Sport in Africa: Essays in Social History*, edited by William J. Baker and James A. Mangan, 272–94. New York: Africana, 1987.

Bale, John. *The Brawn Drain: Foreign Student-Athletes in American Universities*. Urbana: University of Illinois Press, 1991.

Bale, John, and Joe Sang. *Kenyan Running: Movement Culture, Geography and Global Change*. London: Frank Cass, 1996.

———. "Out of Africa: The 'Development' of Kenyan Athletics, Talent Migration and the Global Sports System." In *The Global Sports Arena: Athletic Talent Migration in an Interdependent World*, edited by John Bale and Joseph Maguire, 206–26. London: Frank Cass, 1994.

Barney, Robert K. "The Olympic Games in Modern Times." In *Onward to the Olympics: Historical Perspectives on the Olympic Games*, edited by Gerald P. Schaus and Stephen R. Wenn, 221–41. Waterloo, Ontario: Wilfrid Laurier University Press, 2007.

Beverly, Jonathan. "Lornah Kiplagat: Inventing Herself and a Better World." Runners World, May 2, 2006. https://www.runnersworld.com/.

Binder, Deanna, Roland Naul, and Ludmila Fialova, eds. *Olympic Education: History, Theory, Practice: Proceedings of the 4th Willibald Gebhardt Olympic Symposium, Prague (2017)*. Aachen, Germany: Meyer & Meyer Verlag, 2021.

Block, Melissa. "'I Am a Woman': Track Star Caster Semenya Continues Her Fight to Compete as Female." National Public Radio, May 31, 2019. https://www.npr.org/.

Blutstein, Harry. *Games of Discontent: Protests, Boycotts, and Politics at the 1968 Mexico Olympics*. Montreal: McGill-Queen's University Press, 2021.

Booth, Douglas. "Accommodating Race to Play the Game: South Africa's Readmission to International Sport," *Sporting Traditions* 8 (1990): 182–209.

———. *The Race Game: Sport and Politics in South Africa*. London: Frank Cass, 1998.

Bose, Mihir. *Sporting Colours: Sport and Politics in South Africa*. London: Robson Books, 1994.

Boston City Campus. "Caster Semenya Foundation Partners with Boston City Campus." Careers Portal, January 19, 2021. https://www.careersportal.co.za/.

Bibliography

Boykoff, Jules. *Power Games: A Political History of the Olympics*. London: Verso, 2016.

Brenner, Steve. "Caster Semenya: 'They're Killing Sport. People Want Extraordinary Performances.'" *The Guardian*, April 23, 2021.

Brickhill, Joan. *Race against Race: South Africa's Multinational Fraud*. London: International Defense Aid Fund, 1976.

Budd, Zola, with Hugh Eley. *Zola: The Autobiography of Zola Budd*. London: Partridge, 1989.

"Caster Semenya Says Testosterone Case against IAAF Has 'Destroyed' Her 'Mentally and Physically.'" BBC, July 1, 2019. https://www.bbc.com/.

Catsum, Derek Charles. *Flashpoint: How a Little-Known Sporting Event Fueled America's Anti-Apartheid Protest*. Lanham, MD: Rowman & Littlefield, 2021.

Cazeneuve, Brian. "Running into Trouble." *Sports Illustrated*, December 12, 2011, 22.

Charitas, Pascal. "Anglophone Africa in the Olympic Movement: The Confirmation of a British Wager? (1948–1962)." *African Research and Documentation* 116 (2011): 35–52.

———. "The Birth of an African Olympic Movement between French and English Imperialisms (1910–1965)." In *Historical and Contemporary Issues in Olympic Studies: Proceedings of the Conference Held by the University of Johannesburg and the Olympic Studies Centre of the German Sport University Cologne in Johannesburg, November 30-December 2, 2015*, edited by Cora Burnett, 172–83. Johannesburg: University of Johannesburg Press, 2015.

Charitas, Pascal, and David-Claude Kemo-Keimbou. "The United States of America and the Francophone African Countries at the International Olympic Committee: Sports Aid, a Barometer of American Imperialism? (1952–1963)." *Journal of Sport History* 40, no. 1 (Spring 2013): 69–91.

Chatziefstathiou, Dikaia, Ian Henry, Mansour Al-Tauqi, and Eleni Theodoraki. "Cultural Imperialism and the Diffusion of Olympic Sport in Africa: A Comparison of Pre and Post Second World War Contexts." *Olympic Studies Reader* 1 (2008): 99–116.

Cornelissen, Scarlett. "Resolving the 'South Africa Problem': Transnational Activism, Ideology and Race in the Olympic Movement, 1960–91." *International Journal of the History of Sport* 28, no. 1 (2011): 153–67.

Darby, Paul. "Out of Africa: The Exodus of Elite African Football Talent to Europe." *Working USA: The Journal of Labor and Society* 10 (December 2007): 443–56.

Demak, Richard. "Nowhere to Run." *Sports Illustrated*, February 4, 2008, 18–19.

Diack, Lamine. "The Development of African Sport: Achievements, Obstacles and Future Prospects." *Olympic Review* 26, no. 15 (June–July 1997): 59–63.

Durántez, Conrado. "Africa and Olympism." *Olympic Review* 26, no. 20 (April–May 1998): 71–73.

Bibliography

Echard, Denis, Sylvie Espagnac, Katia Mascagni, Amanda Pingree, and Michéle Verdier. "From Olympic Competitors to IOC Members." *Olympic Review* 25, no. 7 (February–March 1996): 5–45.

Edwards, Harry. "Perspectives on Olympic Sport Politics: 1968–1984." *National Black Law Journal* 9, no. 1 (1984): 38–50.

Espy, Richard. *The Politics of the Olympic Games.* Berkeley: University of California Press, 1979.

Finn, Adharanand. *Running with the Kenyans: Discovering the Secrets of the Fastest People on Earth.* New York: Ballantine Books, 2012.

Goldblatt, David. *The Games: A Global History of the Olympics.* New York: W. W. Norton, 2016.

Goslin, Anneliese, ed. *Inspirational Women in Africa: Making a Difference in Physical Education, Sport and Dance.* Juiz de Fora, Brazil: Universidade Federal de Juiz de Fora, 2016.

Goubadia, B. A. A. *Our Olympic Adventure.* Lagos, Nigeria: Crownbird, 1953.

Guedes, Rui Tavares. "Francis Obikwelu: Nascido para Voar." *Visão,* August 26–September 1, 2004, 80–82.

Guest, Andrew M. *Soccer in Mind: A Thinking Fan's Guide to the Global Game.* New Brunswick, NJ: Rutgers University Press, 2022.

Hendershott, Jon. "Olympic Hurdle Champions: Benita Fitzgerald and Nawal El Moutawakil." *Track and Field News* 37, no. 9 (October 1984): 42.

———. "T & FN Interview: Suleiman Nyambui." *Track and Field News* 35, no. 6 (July 1982): 12–13.

Hill, Christopher R. *Olympic Politics.* Manchester: Manchester University Press, 1992.

Hoberman, John M. "Olympic Universalism and the Apartheid Issue." In *Sport, the Third Millennium: Proceedings of the International Symposium, Quebec City, Canada, May 21–25, 1990,* edited by F. Landry, M. Landry, and M. Yerlès, 523–34. Sainte-Foy: Les Presses de L'Université Laval, 1991.

Ingle, Sean. "Caster Semenya Accuses IAAF of Using Her as a 'Guinea Pig Experiment.'" *The Guardian,* June 18, 2019.

International Olympic Committee (IOC). *Olympic Charter, in Force as from 17 July 2020.* Lausanne, Switzerland: International Olympic Committee, 2020.

"Interview with Lornah Kiplagat: Training for Change." PBS, March 28, 2024. https://www.pbs.org/.

Johnson, William Oscar. "Endurance Test." *Sports Illustrated,* June 24, 1991, 70–80.

———. "It Is Time. It Is Time." *Sports Illustrated,* April 29, 1991, 36–41.

———. "Welcome Back: The Presence of Nelson Mandela Marked the Momentous Return of a Former Pariah." *Sports Illustrated,* August 3, 1992, 26–35.

Judah, Tim. *Bikila: Ethiopia's Barefoot Olympian.* London: Reportage Press, 2008.

Kane, Martin. "A Very Welcome Redcoat." *Sports Illustrated*, December 19, 1966, 78–82.

Kanin, David B. *A Political History of the Olympic Games*. Boulder, CO: Westview, 1981.

Kazeem, Yomi. "Africa Meant a Lot to Muhammad Ali—He Meant Even More to Africa." Quartz, June 5, 2016. https://qz.com/.

Kenya Olympic Association. *The XVIth, Olympiad, Melbourne*. N.p.: Kenya Olympic Association, 1956.

Keys, Barbara J. "Introduction: The Ideals of International Sport." In *The Ideals of Global Sport: From Peace to Human Rights*, edited by Barbara J. Keys, 1–20. Philadelphia: University of Pennsylvania Press, 2019.

Keys, Barbara J., ed. *The Ideals of Global Sport: From Peace to Human Rights*. Philadelphia: University of Pennsylvania Press, 2019.

Kgogome, Koketso. "Caster Semenya Foundation Works for Education." GSport, February 19, 2021. https://gsport.co.za/.

Killanin, Lord. *My Olympic Years*. New York: William Morrow, 1983.

Kirshenbaum, Jerry. "Buzz before the Curtain." *Sports Illustrated*, August 28, 1972, 34–35.

Krieger, Jörg. "'We Don't Want to Be Pushed by Outsiders': The International Association of Athletics Federation's Attempts to Re-Admit South Africa to the Global Athletics Stage." *South African Journal for Research in Sport, Physical Education and Recreation* 39, nos. 1–2 (2017): 171–88.

Lapchick, Richard Edward. *The Politics of Race and International Sport: The Case of South Africa*. Westport, CT: Greenwood Press, 1975.

Layden, Tim. "Cast Aside." *Sports Illustrated*, May 7, 2018, 23.

———. "Engendering Debate." *Sports Illustrated*, August 15, 2016, 33–38.

Leach, Mark, and Gary Wilkins. *Olympic Dream: The South African Connection*. London: Penguin Books, 1992.

Llewellyn, Matthew, and Toby C. Rider. "Dennis Brutus and the South African Non-Racial Olympic Committee in Exile, 1966–1970." *South African Historical Journal* 72, no. 2 (2020): 246–71.

Lomong, Lopez, with Mark Tabb. *Running for My Life: One Lost Boy's Journey from the Killing Fields of Sudan to the Olympic Games*. Nashville, TN: Thomas Nelson, 2012.

Lopez, Shaun. "Football as National Allegory: *Al-Ahram* and the Olympics in 1920s Egypt." *History Compass* 7, no. 1 (2009): 282–305.

Manners, John. "African Recruiting Boom." In *The African Running Revolution*, edited by Dave Prokop, 62–69. Mountain View, CA: World Publications, 1975.

Maraniss, David. *Rome 1960: The Olympics That Changed the World*. New York: Simon and Schuster, 2008.

Mark, Chris. "Running for Economic Development in Kenya." *Stanford Social Innovation Review*, August 3, 2012.

Bibliography

Mason, Courtney W. "The Bridge to Change: The 1976 Montreal Olympic Games, South African Apartheid Policy, and the Olympic Boycott Paradigm." In *Onward to the Olympics: Historical Perspectives on the Olympic Games,* edited by Gerald P. Schaus and Stephen R. Wenn, 283–96. Waterloo, Ontario: Wilfrid Laurier University Press, 2007.

Maule, Tex. "A Flare in the Dark." *Sports Illustrated,* June 3, 1968, 60–74.

———. "Switcheroo from Yes to Nyet." *Sports Illustrated,* April 29, 1968, 28–29.

Mbaye, Kéba. *The International Olympic Committee and South Africa: Analysis and Illustration of a Humanist Sports Policy.* Lausanne, Switzerland: IOC, 1995.

———. *Proceedings of the International Scientific Symposium to Open the African Centre for Olympic Studies (ACOS).* Yaoundé, Cameroon: Eclosion, 2019.

McEwan, Susan. *The Cape Town 2004 Olympic Bid: A Sporting Chance for South Africa.* Johannesburg: Smith Borkum Hare, 1996.

Merwe, Floris J. G. van der. "Africa's First Encounter with the Olympic Games in . . . 1904." *Journal of Olympic History* 7, no. 3 (1999): 29–34.

"Meseret Defar." Global Athletics, accessed March 28, 2024. https://www.globalathletics.com/users/63/65/meseret-defar.php.

"Messeret Defar Renewed Agreement with UNFPA." United Nations Population Fund, Ethiopia, March 10, 2011. https://ethiopia.unfpa.org/en/.

Meyer, Elana. "Olympics: Breeding Ground for Transformative Action." Peace and Sport, August 14, 2016. https://www.peace-sport.org/.

Miller, Geoffrey. *Behind the Olympic Rings.* Lynn, MA: H. O. Zimman, 1979.

Moore, Kenny. "Hero for a Thirsty Land." *Sports Illustrated,* May 30, 1988, 70–82.

Moses, Edwin. "Caster Semenya." *Time,* March 28, 2024.

Mzali, Mohamed. "Mr. Mzali: 'I Am Sorry about the Boycott of the Montreal Olympic Games.'" *Olympic Review* 100 (1976): 463–64.

"Namibian Teenagers Out of Olympic 400m over Testosterone Levels," BBC, Sport Africa, July 2, 2021. https://www.bbc.com/.

Ndee, Hamad S. "Sport as a Political Tool: Tanzania and the Liberation of Africa." *International Journal of the History of Sport* 22, no. 4 (2005): 671–88.

Neff, Craig. "A Runner Runs Home." *Sports Illustrated,* May 23, 1988, 26–31.

Njoroge, Joseph Muiruri, Lucy Atieno, and Daniele Vieira Do Nascimento. "Sports Tourism and Perceived Socio-Economic Impact in Kenya: The Case of Machakos County." *Tourism and Hospitality Management* 23, no. 2 (2017): 195–217.

Nkwocha, Jossy. *Nigeria's Golden Olympics: How the Giant of Africa Conquered the World.* Lagos, Nigeria: Zoom Lens, 1997.

Noden, Merrill. "Catching up with Runners Mike Boit and Alberto Juantorena." *Sports Illustrated,* December 23, 2002, 17–18.

Noronha, Francis. *Kipchoge of Kenya.* Nakuru, Kenya: Elimu, 1970.

Odinga, Oginga. *Not yet Uhuru: The Autobiography of Oginga Odinga.* London: Heinemann, 1967.

208 Bibliography

Oduvale, Amos Tinuayo, Kanayo Onyiliogwu, and Olutola Oduyale. *History of Olympic Movement in Nigeria*. Lagos: Nigerian Olympic Committee, 2009.

"Olympics for Life Project Proves Popular at Olympians Reunion Centre by EY." International Olympic Committee, August 20, 2016. https://olympians.org/.

"Paul Tergat: Ambassador against Hunger." World Athletics, April 9, 2004. https://www.worldathletics.org/.

Price, S. L. "The Longest Run." *Sports Illustrated*, July 25, 2016, 102–11.

Putnam, Pat. "It Was a Call to Colors." *Sports Illustrated*, July 26, 1976, 14–19.

Rahmani, Shane. "Letters to the Editor." *Sports Illustrated*, November 18, 1996, 12.

Rambali, Paul. *Barefoot Runner: The Life of Marathon Champion Abebe Bikila*. London: Serpent's Tail, 2007.

Ramsamy, Sam, with Edward Griffiths. *Reflections on a Life in Sport*. Cape Town: Greenhouse, 2004.

Reavis, Toni. "Meseret Defar Aids Entoto Foundation." *Wandering in a Running World* (blog), March 25, 2011. https://tonireavis.com/.

Richards, Trevor. *Dancing on Their Bones: New Zealand, South Africa, Rugby, and Racism*. Wellington, New Zealand: Bridget Williams Books, 1999.

Roberts, Cheryl. *South Africa's Struggle for Olympic Legitimacy: From Apartheid Sport to International Recognition*. Cape Town: Township Publishing Co-operative, 1991.

Rosen, Armin. "The Olympics Used to Be So Politicized That Most of Africa Boycotted in 1976." *The Atlantic*, August 7, 2012, 23–25.

Saneh, Christel. "Nawal El Moutawakel: The 54 Seconds that Changed Her Life." World Athletics, April 8, 2021. https://worldathletics.org/.

Sarantakes, Nicholas Evan. *Dropping the Torch: Jimmy Carter, the Olympic Boycott, and the Cold War*. Cambridge, UK: Cambridge University Press, 2011.

Senn, Alfred E. *Power, Politics, and the Olympic Games*. Champaign, IL: Human Kinetics, 1999.

Seroney, Kibny'aanko. *From Strength to Strength: The Story of Ambassador Peter Kipchumba Rono*. Nairobi: Mvule Africa, 2009.

Shropshire, Mike. "Heavy Lifting." *Sports Illustrated*, September 20, 1999, 69–81.

Sikes, Michelle. "The Enemy of My Enemy Is My Friend? A Clash of Anti-Apartheid Tactics and Targets in the Olympic Movement of the Early 1960s." *International Journal of the History of Sport* 37, no. 7 (2020): 520–41.

———. "From Nairobi to Baden-Baden: African Politics, the International Olympic Committee, and Early Efforts to Censure Apartheid South Africa." *International Journal of the History of Sport* 36, no. 1 (2019): 7–23.

———. "Ousting South Africa: Olympic Clashes of 1968." *Acta Academica* 50, no. 2 (2018): 12–33.

Bibliography

Skinner, Robert. "Antidiscrimination: Racism and the Case of South Africa." In *The Ideals of Global Sport: From Peace to Human Rights*, edited by Barbara J. Keys, 47–67. Philadelphia: University of Pennsylvania Press, 2019.

Smith, Maureen Margaret. "Revisiting South Africa and the Olympic Movement: The Correspondence of Reginald S. Alexander and the International Olympic Committee, 1961–86." *International Journal of the History of Sport* 23, no. 7 (November 2006): 1193–216.

Sotomayor, Antonio, and Cesar R. Torres, eds. *Olimpismo: The Olympic Movement in the Making of Latin America and the Caribbean*. Fayetteville: University of Arkansas Press, 2020.

Stevens, Simon. "Why South Africa? The Politics of Anti-Apartheid Activism in Britain in the Long 1970s." In *The Breakthrough: Human Rights in the 1970s*, edited by Jan Eckel and Samuel Moyn, 204–25. Philadelphia: University of Pennsylvania Press, 2014.

Stidwill, H., and A. Flatah, "The Internationalization of Track and Field at American Universities." *Journal of Comparative Physical Education and Sport* 7, no. 2 (1985): 26–42.

Sustar, Lee, and Aisha Karim, eds. *Poetry and Protest: A Dennis Brutus Reader*. Chicago: Haymarket Books, 2006.

Swarr, Amanda Lock, Sally Gross, and Liesl Theron, "South African Intersex Activism: Caster Semenya's Impact and Import." *Feminist Studies* 35, no. 3 (Fall 2009): 657–62.

Tshisalive. "Caster Semenya's Foundation Aims to Raise Funds for Menstrual Cups." Sowetan Live, November 3, 2016. https://www.sowetanlive.co.za/.

"Uganda and Olympism." *Olympic Review* 157 (1980): 657–63.

Underwood, John. "Games in Trouble." *Sports Illustrated*, September 30, 1968, 45–50.

———. "Lost Laughter." *Sports Illustrated*, September 30, 1968, 90–104.

———. "The Number Two Lion in the Land of Sheba." *Sports Illustrated*, April 12, 1965, 86–105.

"UNFPA National Honorary Ambassador Wins Gold at London 2012." United Nations Population Fund, August 17, 2012. https://www.unfpa.org/.

Wacker, Christian. "Egypt Goes Olympic: 1914 to 1932." *South African Journal for Research in Sport, Physical Education and Recreation* 39, nos. 1–2 (2017): 155–70.

Watta, Evelyn. "Caster Semenya: Seven Things You Should Know about the Double Olympic Champion." International Olympic Committee, February 11, 2021. https://olympics.com/en/.

Weisbord, Robert G. *Racism and the Olympics*. New Brunswick, NJ: Transaction, 2015.

Werner, M. R. "More Fun Than Games at the Games." *Sports Illustrated,* August 15, 1960, EM5–EM8.

Wise, Mike. "The Man South Africa Forgot," ESPN, August 5, 2015. http://www.espn.com/.

Witherspoon, Kevin B. *Before the Eyes of the World: Mexico and the 1968 Olympic Games.* DeKalb: Northern Illinois University Press, 2008.

Wolff, Alexander. "Run the World, Girls." *Sports Illustrated,* August 13, 2012, 40–45.

Zaoui, Maha, and Emmanuel Bayle. "The Central Role of the State in the Governance of Sport and the Olympic Movement in Tunisia, from 1956 to the Present Day." In *The Olympic Movement and the Middle East and North Africa Region,* edited by Mahfoud Amara, 39–59. London: Routledge, 2019.

Index

Page numbers in *italics* refer to figures and maps.

Abdesselam, Rhadi Ben, 4
Abdul-Jabbar, Kareem, 80
Abebe Bikila Project, 151
Adedoyin, Adegboyega, 33
Ademola, Adetokunbo, 26, 48, 72, 77, 187n38
Afghanistan, Soviet invasion of, 114–22
Afghanistan Olympic Committee, 16
Africa: map of, *xiv*; marginalization of, 9; possible Olympic host cities in, 2, 178n13; regional conflict in, 6, 142–44; social, political, and economic change in, 1–9, 21–24 (*see also* anti-apartheid movement; anti-colonialism; boycotts; independence; national unity; personal improvement strategies; social-development programs). *See also specific countries*
African athletes: impact of boycotts, 102, 110–14; quality of life, 2–3, 158 (*see also* personal improvement strategies); social-development programs, 23, 126–56; "winning away from the podium," 2–9, 42, 55, 57, 92, 114, 121, 152, 175–76. *See also* professional athletes; women athletes
African Games, 11–14, *13,* 179nn18–19
African National Congress (ANC), 58, 86–87, 89–90
Afrikaners, 5, 94, 178n5, 188n61
Akii-Bua, John, 111
Akioye, Isaac, 110
Alexander, Reginald, 26, 37–38, 48, 73, 77, 107, 181n4

Algeria, 10, 13, 78, 109
Ali, Muhammad, 117–19
Ali, Ramadhan, 20, 56
All-Africa Games, 140, 173
All Blacks (New Zealand national rugby team), 5, 94, 103–4
Amin, Idi, 191n29
Andrianov, Constantin, 82
Angola, 47, 116, 122, 124
anti-apartheid movement, 1–2, 22, 43–44, 57–92, 94, 186n21; Gleneagles Agreement and, 5, 94, 112–13, 192n42; international, 60, 64, 94; Soviet support for, 46; Zola Budd case and, 163–66
anti-colonialism, 27–28, 40, 42–44, 47, 66–67, 118, 186n21. *See also* decolonization; independence
Aouita, Saïd, 197n43
apartheid, 4–5, 22, 44, 59–64, 86, 105–6, 125, 186n21, 187n51. *See also* anti-apartheid movement; South Africa
Arap Moi, Daniel, 120
Ashe, Arthur, 81
Asian Games (1962), 68
Association of National Committees of Africa (ANOCA), 87, 123
athletes. *See* African athletes; professional athletes; women athletes
athletic-development programs, 127–28; for African women and girls, 140, 147–50
Austria, 4, 17
Awori, Aggrey, 199n19

Index

Ayele, Tsegaw, 108

Ba, Lamine, 192n46
Bach, Thomas, 132
Bahrain, 6, 158–59
Bailey, McDonald, 39
Baker, William J., 18, 49, 52
Barbados, 181n1
Barry, Amadou, 73
Bayi, Filbert, 111, 174
Bayle, Emmanuel, 42
Benin, 122
Benjelloun, Hadj Mohammed, 48
Berlin Conference (1884), 27
Bermuda, 181n1
Biel, Yiech Pur, 133, 144
Bikila, Abebe, 4, 49–53, 50, 79, 81, 151, 184n58
Bile, Abdi, 175
Biwott, Amos, 55
Black Power, 80–81
Blutstein, Harry, 82, 96
Bohemia, 17
Boit, Mike, 110, 127–28, 170, 195n3
Bolanachi, Angelo, 30–32
Booth, Douglas, 65, 88–89
Boston City Campus, 154
Bouabid, Maati, 121
Bourguiba, Habib, 42
boycotts: 1956 Melbourne Games, 189n1; 1964 Tokyo Games, 68; 1972 Munich Games, 22, 83, 93–94, 97–103, 195n2; 1976 Montreal Games, 5, 17, 22–23, 92, 94, 103–16, 111, 123, 173, 190n20, 191n29, 195n2; 1980 Moscow Games, 95, 114–22, 150, 192n46, 192n48, 193n61, 194nn67–68; 1984 Los Angeles Games, 114, 122–25, 194n69, 195n71; 1988 Seoul Games, 195n75; African American support, 80–81; Cold War, 95, 114–25; impact on African athletes, 102, 110–14; strategy against racial discrimination, 18, 75–81, 84, 93–114, 125
Braun, Frank, 71, 84, 187n38
"brawn drain," 159, 171
Brazil, 65
Brickhill, Joan, 61
Brigham Young University, 169
British Nationality Act, 34
British Olympic Association, 123
Brundage, Avery: amateurism, 175; CIOA,

15, 47; correspondence, 38, 48; fear of African voting bloc, 46; Kenya, 68; NOCs in colonies, 34–35; purpose of Olympic Movement, 1; racial attitudes, 15, 41, 63–64; Rhodesia, 97–98, 100, 102–3, 190n15; separation of sports and politics, 17–19, 63–64, 74, 78; South Africa, 22, 60, 62–64, 73–74, 77–81, 85, 188n70; Tunisia, 41
Brutus, Dennis: anti-apartheid activism, 58, 60, 62–66, 72, 74–79, 76, 88; arrest and shooting, 69–70, 186n26; Montreal boycott, 104, 112; racial heritage, 62–64; Rhodesia, 100–101; SANROC, 60, 65–66, 76; SASA, 62
Budd, Zola, 24, 123–24, 163–66
Bulgaria, 4
Burghley, David (Marquess of Exeter), 26, 46, 70
Bush, Jim, 170

Cameroon, 109, 166–67
Carlos, John, 6
Carter, Jimmy, 115, 117–19
Chamberlain, Wilt, 80
Chaplin, John, 171
charitable initiatives and foundations: in African countries, 6, 23, 127, 134–44, 155–56; for women and girls in Africa, 144–52
Charitas, Pascal, 26, 44
Chemtai, Lonah, 8
Cheruiyot, Abraham, 137
child marriage, 145, 151–52
China, 191n27
coaches and training staff, 39
Cold War alignments: 1980 Moscow boycott and, 95, 114–22, 125; 1984 Los Angeles boycott and, 114, 122–25, 194n69, 195n71; Committee for International Olympic Aid and, 47; Olympic participation and, 27–28, 40–41, 45–46; South African, 59, 71
colonialism, 27, 59; African athletes integrated into metropolitan Olympic squads, 10, 13–14, 27, 33–34, 40, 181n1, 182n23; Olympic teams from African colonies, 3–4, 11, 21, 26, 29–39; promotion of sport in Africa, 11–14; sporting autonomy as threat, 34–35

Index

213

(*see also* anti-colonialism). *See also* neocolonialism; Rhodesia; South Africa; White minority regimes
Committee for International Olympic Aid (CIOA), 15, 47
Commonwealth Games, 34, 112–13, 168, 173
Commonwealth nations, 5, 94
Congo (DRC), 132, 167, 190n20
Congo-Brazzaville, 75, 122
Cook, P. H., 26
Copa Mutola, 140
Cornelissen, Scarlett, 59, 71–72, 75, 88, 92
Côte d'Ivoire (Ivory Coast), 48, 109
Coubertin, Baron de (Charles Pierre de Frédy), 9–12, 10, 179n18
Cross, Lance, 104

Daily Graphic (Ghana), 121
Daily Mail (UK), 163–64
Daily News (Tanzania), 117
Daily Times (Nigeria), 34, 37–38, 99
Danin, Amina, 147
de Broglio, Chris, 65
Decker-Slaney, Mary, 24, 123, 163–65
decolonization, 26–28, 48, 95; Soviet support for, 45; in sports, 34, 54–55. *See also* anti-colonialism; independence
de Costa, Norman, 157
Defar, Meseret, 144–45, 150–52
defection, 158, 166–67
de Klerk, Frederik Willem, 86, 87
Demak, Richard, 56
democracy, 87, 90
differences of sexual development (DSD), 23–24, 152–55, 198n72
distance runners, elite East African, 2, 4; changing nationalities, 6–8, 147, 158–62; charitable initiatives and foundations established by, 6, 23, 127, 134–52, 155–56; economic opportunities for, 8–9; medals won by, 49–57; national unity and, 48–57; on US NCAA track teams, 167–76
Durántez, Conrado, 11
Dykov, Alexei, 45
Dzoma, Bernard, 97

Eastern New Mexico University, 128, 170
education: gender equity, 140, 153–54, 174; programs in Africa, 6, 135;

scholarships at US colleges and universities, 23–24, 128, 134, 136–38, 157–58, 167–76, 200n33
Edwards, Harry, 81
Egypt: anti-apartheid activism, 85; boycotts, 109, 118, 120, 189n1, 195n75; colonial-era sports and nationalism, 3, 11, 29–33, 181n8; independence, 11, 30–31; IOC representatives, 48; medals won, 32; National Olympic Committee, 11, 30–32; Pharaohs of Antwerp (football team), 30–32, 31, 182n14, 182n17
Ehizuelen, Charlton, 111
Elizabeth II (UK), 54
El Moutawakel, Nawal, 144–47, 174, 175
El Ouafi, Boughéra, 13
Entoto Foundation, 152
Eritrea, 167
Eswatini, 69
Ethiopia: 1956 Melbourne Games, 3, 27; 1960 Rome Games, 4, 49–52; 1964 Tokyo Games, 52; 1968 Mexico City Games, 52, 78; 1980 Moscow Games, 121; 1992 Barcelona Games, 91–92; athletes changing nationality, 158–60; boycotts, 78, 98, 122, 124, 195n75; colonialism, 51; education, 144; elite distance runners, 4, 49–53 (*see also* distance runners, elite East African); human rights abuses, 6; National Olympic Committee, 108, 194n67; programs for women and girls, 145, 150–52; refugee athletes, 132
Ethiopian Sports Confederation, 76
European Athletics Championship (2018 Berlin), 8
European Court of Human Rights, 153
Evans, Lee, 110
Exeter, Marquess of (David Burghley), 26, 46, 70

Far Eastern Games, 11
Farleigh Dickinson University, 138
Federation of Rhodesia and Nyasaland, 4, 27
FIFA, 9, 14, 59, 178n4, 178n9
Finland, 17
5K Courir pour le Plaisir (Run for Fun), 147

214   Index

Florida Southern College, 138
food insecurity, 126, 141–42
football. *See* soccer
Foreman, George, 118
4 South Sudan (organization), 136
France: colonies, 10, 13, 27, 34, 40, 181n1,
    182n23; neocolonialism, 44–45
Friendship Games, 179n19, 194n69

Ganga, Jean-Claude, 17–18, 75, 80, 81–82,
    84–85, 87–89, 98, 100, 104, 106, 112–13
gender equity, 23–24; in education, 140,
    153–54, 174; for intersex athletes,
    23–24, 152–55, 198n72; for Muslim
    women, 145; in sports, 148, 152, 154–
    55. *See also* women and girls
George Mason University, 175
Germany, 4, 101–2
Ghana, 45, 118–19, 121. *See also* Gold Coast
Ghebresilasie, Weynay, 167
Gleneagles Agreement, 5, 94, 112–13,
    192n42
Gold Coast, 3, 26, 34. *See also* Ghana
Goslin, Anneliese, 147
Goubadia, B. A. A., 25, 39
Great Britain: 1900 Paris Games, 10; 1948
    London Games, 33–34; athletes from
    colonies integrated into Olympic
    squad, 33–34; British colonies, 11, 33,
    181n1; citizenship, 163–65; neocolo-
    nialism, 44; Rugby Football Union,
    123–24; South Africa relationship, 83
Griffiths, Edward, 90
Guinea, 45
Guirandou-N'Diaye, Louis, 48

Halim, Abdel Mohamed, 48
Hamza, Mohammed, 117
Hardman, Dennis, 192n48
Harvard University, 199n19
Hassan II (Morocco), 145
Hefferon, Charles, 177n3
Heyns, Penny, 131
high-altitude training centers, 8–9,
    147–50, *149*
HIV/AIDS prevention, 145, 151
Hlongwane, R., 83
Hoberman, John M., 14, 78
Hombessa, André, 75, 80
Honey, Reginald, 48, 62, 72, 107, 188n70

Howard University, 169
human rights, 6, 80–81, 115, 117, 128, 132,
    153, 155
Hungary, 4, 17
hunger, 126, 141–42

independence, 4, 21–22, 59, 94; National
    Olympic Committees and, 14–16, 39–
    48; Olympic Games and, 25–57. *See
    also* anti-colonialism; decolonization
India, 33
Indonesia, 68
International Amateur Athletic Federa-
    tion (IAAF), 34, 163, 199n8
International Institute for the Develop-
    ment of NOCs, 47
International Labour Organisation, 67
International Olympic Committee (IOC):
    Committee for International Olympic
    Aid and, 15, 47; Executive Committee,
    9, 16, 81; formation of, 9; members of,
    9, 14–16, 21, 26, 48, 62, 84–85, 181n4;
    on professional athletes at the Games,
    175; proposed meeting in Nairobi, 47,
    66–69; racist and imperialist attitudes
    in, 15, 21, 28, 34–36, 41, 46, 63–64, 78;
    refugee athletes and, 132; Rhodesian
    commission and, 97–98; South
    African apartheid and, 62, 73–74,
    86–88, 186n35 (*see also* South Africa).
    See also Brundage, Avery
intersex athletes, 23–24, 152–55, 198n72
Iowa State University, 137, 146, 173, 175
Israel, 8, 19, 68, 102, 191n29
Italian colonies, 51
Ivory Coast. *See* Côte d'Ivoire

Jamaica, 181n1
Jamal, Maryam Jusuf, 158
Japan, 4
Jebet, Ruth, 6, 158–59
Jipcho, Ben, 171
Johnson, William Oscar, 166
Joseph, Amuam, 167

Kalasa, Benoit, 151
Kanin, David B., 16, 49, 55, 120, 127
Kasyoka, John, 93, 107, 191n29
Kazeem, Yomi, 118
Keino, Kipchoge "Kip," 54–56, 56, 78, 81

Index

Kenya: 1952 Helsinki Games, 26; 1956 Melbourne Games, 3, 26, 38; 1960 Rome Games, 38–39; 1964 Tokyo Games, 53, 68–69; 1968 Mexico City Games, 54–56, 78–79, 168; 1972 Munich Games, 56; 1976 Montreal Games, 111; 2000 Sydney Games, 160, 162; 2004 Athens Games, 160, 162; 2008 Beijing Games, 56; anti-apartheid activism, 47, 66–69, 83; anti-colonialism and independence, 47, 66–69; boycotts, 68, 78–79, 93, 110–11, 120, 191n29, 193n61, 195n2; colonial era, 53–54; elite distance runners, 53–57 (*see also* distance runners, elite East African); food insecurity, 141–42; high-altitude training centers, 147–50, *149*; IOC representatives, 48; Liberty Bell Classic, 193n61; migration, 158–59; multiracial Olympic squads, 38–39; National Olympic Committee, 37–39, 171; National Sports Council, 107; programs for women and girls, 145, 147–50; regional conflict, 142–44; students on athletic scholarships in United States, 137–38, 168–72

Kenyan Amateur Athletics Association, 172

Kenya Athletics Federation, 128

Kenya National Sports Council, 76

Kenya Scholar Access Program (KenSAP), 128

Kenyatta, Jomo, 53, 56, 66, 120

Kenyatta University, 128

Killanin, Lord, 19, 38, 73, 77, 104, 109

Kimeto, Joshua, 111

Kiplagat, Lornah, 144–45, 147–50

Kiprugut, Wilson, 53

Knight, Tom, 147

Koch, Jael, 138

Korir, Julius, 175

Kuriungi, Wilson, 8–9

Lagat, Bernar, 160–62, 199n5

Latin American Games, 11

Leserwane, Joseph, 82

Lesotho, 93

Liberia, 3, 27, 119

Liberty Bell Classic, 193n61

Libya, 122, 194n68

Lilesa, Feyisa, 6, 7

Llewellyn, Matthew, 70, 78

Lohalith, Anjelina Nadai, 133

Lokeris, Peter, 143

Lomong, Lopez, 126, 134–36

Longman, Jeré, 162

Lopez, Shaun, 30

Lopez Lomong Foundation, 135–36

Lornah Kiplagat High Altitude Training Centre (HATC), 147–50, *149*

Loroupe, Tegla, 6, 137, 142–44

Los Angeles Games (1984), 24, 145, 163–65, 175, 194n67; Los Angeles Olympic Committee, 124, 194n69; Soviet boycott of, 114, 122–25, 194n69, 195n71

Lugonzo, Isaac, 76, 107

Lux (company), 155

MacDonald, Malcolm, 66

Macharia, Allan, 143

MacPherson, John, 37–38

Madagascar, 195n75

Mais Escola para Mim (More School for Me), 140

Mandela, Nelson, 2, 60, 69, 86–87, 129–32

Manners, John, 128, 150

Masai Athletics Club, 154

Masiana, Jan, 2, 3, 4, 177n2

Mason, Courtney, 113

Massard, Armand, 34

Matthia, Anani, 123–24

Mayer, Otto, 15, 26, 34–35, 41, 44, 47, 63, 68

Mbaye, Kéba, 19, 87

Mbaye Mission, 87–88

medals: national unity and, 129–34; Olympic Movement goals and, 1; Refugee Olympic Team and, 133–34; won by African Olympic teams, 2, 4, 32, 40, 49, 121, 128–32, 136, 138, 141–42, 145, 150–51, 170, 174, 176, 177n1; won by elite East African distance runners, 49–57; won by Muslim women, 145; won by South African athletes, 4, 91; won for adopted countries, 6, 158–59

Mesfin, Woizero Azeb, 151–52

Mexico City Games (1968), 6, 25, 44, 49, 52, 54–56, 168; African boycott of, 18, 75–81, 96–97; exclusion of Rhodesia, 22, 96–97; Organizing Committee, 97; protests at, 110

Meyers, Elana, 91
migration: defection and, 158, 166–67; due to insufficient domestic support, 158–60, 176; and educational scholarships at US colleges and universities, 23–24, 128, 134, 136–38, 157–58, 167–76, 200n33; by elite East African distance runners, 6–8, 147, 158–62
military service, 52
Miller, Geoffrey, 113
Mimoun, Alain, 13
Montreal Games (1976): African boycott, 5, 17, 22–23, 92, 94, 103–16, 111, 123, 173, 190n20, 191n29, 195n2; impact of boycott on African athletes, 110–14
Moorosi, Motsapi, 93
Morocco: 1960 Rome Games, 3–4, 27; boycotts, 109, 121; independence, 45; IOC representatives, 48; migration, 174; Minister of Youth and Sports, 146; programs for women and girls, 145–47; Soviet Union relationship, 45
Morris, James T., 142
Moscow Games (1980), 123, 174; Western bloc boycott of, 95, 114–22, 150, 192n46, 192n48, 193n61, 194nn67–68
Moses, Edwin, 152
Mota, Fernando, 160
Mount St. Mary's University, 136
Mozambican Football Federation, 140
Mozambique, 47, 138–41; boycotts, 122; independence, 116, 196n26
Mugabe, Robert, 193n48
Muldoon, Robert, 105–6, 112–13, 190n19, 192n42
Mundia, Nalumino, 115–16
Munich Games (1972), 19, 56, 98, 128, 169–70; African boycott of, 22, 84, 93–94, 97–103, 195n2; terrorist attack on Israeli team, 19, 102
Murei, Mike, 170
Muslims, 120, 122, 145–46
Mustafa, Ibrahim, 32
Mutala, Jackson, 78–79
Mutola, Maria de Lurdes, 138–41, 139
Mutola Foundation, 140
Mwiru, Ngombale, 27–28, 43–44
Mzali, Mohamed, 48, 103–5

Nandi Education and Training Centre, 137–38
Nation (Kenya), 115
National Association of Intercollegiate Athletics (NAIA), 169–70
National Olympic Committees (NOCs): aid for, 15, 47; anti-apartheid activism by, 76–77; in colonial Africa, 11, 21, 29–39; IOC membership and, 16; in newly independent African nations, 14–16, 26, 39–48. *See also specific countries*
National Sunday Times (South Africa), 90
national unity, 23, 27–57; colonial-era Olympic participation and, 21, 29–39; elite distance runners and, 48–57; Olympic success and, 129–34; postcolonial Olympic participation and, 39–48
nation building, 27, 57
Nazis, 17, 74, 78
NCAA (National Collegiate Athletic Association), 134, 192n38; African athletes on track teams, 167–76; overage policy, 169–70, 174
Ndee, Hamad S., 102
neocolonialism, 41, 44–45
Netherlands, 147
New Balance (company), 138
Newham, C. E., 37
New York Times, 79, 173
New Zealand: African boycott of Montreal Games, 5, 17, 22–23, 92, 94, 103–15, 173; National Olympic Committee, 104; national rugby team (All Blacks), 5, 94, 103–4; SCSA, 103–7, 190n19; sporting ties with South Africa, 5, 94, 103–14, 192n42
New Zealand Rugby Union, 104
Nigeria: 1948 London Games, 33; 1952 Helsinki Games, 3, 25–26, 34, 36–39; 1956 Melbourne Games, 26; 1976 Montreal Games, boycott of, 110–11; 2000 Sydney Games, 159–60; athletes changing nationality, 159–60; boycotts, 118–19; colonial-era Olympic participation, 3, 25, 33, 39–40; independence, 40; IOC representatives, 48, 73; multiracial coaching squads, 39; National Olympic Committee, 34–35, 37–40, 159–60;

Index

size of Olympic squad, 176; "sporting decolonization," 34

Nigeria Standard, 116, 117

nongovernmental organizations (NGOs), 134, 136, 140

Norfolk State University, 134

North Carolina Central University (NCCU), 168, 171–72

Northern Arizona University, 134

North Korea, 195n75

Nyambui, Suleiman, 173

Nyangweso, Francis W., 36–37

Nyerere, Julius, 42–43, 118, 183n42

Nzminade, Tshakile, 90–91

Obane, Osinde, 143

Obikwelu, Francis Obiorah, 159–60, *161*

Odinga, Jaramogi Oginga, 66–67

Olympians for Life, 144

Olympic Games: ancient Greece, 10, 178n10; list of Summer Olympic Games, xi–xii; 1896 Athens, 2, 10; 1900 Paris, 10, 177n2; 1904 St. Louis, 2, 3, 4, 11, 177n2; 1908 London, 4, 17; 1912 Stockholm, 3, 11, 17, 181n8; 1916 Berlin, 11, 182n8; 1920 Antwerp, 3, 4, 11, 29–32, *31*, 182n8; 1924 Paris, 4, 31–32; 1928 Amsterdam, 13, 32, 95; 1932 Los Angeles, 32; 1936 Berlin, 17, 74; 1948 London, 4, 33–34, 39; 1952 Helsinki, 3, 25–26, 33, 34, 36–39; 1956 Melbourne, 3, 13, 26–27, 36, 38, 189n1; 1960 Rome, 3–4, 27, 37–39, 45, 49–52, 63, 199n19; 1964 Tokyo, 43, 49, 52, 53, 59, 68–69, 96; 1968 Mexico City, 6, 18, 22, 25, 44, 49, 52, 54–56, 75–81, 96–97, 110, 168; 1972 Munich, 19, 22, 56, 84, 93–94, 97–103, 128, 169–70, 195n2; 1976 Montreal, 5, 17, 22–23, 92, 94, 103–16, *111*, 123, 173, 190n20, 191n29, 195n2; 1980 Moscow, 95, 114–23, 150, 174, 192n46, 192n48, 193n61, 194nn67–68; 1984 Los Angeles, 24, 114, 122–25, 145, 163–65, 175, 194n67, 194n69, 195n71; 1988 Seoul, 136, 138, 165, 195n75; 1992 Barcelona, 4, 60, 86, 88–92, 142, 157, 166; 1996 Atlanta, 129–31, *130*, 138, 142; 2000 Sydney, 138, 142, 159–60, 162; 2004 Athens, *139*, 147, 150, 160–62, *161*; 2008 Beijing, 56, 135, 138, 147, 150, 160;

2012 London, 141, 147, 150, 152, 158, 160, 166–67; 2016 Rio de Janeiro, 6, *7*, 23, 132–33, 144, 152, 158, 160, 162; 2020 Tokyo, 2, 134, 176, 200n35. *See also* African athletes; medals

Olympic Movement: goals of, 1; history of Africa's engagement with, 9–16; nation-states as organizing structure in, 16; participants, numbers of, 10–11, 176, 200n35; politics and, 4, 16–19, 63–64, 74, 78, 84, 110–11; as vehicle for social, political, and economic change in Africa, 1–9, 21–24

Olympic Museum, 10

Olympic Project for Human Rights (OPHR), 80–81

Olympic Solidarity campaign, 15, 47

Opperman, Rudolph W. L., 72

Ordia, Abraham, 84–85, 98, 100, 102, 105–6, 112, 188n70

Organization of African Unity (OAU), 17–18, 67, 75, 80, 106, 186n21

Oshikoya, Modupe, 111

Osotimehin, Babtunde, 151

Ouko, Robert, 168–72

Oxfam Ambassador of Sport and Peace, 143

Pakistan, 33

Parienté, Robert, 50

Paton, Alan, 62

Peace Race, 143

personal improvement strategies, 2–3, 24, 157–76; economic opportunities and financial success, 6, 8–9, 24, 157–58, 160–62, 166; professionalism, 24, 175; scholarships at US colleges and universities, 23–24, 128, 134, 136–38, 157–58, 167–76, 200n33. *See also* migration

Petrusenko, Vitali, 45

Pharaohs of Antwerp (Egyptian football team), 30–32, *31*, 182n14, 182n17

Pieterse, Zola. *See* Budd, Zola

Piétri, François, 34

Plaskitt, Ossie, 99

politics, 2, 87; separation of sports and, 17–19, 63–64, 74, 78, 84, 110–11. *See also* anti-apartheid movement; anti-colonialism; boycotts; decolonization; independence

218 Index

Portugal: 2004 Athens Games and, 160, 161; African athletes in, 159–60; colonies of, 17, 47, 138, 186n21, 196n26; Kenya and, 47, 66–69
Portuguese Athletics Federation, 160
Powell, V. B. V., 39
professional athletes, 24, 140, 167, 175
Punch (Nigeria), 116

Quax, Dick, 110

racialism and racism: in colonial Africa, 28; in Olympic Movement, 11–15, 21, 28, 35–36, 41, 63–64, 78; protests against, 6, 23, 110 (*see also* anti-apartheid movement; anti-colonialism; boycotts); in the United States, 168, 170–72; violence and, 71, 103, 109. *See also* Rhodesia; South Africa
Rambali, Paul, 184n58
Ramsamy, Sam, 87, 89, 100, 106, 112, 123, 164
Rand Daily Mail (South Africa), 70
Refugee Olympic Athletes Team, 23, 127, 132–34, 144, 179n28
regional conflict, 6, 142–44
Reid, Graeme, 153
Reinhold, Robert, 173
Rhadi, Ben Abdesselam, 50, 50
Rhodes, Cecil, 11
Rhodesia, 17, 47, 67, 117; African efforts to ban from Olympic Games, 22, 92–103, 190n15; National Olympic Committee, 96; Unilateral Declaration of Independence (UDI), 95, 99, 101; White minority regime, 22, 67, 92, 94–103. *See also* Zimbabwe
Richards, Trevor, 191n27
Robben Island Prison, 69–70
Roberts, Cheryl, 63
Robinson, Clarence, 169
Robinson, Jackie, 81
Rono, Peter Kipchumba, 136–38, 196n22
Rugby Football Union, 123–24
Rugby World Cup, 129
runners. *See* distance runners, elite East African
Run with Kenyans (company), 8–9
Russia, 17

Said, Muhammad Pasha, 30
Sakaba, Yenyi, 116
Salpeter, Dan, 8
Samaranch, Juan Antonio, 86, 123
Sang, Julius, 168–72
Sang, Patrick, 137
Sarantakes, Nicholas Evan, 121
scholarships. *See* education
Selassi, Haile, 50–52
Semenya, Caster, 23–24, 141, 152–55
Semenya Foundation, 153–54
Senegal, 27, 109, 192n46
Senn, Alfred E., 40, 122
Seychelles, 195n75
Seye, Abdul, 27
Shapa Soweto (training center), 154
Sharpeville massacre, 71
Sikes, Michelle, 66, 67, 186n21
Siraj, M. Faroq, 16
Skinner, Robert, 28, 57, 60
Smith, Ian, 96, 97, 99, 101
Smith, Maureen Margaret, 27
Smith, Tommie, 6
soccer (football), 159, 167; Egyptian team, 30–32, 31, 182n14, 182n17; programs for women and girls, 140. *See also* FIFA; World Cup
social-development programs, 23, 126–56. *See also* athletic-development programs; charitable initiatives and foundations; education; food insecurity; gender equity
socialism, 40, 43, 45
social mobility, 2, 158–62
Somalia, 122, 190n20
South Africa, 58–92; 1908 London Games, 4; 1960 Rome Games, 63; 1992 Barcelona Games, 60, 88–92, 157, 166; 2012 London Olympics, 152; apartheid regime, 4–5, 22, 44, 59–64, 86, 105–6, 125, 186n21, 187n51; colonial era, 2, 11; expulsion from Olympic Movement, 21–22, 57, 83–85, 92, 163; FIFA ban, 178n4; Interim National Olympic Committee of South Africa (INOCSA), 88; IOC representatives, 48, 188n70; Kenya relationship, 47, 66–69; national identity, 82; Nationalist Party, 59, 61; National Olympic Committee

Index 219

(SANOC), 11, 65, 70–72, 88–90, 187n38; national unity (after apartheid), 129–32; readmission efforts, 18, 58, 70–83, 187n38; rugby, 5, 94–95, 105–6, 113, 123, 129, 192n42, 194n71; Sharpeville massacre, 71; Soweto Uprising, 103, 109; Suppression of Communism Act, 64; suspension from Olympic Games, 4–5, 19, 21–22, 57, 59–61, 64, 70–83, 92, 94; United States relationship, 117, 119; White athletes (*see* Budd, Zola); White subpopulations, 188n61

"South African Games" (1969), 83–84

South African Non-Racial Olympic Committee (SANROC), 4, 59–60, 65–66, 68, 71–72, 74, 76, 77, 87–88, 104, 164, 186n35

South African Olympic and Commonwealth Games Association (SAOCGA), 61–63

South African Olympic and National Games Association (SAONGA), 61, 65

South African Sports Association (SASA), 62–65

Southeast Asians, 38–39

Southern Rhodesia, 99. *See also* Rhodesia

South Korea, 195n75

South Sudan, 126, 132–36, 144

Soviet Union (USSR): 1976 Montreal boycott and, 114; 1980 Moscow Games boycott and, 114–22; 1984 Los Angeles boycott and, 114, 122–25, 194n69, 195n71; invasion of Afghanistan, 114–22; South Africa and, 65, 82; support for African independence movements, 40, 45, 116

Soweto Uprising, 103, 109

Sports Illustrated, 54, 56, 131

Springboks (South African national rugby team), 5, 94–95, 105–6, 129, 194n71

Stanford University, 128

Stevens, Simon, 68

Stop Early Marriage Campaign, 151–52

Sudan: 1960 Rome Games, 3–4, 27; defection, 167; IOC representatives, 48; regional conflict, 144. *See also* South Sudan

Summer Olympic Games, 20; by year and location, xi–xii. *See also* Olympic Games

Supreme Council for Sport in Africa (SCSA), 17–18; Los Angeles boycott and, 125; Moscow boycott and, 115, 192n46; New Zealand and, 103–7, 190n19; Rhodesia and, 96, 98–100, 102; South Africa and, 74–75, 78–80, 83–85, 113, 115

Swaziland, 69

Taiwan, 68, 191n27

Tanganyika, 183n44; National Olympic Committee, 35, 43. *See also* Tanzania

Tanui, Moses, 57

Tanzania: 1964 Tokyo Olympics, 43; 1968 Mexico City Games, 44; 1972 Munich Games, 102; 1976 Montreal Games boycott, 111; 1980 Moscow Games, 121; 1984 Los Angeles Games, 174; anti-apartheid movement, 75; anti-colonialism and Olympic participation, 27–28, 40, 42–44; athlete migration, 173; boycotts, 99, 109, 111, 117, 118, 190n20; independence, 42; National Olympic Committee, 43–44. *See also* Tanganyika

Tass (Soviet news service), 124

Tau, Jan, 90

Taunyne, Len, 2, 3, 4, 177n2

Tegla Loroupe Peace Academy, 144

Tegla Loroupe Peace Foundation, 6, 142–43

Temu, Naftali, 55

Tenga, Sendeu Titus M., 43

Tergat, Paul, 126, 137, 141–42

Tessema, Ato, 76

Tessema, Ydnekatchev, 194n67

Thabede, Fred, 82–83

Thugwane, Josia, 129–32, 130

Touny, Ahmed Eldermerdash, 48

Toure, Sékou, 45

tourism, 8–9, 42–43, 67, 183n42

Track and Field News, 171

"track drain," 171–72

Trinidad and Tobago, 181n1

Tshwete, Steve, 89

Tulu, Derartu, 91–92

220   Index

Tunisia: 1960 Rome Games, 3–4, 27; boycotts, 104; independence, 45; IOC representatives, 48; National Olympic Committee, 41, 44–45; National Olympic Day, 42; postcolonial national identity, 41–42; Soviet Union relationship, 45
Turkey, 4, 158
Tusun, 'Umar, 30–31

Ueberroth, Peter, 124
Uganda: 1952 Helsinki Games, 26; 1956 Melbourne Games, 3, 26, 36; 1960 Rome Games, 37, 199n19; 1968 Mexico City Games, 25, 78; 1976 Montreal Games boycott, 111; 1980 Moscow Games, 121; boycotts, 78, 99; Israeli hostages, 191n29; National Olympic Committee, 34–36; regional conflict, 143–44
Underwood, John, 54
UNICEF, 140
United Nations: African members of, 47; Ambassador of Sport, 143; Goodwill Ambassadors, 138; marginalization of Africans in, 9; resolutions against Rhodesia, 22, 96–97; sporting embargo against South Africa, 94; World Food Programme (WFP), 121–22, 126
United Nations Population Fund (UNFPA), 151
United States (US): athletic scholarships in (see education); Fourteenth Amendment, 169; Montreal boycott and, 115; Moscow boycott and, 114–22, 194n67; National Olympic Committee, 168; Olympic squad, 24, 123, 134–35, 160, 162, 163–65; racism in, 168, 170–72; South Africa and, 71, 117, 119, 194n71; Title IX of Education Amendments Act, 174; Unaccompanied Refugee Minor Program, 134
University of California Los Angeles (UCLA), 170
University of Oklahoma, 174
University of Oregon, 128
University of Pennsylvania, 193n61

University of Texas at El Paso (UTEP), 173, 174
University of Wisconsin, 170
Upper Volta (Burkina Faso), 122
USSR. See Soviet Union

Velzian, John, 53–55
Visa Humanitarian of the Year Award, 136
Vorster, B. J., 77

Walker, John, 111
Walker, Leroy, 168, 171
Walters, Reg, 4
Wambua, Jim, 172
Washington State University, 160–62, 170–71, 173, 175
WaterAid (NGO), 140
Weisbord, Robert G., 96
West Indies, 39
White minority regimes, 4, 22, 59–61, 67, 92, 94, 96, 98, 101, 125, 186. See also colonialism; Rhodesia; South Africa
Wint, Arthur, 39
Winter Olympic Games, 20
Wise, Mike, 129–31
women and girls: charitable initiatives for, 23, 144–52; sports programs for, 140, 147–50. See also gender equity
women athletes, 4, 10, 23–24, 145, 152–55, 173–74, 198n72. See also specific athletes
Women First Run, 152
Worden, Minky, 132, 153
World Athletics, 153, 199n8
World Cup, 9, 178n9
World Food Programme (WFP), 121–22, 126
World's Fair, 177n2
World Trade Organization, 9
World Vision (NGO), 136
World Wars I and II, 4, 11, 30, 33, 182n8

Zaire (Congo), 118–19
Zambia, 98, 99, 115–16
Zanzibar, 183n44
Zaoui, Maha, 42
Zerguini, Mohamed, 109
Zimbabwe, 94, 116, 121, 125, 192n48. See also Rhodesia